A Handful of Earth

A Handful of Earth

A Year of Healing and Growing

BARNEY BARDSLEY

ISIS
LARGE PRINT
Oxford

Copyright © Barney Bardsley, 2007

First published in Great Britain 2007
by
John Murray (Publishers), a division of Hodder Headline

WORCESTERSHIRE COUNTY COUNCIL	
922	
ULVERSCROFT	31.3.08
	£19.95
EV	

Published in Large Print 2008 by ISIS Publishing Ltd.,
7 Centremead, Osney Mead, Oxford OX2 0ES
by arrangement with
John Murray (Publishers), a division of Hodder Headline

British Library Cataloguing in Publication Data
Bardsley, Barney
    A handful of earth: a year of healing and growing.
    – Large print ed.
    1. Bardsley, Barney – Diaries
    2. Gardening
    3. Allotment gardens
    4. Widows – Great Britain – Diaries
    5. Loss (Psychology)
    6. Large type books
    I. Title
    635'.092

ISBN 978–0–7531–9480–5 (hb)
ISBN 978–0–7531–9481–2 (pb)

Printed and bound in Great Britain by
T. J. International Ltd., Padstow, Cornwall

For Tim McGee, who wanted the truth told

Contents

Introduction

I walk in this garden, holding the hands of dead friends . . .

Derek Jarman, *Derek Jarman's Garden*

One morning, in May 2005, I took an early walk with my dog in Roundhay Park, a beautiful piece of cultivated green and woodland in north-east Leeds. As I walked, watching the sharp sunlight glitter on the lake, and following the winding paths through groves of trees, lime-green with fresh growth, I realized I was not alone even though the park was deserted. I had by my side the ever-present dead: my mother, my husband, my grandmother, my aunt . . . and various beloved friends, cut down in their youth, way before their time.

It had not struck me so clearly before, but something about the stillness of this particular morning illuminated the fact: whenever I am outside, these days, in the wild, or in my own garden and allotment, I am always retrieving lost souls. Nature has become the meeting place and playground of those taken away from me. When I garden, I also search for things no longer mine — times, experiences, feelings, as well as people, from the past. And the strange thing is, I seem to find them.

1

The garden has become a place I go to, to heal my wounds, my sense of loss. Over the past decade — throughout my late thirties and forties — these wounds have been considerable, but the garden is generous. Whether contained in a window box or spreading out like a meadow, it gives and gives. And I am greedy now.

I have come late to the garden, as with most things in my life (dance training at thirty, first and only child at thirty-six, first real garden at forty), and it is the symbolism, the philosophy of the process, which intrigues me as much as the hands-on sensuality. Love of the outdoors, and, in particular, my little garden and wilful, sprawling allotment, has become a search for meaning: how to live, when the only certainty is death? With its endless cycle of blossoming and withering; its withstanding of cruel winters, of winds and cold, as well as the rush of spring growth and lovely summer profusion, the garden points me forward.

Gardening — and the great outdoors — as an aid to self-healing, is by no means a new or startling concept. What could be more therapeutic than to work outside in the fresh air, feeling wind, sun or rain beating on your skin, and driving the real, lovely world into your heart? Is there any symbol more redolent of regeneration than a seed, planted in rich compost, watered and warmed, to produce a new shoot of green in the spring, crowned by two perky, embryonic leaves? A tiny start, with the promise of plenty. It has taken me a long time to learn to look at those little leaves, and appreciate their significance, but I understand it now. And it has saved me from depression, even despair.

2

My initial compulsion to garden was triggered by a life-threatening crisis. I was in my thirties, with a very young child, living in a top-floor flat at the poorer end of Stockwell, south London. Not a hint of green in sight. My husband — sturdy, reliable Tim — had, out of the blue, been diagnosed with an advanced cancer, and would need prompt and extensive surgery. There was a chance he might not survive the operation, and even if he did, the long-term prognosis was grim. So what did I do? I started to plant pots and window boxes obsessively, interspersing my visits to the intensive care unit with tending my flowers, and gazing at them, as fiercely protective as a mother bird on a nest of fledglings. The desire to garden felt almost atavistic: as if I were planting myself in the soil, rooting myself in, so that I, at least, would not be swept away by the storm of suffering that had blown into my life.

This was 1994. The south London arts community I lived in — with a high percentage of young gay men, actors, dancers, writers and teachers, my friends — was in the middle of a deep and trenchant battle against HIV and AIDs. Three close friends had died, and many more were HIV-positive. A significant proportion of other people my age had contracted cancer. Now Tim, my rock in a hard place, was ill too. After rollicking through the carefree college era of punk, and the grassroots radicalism of alternative London in the 1980s — when there was a chaotic but real sense of community among the dissenting young — we suddenly seemed to be a stricken generation. An atmosphere of fear and prejudice arose. And death came stalking us.

Out of this darkness came a push towards colour and light. The funerals of the young men who died of AIDs were vivid and brilliant testimonies of hope, with decorated coffins, embroidered quilts, big explosions of music and poetry — followed, later, by the traditional dedicated benches and ritual planting of trees. We needed to feel, much as the survivors of any disaster, that life, in all its myriad confusions, would go on. Babies were born — including my own. New life: a vital link to the future. And for me, came the enduring impulse to create a garden.

I finally inherited a patch of earth of my own when we left London in 1996, to set up home in Leeds. We rented a house with a shared space at the back, and a tiny plot at the front. This became my sole domain, haphazardly cultivated, but jealously guarded. Tim had recovered from his surgery by now, and was back at work. It was a brief reprieve. Soon the dreary round of chemotherapy, radiotherapy and hospital confinements began again: and it went on for many years. But something fruitful had entered the equation, and in time the garden blossomed, even if Tim could not. We lived from day to day, not knowing what the future would bring. But each spring, the garden burst reliably forth, with foliage, blossom, berries and fruit. A palpable symbol of renewal and change.

It was another seven years before I was confident enough to take on a bigger piece of ground, in the shape of an allotment. This was 2003. By now, my back was really against the wall. Nearly ten years after his diagnosis, Tim's time was running out. He was sick and exhausted — and what he felt in his body, I felt in my heart. We went nowhere that summer, since Tim was far too ill to travel, and our finances were at an all-time low. We were miserable. One day I wandered past our local health food shop, and saw a notice about allotments to rent a mile or so away from our home. On impulse, I rang up the secretary, and arranged a visit the next day.

The allotment is situated on a strip of land hidden away between a block of municipal flats and the local leisure centre. There are padlocked gates and barbed wire — fortification against the local delinquents — and a private drive, which winds past the first few plots to a communal shed and storehouse. Then, all goes quiet. It is like a piece of countryside bang in the middle of an urban sprawl. The atmosphere is almost medieval: people working their strips of land with spade, fork and trowel to produce the same fruits and vegetables that have been grown for generations. I signed up immediately. Our plot was basically a small field, with a lovely old shed at the top end, and a splendid pond created by the previous incumbents. I think it was this pond, complete with family of frogs, which swung it for me. Although I did very little to begin with — except cover the ground, to kill off the thick infestation of weeds beneath — just the existence of this other space, away from home and hardship, saved our summer. It was to be Tim's last.

In October 2003, he was admitted to a local hospice, and died there in January 2004. Some pain cannot be penetrated, even by the richness of the earth; it must simply be endured. For most of the year following Tim's death, I felt too weak and shocked to do anything much, and certainly could not garden. Apart from an eccentric latticework of paths, and some roughly shaped beds marked out with mouldy carpets and rocks, and a few desultory broad beans and broccoli planted in a tiny strip by the shed, my plot lay fallow, and even the little garden at home became shaggy, sad and overgrown.

In January 2005, all this changed. The first anniversary of Tim's death passed, and I began to DIG, with a vengeance, for the future.

January

In every winter's heart,
there is the seed of spring.

Richard Kirsten Daiensai, *Smile*

1 January I do not enjoy New Year's Eve: the compulsion to socialize when every fibre of my being is straining towards silence and contemplation. It makes no sense, ending the year in noise and oblivion. Stillness is all. The garden is with me on this. I have hardly any evergreens in my little patch, and so, at this dark turning of the year, I am left with a collection of raw, resentful sticks poking out from the bare ground. Sumach, smoke bush, weeping pear: in midsummer, these are all froth, and filmy, laced foliage. Today they sing a funeral note. Everything is fallen to earth. I feel like one of the fallen too, since I have some strange stomach bug, and am practically confined to the bedroom.

Last year, on 1 January, my husband Tim was still alive, but only just. He had exactly one more week to live, having hung on, by an increasingly slender thread, as a hospice in-patient, since the previous October. The struggle of that final week, as, little by little —

7

sometimes peacefully, sometimes painfully — he relinquished his hold on life, is etched in my memory as a series of timeless monochrome tableaux. Tim, sitting back, head drooped in unimaginable weariness, body propped up by a barrage of pillows; Tim, sleeping curled on his side, knees to chest protectively, blissfully unconscious; Tim, perched on the edge of his high hospice bed, balance precarious, big body light as a feather, centre of gravity gone, disorientation in the gaze, but dignity — even hauteur — in his demeanour.

Strong and subtle waves of feeling arise, as I think of those last days. There is awe, at the infinite care the nurses took to make their (sometimes demanding) patient more comfortable. And wonder at the tenderness and ferocity that Tim showed in his dying — bewilderment, shot through with moments of piercing clarity. It takes courage to die, and though his mind was cloudy with narcotics, his heart was big. Above the bed covers, the bare bones of his arms and hands rested, body and soul pared down to a deep, essential humanity. Outside his balcony window, the branches on the trees were bare too; winter — the inevitable death in nature — reflecting, without compunction, the death of an individual man.

One year later, all this seems very far away, almost a dream. Memory of it puts my current sickness into sober perspective. But being laid up for a few days, spending my time mostly in bed, in solitude, brings me closer, somehow, to Tim. Or at least, to the space that he leaves behind.

My daughter Molly goes off for a wild coastal walk with friends. I was invited too, but am too weak to make it. The North Yorkshire Moors and the North Sea will have to do without me. Still, the dog needs walking, and I must stagger out somehow, later in the day, past my bleak garden, and off to the local wood. The trees carve skeletal shapes against a bilious sky. It is a sullen, unforgiving scene, stark in mood, yet somehow bracing and necessary. The absence of decoration fits the energy of the season. All is in abeyance — is gone. Yet without January, how could we ever have July?

The beat of your foot on the earth, that is what counts. Get outside. If winter is in your heart, and not just outside the window, there will always be something in nature to soothe you. It's just the way it is. A garden lives and breathes: it offers stamina for a tired body and a soul worn thin with strain. But you have to work for it. And this is where the work starts — in the dead of January, when nothing grows, and everything has gone under. The work? Believing that life will resurface — that what is lost will return. Becoming a gardener is, first and foremost, an act of the imagination, of hope. And hope is not just a feeling, it is a muscle which can be developed, even in the most wintry of spirits. So go walking. And as you do so, think deep, and dream the garden back to life, right where it matters, in the dark of your mind. These are the messages I sing to myself.

4 January The last light started to fade at 4.25p.m. How eagerly I watch the clock at this time of year, clawing back for myself the pale minutes of sunshine; the faint, distant whisperings of spring. Molly went back to school today, after the Christmas break, and I ventured briefly into the front garden, to cut back some dead wood on last year's plants. The secateurs made a satisfying snap, as the curved blades sliced through stem and branch. It may be wet underfoot, too wet to weed, but there is always a need for a little light grooming.

Anyone can make a garden — truly — and make it anywhere. Pot on a window ledge. Pocket handkerchief piece of earth outside the front door. Scrappy, grass-infested plot, gone to wild, calling only for time and a bit of attention to become productive again, even beautiful, in a ragged kind of way. Over the past ten years, this has been my particular journey, from window box, to little garden, to allotment — not in a perfect measured progression, but in a wild weave of wanting. The garden came to me, because I needed it.

I have a friend and teacher, Andreas Demetriou, who, over the expanse of a decade, revealed to me the intricacies of T'ai Chi, its philosophy and subtle movements, its attention and reference to the natural world, and to the necessity and joy of the changing seasons, both inside and outside of us. Not only a teacher, but a gardener, he is a man who has brought his love of earth all the way from a small village in Greek Cyprus, to rough old Railton Road in London —

10

Brixton's notorious front line — where he has made an exquisite tapestry of plants and flowers, practically on top of a brick wall in front of his little terraced house. He says, and how I applaud his words: "I don't have much of a garden, it is just a yard, but that didn't put me off. I'd grow plants in the palms of my hands if I had no other place to put them."

The worse things get, the greater the need to see something flourish — that is my experience. So I took on an allotment at the lowest point in my life: in August 2003, when my husband had only six months to live.

Tim had been extremely ill all year: his appetite was gone, and he had a permanent hacking cough. He could not walk very well, was often sick or nauseous, and spent a lot of time lying down, gaunt and withdrawn. It fell to me to watch this slow decline, day and night — the impotent witness of a process set in motion by his cancer diagnosis nine years before, now spiralling down to its inevitable conclusion. I felt hopeless and lonely — and badly in need of nourishment, which other people could not easily provide, given their own fears and inadequacies in the presence of terminal illness and death.

A local allotment seemed an unlikely source of help: an overgrown piece of land, which would need time, attention and determination to cultivate. Surely it would only demand more of me than I could offer? Another responsibility, on top of my many pressing concerns? But I found the opposite to be the case. The allotment, even when visits to it were precious and few, became both escape and refuge.

It was the simple existence of this other place — this impartial, insouciant elsewhere, unconnected to house or illness, or the burdens of care — that kept me going. Although we judge ourselves and our gardens remorselessly (have we weeded the borders . . . do the bushes need pruning . . . are our flowers as colourful, vegetables as bountiful, as those next door?) they never judge us. If we use them well, our gardens can set us free.

In my case, even *thinking* of the garden did the trick. As Tim's illness grew worse, through the autumn of 2003, and he made the inevitable journey from home to hospice, from life slowly towards death, I couldn't do anything much, except support and survive. For a while there was no time for the house, for the garden, for ordinary life. The allotment — after an initial burst of energy that first summer, to start it off, with some digging and planting and covering of the ground — was left largely to its own devices.

But down in my subconscious, the fact of the earth remained. One day I would re-enter the green spaces I had abandoned. It took a long while to find my way back — 2003 . . . 2004 . . . 2005. Now is the time. Begin again. Make something grow.

5 January I went digging today: my first visit to the allotment this year. It was cold and wet. I felt very virtuous. I am making a new start.

I peeled back the last piece of old carpet on the upper part of my land (put there to kill off the grass, and soften the soil), and can see the shape of two rectangular beds, covered in the yellow-grey remains of dead vegetation. It is not pretty, but promises much. I now have ten growing beds, cut out higgledy-piggledy from the overgrown grassland of my blunt, wide plot. It is eighteen months since I first signed up to Oakwood Lane Allotments, and here I am, still working on making the top half habitable to something other than couch grass, bindweed and dandelions. I am not the most diligent or dedicated of tenants . . . Still, maybe something will flourish here soon, other than weeds, and my colourful imagination.

6 January Why do all the big bills come in January, just when my pockets are most empty? The gas bill, car tax and television licence line up, waiting to be paid. Still, it is an excuse to get out of the house and walk through the woods to our little local post office at Oakwood. The man who runs the place is a jolly, buzzing bee of energy. He whistles and hums constantly, but his relentless good humour is infectious. I invariably come away with a smile on my face. The dog is parked in her usual place by Oakwood Bookshop, looking forlorn. But she cheers up too, after chasing a few squirrels up trees on the muddy hill walk home.

7 January It is a calm winter's day. Later, Molly and I will drive out to the coast, taking the Scarborough road east, and then veering north, over the Yorkshire Moors, ready to mark the day Tim died, exactly one year ago, with a scattering of ashes over the cliff edge at Whitby Abbey.

This time last year, Molly and I — together with our dog Muffin — paid Tim a visit early in the evening. His sisters and parents had been coming in regularly. But today it was just us. And, although we did not know it then, this was to be the last time anyone came calling. He died the following morning.

His balcony room overlooked an elegant, calm garden, with a cool rill of water describing the length of the building, and a tangle of wild grass curving at its far edges. Around the side of the hospice were delicate pathways, with beautiful mosaics set into the earth and, in the corner, a still pool to sit beside. This garden had been newly enlarged and redesigned, and was both comforting and graceful, for patients and visitors alike. I envied the amount of skill which went into its making. How different to my own scruffy allotment and neglected garden, languishing under the weight of Tim's illness, and the conflicting demands of his final, difficult few months. Never mind. For the time being, this hospice space was a welcome and peaceful surrogate.

Tim's death was scarcely a surprise. It had been a long time coming, since he had first been diagnosed with a rare cancer of the thymus gland (which sits below the throat, at the entrance to the lungs and upper chest) a full ten years before. Even at the initial diagnosis, he knew it was ultimately incurable. The tumour had already been growing stealthily, probably over many years, and was comfortably established in his body. Medical intervention might slow its growth, but eradication was out of the question. But Tim was only thirty-six. We had been together barely five years, and our daughter was only a year and a half old. He was not about to take notice of sell-by dates; there was still too much to live for.

Indeed, he was revived countless times during the ensuing decade between diagnosis and death. He came through his initial operation, despite the gloomy warnings of the spectacularly robust consultant who opened him up. He survived massive doses of sickening chemotherapy the same year, and then a prolonged regime of radiotherapy some years later. His disease became officially terminal in 1999, leaving palliative care his only option. Still he lived on, for another five years after that. My husband was a stubborn man.

There were plenty of crises, midnight dramas, emergency visits to GPs and hospitals during those final five years, plus two close flirtations with death itself. The first of these was in 2001, when he seemed to be slipping away in front of us, silently, inexorably. He stopped eating, whilst the cancer ate at him, and lost so much weight he was like a tall, quiet shadow, hardly able to stand or walk. But he recovered, slowly, with a dazzling armoury of chemical stimulants and opiates to help him on his way.

The second, even closer shave, was in the autumn of 2003, when he was already a hospice in-patient. By November, doctors were convinced he would die of a pneumonia-like chest infection. A last-minute switch to a draconian antibiotic, administered in high, intravenous doses, turned him around yet again. He had been within hours of death. Now he had a few weeks of relative peace and comfort in which to read, reflect and dream.

But in the dark days of January 2004, having celebrated Christmas and seen in the New Year, he knew there was no more cheating the inevitable — the fight was gone, from mind and body. It was time to let go. Despite all the preparation — all the dramas of his complex journey through the long cancer years — his death was devastating.

In the weeks leading up to his death, this quintessential Yorkshire man, normally so reticent emotionally, so stoical and silent, became loosened, even liberated, by its imminence. He spent hours quietly listening to music or watching favourite films; and enjoyed lengthy telephone conversations and meetings with friends and family, in which he became uncharacteristically expressive. The emotional floodgates swung open as his physical life ebbed away.

The biggest gift he prepared was for our daughter Molly, then eleven years old, in the form of a remarkable Memory Box: this was filled with writings, a video of him speaking directly to camera from his hospice room, and various treasures from his life, which he compiled in his final weeks. His guide through such a difficult process was a social worker called Annie, who worked tirelessly with the whole family, integrating his dying into our lives in a way which felt rich and gentle.

Molly repaid her father's diligence with a steadfast presence at his bedside. By now, worn out from years of being Tim's sole carer, my own compassion had drained away, leaving me exhausted and hollow. Molly stepped in for me, with exquisite gestures of affection which I know soothed her father immensely. How often our children fill the gaps for us.

All through my childhood I worried that my parents might die. When my older brothers became teenagers and started staying out at night, I absorbed the anxiety my mother felt, and, like her, lay in bed waiting for their safe return. They always came back. No one was left lying in a ditch. No one died.

But the fear that every child has — the death of a parent — came true for Molly. She has come through it all with strength and grace, though what she felt is hard to imagine. Through the years, I had tried to protect her from the worst of Tim's illness. Still, she saw more than any child should ever see. From the age of two to eleven, she lived with the reality of advanced cancer, in all its ugly manifestations. She is, however, her father's child. She keeps her own counsel, and does not invite intrusion into the privacy of her own mind. The best way to help her, I have found, is to stand well back and wait. Her own wisdom does the rest — the innate wisdom all children possess, should the fussiness of adults not cloud and confuse it.

With her instinct for the right action, Molly bought Tim the last thing he would ever eat, on the night before his death — a double chocolate chip muffin from Marks & Spencer, which he said tasted "wonderful". At 9.50 a.m. the next morning, 8 January 2004, he died.

With typical self-effacement, he chose a time when we were not around as his moment for leaving, without us there to hold him back. I understand from hospice workers that this is far from uncommon. Relatives can keep vigil for hours, days, weeks, and then find that their beloved has died in the moment they took to slip to the bathroom, or to go outside for a coffee or a cigarette.

After Tim had died, the only flowers left in the meticulous hospice bedroom were a little posy of pretty yellow tulips, chosen by Molly. These flowers — a species of which I had always been rather dismissive until that day — have a particular resonance for me now, with their proud long necks, their fleshy leaves, and vivid waxy blooms, which seem to move from tight control to blowsy abandon in an instant, and which look most beautiful just when they are falling apart.

Perhaps the most useful thing a garden can do is the least obvious, and certainly the least glamorous. It teaches us about loss. Since I started gardening in miniature form in 1994, I have regularly "lost" my gardens. Plants die. Pots are neglected. Plans on paper, made in the lazy indoor days of winter, go awry in the hectic action of spring. Colour schemes — those careful combinations of matching shades — are abandoned, in the desperation to get *anything* in the ground to fill the unexpected gaps in the border.

For something so tangible, so beautifully three-dimensional and robust, the garden is also infuriatingly elusive, constantly changing and refusing to do as it's told. Within its confines, it embraces not just the fullness of life, but also its empty dying notes. Tidy

18

gardeners, those who delight in topiary, cropped turf and clinical rows of obedient shrubs and flowers, of whom I am NOT ONE, will always fight nature's chaos. But I am learning, slowly, painfully, to accept it. Nature will win. Death happens. Yet the brightness of new life, of fresh possibility, is already germinating underneath.

8 January Tim's first anniversary. Here we are in Whitby, where the storms have been raging — leaving residual blusters of wind in their wake. Tim loved the Moors, and the quaint little fishing port of Whitby in particular. It was the first place he showed me in Yorkshire: a proud gift to his new girlfriend, in 1989. So, this pilgrimage felt very special, and, oddly, rather joyful.

Last night, on arrival, we booked into a big Bed and Breakfast hotel a few miles north of the town, in Runswick Bay: a place right on the cliff edge, very exposed. When the wind started to blow hard, in the dead of night, I assumed it was always like this, in such a high, open place, and turned over and went back to sleep. But this morning, I could hardly open the main door to let the dog out, such was the force of the gale blowing outside. I nearly collided with a woman cleaner, who came tumbling in as I went out, telling me, breathlessly, that she had never known winds like it in all the years she had lived in the village. People could hardly stand upright in the street. Trees had been blown across roads all over the area, and many routes in and out of Whitby were completely shut off. It was a major incident.

Then, between 9 and 10a.m., just as we had cancelled all our plans, and were sitting indoors hoping the roof would not cave in, all fell silent. The storm left — as abruptly as it had begun — at the exact hour Tim died, one year before.

Later, tentatively, we drove into Whitby, taking a few detours to avoid the debris, and walked the 199 steps up the south cliff, past the ruins of Whitby Abbey to St Hilda's Church. At the far end of the high ancient graveyard, beyond its holy perimeters, I opened a jar of Tim's ashes, and they swirled out in a great gleeful rush, settling quickly amidst the grass and stones and rough earth of the cliff edge, high above the sea itself. Free at last. A dousing of whisky, Tim's favourite tipple in his last years, and a fistful of rosemary from my front garden, thrown after.

Ophelia's words in *Hamlet*: "There's rosemary, that's for remembrance." Nothing has such a powerful, bracing effect on my nose, and my mood. I plant rosemary all over the place, use it liberally in cooking, and cannot resist rubbing stolen sprigs of it between thumb and finger, and inhaling its pungent aroma wherever I find a stray bush. It's a native of the Mediterranean — accustomed to salt, drought and a poor, stony coastal soil — rather than the cold wet clay of inland Yorkshire. The Latin name, *Rosmarinus*, in reference to its natural habitat, translates beautifully as "dew of the sea", with tiny blue flowers gracing its branches in dull old January like stray drops from a far-off sunlit ocean. But still, it seems to thrive here: and what a bracing companion it makes.

The folklore which surrounds rosemary runs deep and long. First recorded in England as far back as 1340, it has been a powerful symbol of friendship and remembrance down through the centuries, used at weddings as well as funerals, in bouquet and in wreath. But I had no conscious notion of this when I started to put it in the ground, in my first little garden in Leeds. I knew spontaneously it was a kind of memory-tree, and thoughts of dead friends came springing to mind as I planted it.

Patrick — a dancer — who died in 1990. John — a singer — and Stewart — a writer and cook — who both died in 1993. All three from AIDs, in the days when the drugs didn't work. And Ria — a Hungarian writer and dramaturg, who died in 1994 of breast cancer. This was a dying decade for many people I loved. Tim — who also became ill in the 1990s — was still very much alive when I started planting my rosemary. Often, he would be sitting in the front room watching his beloved football, whilst I wandered back and forth outside the window, heaving bushes and shrubs and small trees for planting. Did I think of a time when he would not be there? When trees would be planted in his name, too? The truth is, I tried not to think at all. The future was blank. If I dug in my rosemary to remember others, I dug it in, too, to keep Tim, and my hope, alive.

Now I learn that students in ancient Greece wore whole garlands of rosemary around their necks at examinations, to improve their recall, and that a bunch under the pillow at night will stop troublesome dreams. It is vigorous, and encourages those around it to be the same. Rosemary speaks to the brain, rather than the heart. "Miss Jessop's Upright", my favourite variety, reveals its quality in the name. It is sturdy, uncompromising, deep green needles pointing to the skies in uplift and exhortation; the gnarled roots and branches of older specimens acting as a doughty reminder of how to survive in difficult circumstances. Dig deep, toughen up.

The chance of renewal, of a fresh start — this is the gift of a garden. Nothing soothes my agitated spirit more than clean air, rich soil and fresh flowers. Any threat of trouble, or chaos of any kind, and I start to scrabble around in the dirt, trying to make something lovely out of an ugly omen. Nothing in my life had felt uglier than Tim's cancer diagnosis in 1994.

It started with vague fatigue; with urine infections, which made the doctor suspicious when they regularly recurred; with a shadow on the lung, unexpectedly revealed by a prudent X-ray; with a tunnel of darkness, as the tests and waiting began — before a definite diagnosis of Thymoma, cancer of the thymus gland, on the first anniversary of my best friend John's death, 21 April 1994.

Only something as mute and vivid as a flower could allay some of the fear I was living with. So that is why window boxes on the rickety ledges of the upstairs windows where we lived, in our tiny top-floor south

London flat, were suddenly filled with saucy petunias in pink, purple and white; and new pots outside the front door shone with miniature sunflowers. While Tim lay under the surgeon's knife, I was messing about with half hardy annuals! I simply did not know what else to do . . . Without realizing it at the time, I had found a way of symbolizing my trauma even as it unfolded: planting both hope and supplication in amongst the flowers. I set myself a precedent that day. Since then, whenever a crisis occurs in the health of someone close, I go back to the earth and plant something.

When I swapped my pots for a real — though tiny — garden in north Leeds two years later, I immediately set about filling my coveted outside space with living mementoes of dead friends: specifically, a sumach tree — with its long, lacy leaves and graceful arching habit — and rosemary bushes, for those young men I knew who had died young. Into the garden came constant reminders of the living, too — with cuttings from all the keen plantswomen I knew, who wanted to start me off. Cousin Rose gave me ivy to clothe the bare grey walls of the house, and — for the shady hedge — tough woodland loosestrife, with its canary yellow flowers, and the indomitable habit of returning from ground level every spring, more lush and abundant than ever. From Sumi, a new friend in Leeds with an artist's eye for colour and texture, came some spiky mauve-blue globe thistles, and a swishy, coppery pheasant's tail grass, which has self-seeded, with profligate ease, even in the concrete cracks of the drive. The same year we moved to Leeds, my mother gave me money for a plant, and I bought a beautiful small smoke bush, *Cotinus* "Grace". It was barely nine inches tall when I planted it, just two small branches sticking out of the earth. Now it reaches twelve feet and over: its purple radiance, and big, robust, leafy branches, a fitting testimony to my mother's vibrant personality.

9 January In my opinion, tiny spaces need BIG plants. Large spaces need them too. Where flowers and shrubs are concerned, I am not yet subtle enough to appreciate fully the small of the species. Is this because I am nearly six foot tall myself? I have, however, made significant errors of judgement in my greed for growth. Given an empty new garden, as I was in 1996, it was all too easy to go for the biggest gobstoppers in the sweet shop, and to succumb, as I did, to the cheap, eager charms of these particular monsters: Russian vine, which I planted by our front door (within a few months we almost needed a machete to force entrance to the house); lavatera, which quickly billowed up to twelve feet tall, with its cheerful pink flowers, big as saucers, and branches which thickened, almost as I watched, to the size of small tree trunks; and my cousin's evergreen ivy, which brooded for a season or two *in situ*, and then assumed triffid-like proportions as it sprinted — with its tenacious millipede suckers — to the top of the house, over the roof, and in through the bedroom windows, its waxy green foliage ceasing to clothe the house front, as I had intended, and starting to menace the householders inside! So beware the quick growers, particularly close to the house. You may be repenting for a long, long time.

There are other giants in the plant world which behave themselves rather better. I have had great success, even in such a tiny front garden, with my tall, over-arching butterfly bush (*Buddleja davidii* "Lochinch"), which does just as its common name suggests, and brings beautiful insects to flutter contentedly around it all summer; a self-containing bamboo, which has formed an elegant swaying curtain in the corner nearest the road, offering some much-needed privacy and grace; and a beautiful deciduous wall climber, Boston ivy, which attaches delicately to the side wall of the house, and which, after five years, is yet to invade the bathroom or kitchen. It boasts the most beautiful New England shades of ochre, red, green and copper in autumn, before discreetly shedding everything in December. Come January, there is nothing but the etching of its former growth, pressed into the masonry like a fossilized memory of lost summers.

10 January I think of last year as a barren one — like an abandoned field, littered with weeds and stones — but that is not strictly true. Things got done; the world, my shattered one included, moved on. I was so used to *not* having plans — never to think of the next month, the next year of Tim's illness, of the inevitable end, and how I might live then — that when the future did arrive — with his death, its aftermath and the passing of time — I was left in a strange limbo. The world happened, but I was not quite in it.

25

Apart from Molly — her growing and developing, her child's demands and daily needs, which saved me from sinking into inertia and kept me going — it was the three dimensions of the garden and allotment which brought me to my senses. Struggling with the earth — putting up arches, and erecting tripods of canes, messing about with a spade and a trowel, to make tiny inroads into a tentative future — began to give me new roots. I even managed to plant some broad bean seeds and onion sets, red and white, in the cold, unwelcoming November ground. They have survived! Small, green, sassy growing tips are popping up here and there, in the two little beds close by the shed. I admired them when I visited the allotment today. I feel absurdly proud.

I find the red onion particularly lovely to look at, modest in size, and a deep crimson-purple in colour (not red at all). Unwrap its papery exterior, and the tightly packed rings of flesh beneath gleam with good health and humour. In January, the over-wintered Japanese onion is one of the few signs of growth and vigour on a waterlogged allotment. What a relief that something has come through the winter. Birds — pesky pigeons — love to nibble the growing tips, so they should really be protected with a net, although I usually forget, and they still seem to survive. Indomitable.

It's no surprise that the onion originated in Asia, and dates back to antiquity. It is one of the few foods that did not spoil in the winter, was therefore highly prized, and remains ubiquitous in Indian cooking. There is a large Asian community in my part of Leeds, so the air is constantly filled with the rich aroma of garlic and onion being gently fried. (Garlic, another fearless survivor of the frost, grows in my neighbour's garden throughout the dark winter as jauntily as the onions on my allotment.) Such a pleasing and useful vegetable — the ancient Egyptians even worshipped it (it was the only vegetable allowed to be cast in pure gold by their artists), believing that its perfect spherical shape and concentric rings were a symbol of eternity. Eat an onion. Live for ever.

Onion is a major ingredient in my favourite comfort food for winter: lentil soup. It is my ambition to grow all three vegetables in this simple brew — carrots, onions and potatoes; I am happy to keep buying the lentils. After a hard morning's graft on a cold allotment, this easy recipe fits the bill for filling a yawningly hungry stomach. Just grate one onion, one carrot, one potato, and sauté them in olive oil (extra virgin) for a few minutes. Then add a pint or so of vegetable stock and a handful of red lentils and simmer for half an hour. Eat with home-made bread. And maybe a glass of red wine, if you really need warming up! Then snooze. Perfect.

11 January It is not the piercing cold which infects the bones of January and inspires such deep gloom: it is the grey, dark damp. Those skies are so sulky and full. I stumble through our little local wood in the morning dark — walking with my daughter and dog up to school

— and find everything enveloped in a miasma of decay. The leaves are dank and rotten underfoot. They form a greasy carpet, several inches thick, littering the paths and sticking like shit to the bottom of my shoes. The dog comes home smelly and wet, and needs to be dried. Shoes should be cleaned — although they usually remain on the rack, going crusty and resentful. Getting out of bed at all on days like this, let alone at 6.30a.m. on a cold, black morning, is a hateful business.

During the long years of Tim's illness, he found winters particularly hard, and could barely wake up at all during January and February. Like the heavy winter skies, his illness fell like a ton weight on the household, and enveloped us all in a sickly torpor. Nothing got done, no letters written, no phone calls made. I was supposedly the healthy, functioning adult — the wife, mother and carer, responsible for taking us all forward — and yet I too felt drained and exhausted. It was a kind of death, year after year.

I realize, looking back, how vital a role our daughter played in giving both Tim and me a reason to go on, just as she has inspired me, since his death, to persevere. Molly did not take no for an answer from Tim. She insisted he play with her, even in those cold winter days, when his face was turned to the wall. Sometimes she could not rouse him. Sleep and oblivion had taken hold. But often she could. If he would not crawl out of bed, she crawled in with him, and lugged a thousand soft toys in beside her to make a lively crowd. What little energy Tim could muster was always poured into her. He loved his only daughter with a deep, quiet pride: she was his future. My own strength came in the simple repetitive acts of mothering: getting breakfast, walking to school, the bedtime story, the cuddle in the night.

Quite what Molly's reward was in all this remains to be seen. Except that she has been loved, consistently, in the best and worst of times. I do know, too, that she wanted to be born. A year before her conception, I dreamed, out of the blue, of a two-year-old boy, with blond hair and serene, smiling face. Three years later, when Molly was two, she looked identical in every way (except gender!) to the little boy in my dream. Tim had wanted to wait a year or so before having children, but I wanted to go ahead in 1992, and Molly was born that autumn. Not much more than a year later, and Tim had cancer: the chemotherapy high doses, and deadly toxic — immediately made him infertile. We were Molly's chance — and she was ours. I am glad we all took it.

12 January What a difference a day makes. Up on our high hill, in north-east Leeds, the winds can whip up a storm. They create havoc among the plant pots and empty wheelie bins, which go skeetering across roads in a crazy dustbin dance, landing drunk and upside down half a mile away in someone else's garden. So it was last night. But these winds have a supreme higher purpose: they clear away the grey blanket of clouds at a stroke, leaving a bright, high blue sky in their place. At last we can all see again. With the brightness comes a new sense of direction and vigour. Amidst the deep depression of illness, loss and the psychic chaos of grief, the weather becomes a tangible way through; a window out of a beleaguered mind into the beautiful living world. For me, sunshine in January is a small miracle.

Even to walk out of doors into the garden, on a fine winter's day like today, puts me in a better frame of mind. Ceilings and walls can dull and dampen my connection with life — particularly the walls of this house, which have absorbed a lot of pain and anxiety. The movement of the air, the solid support of the earth, work alchemically on my body — uplifting and grounding me, all at the same time. Gardening is hard work, but the work is nearly always productive. The work of grief is intangible, and hidden, usually behind closed doors. No flower will grow from a wounded heart: it takes a physical act — a seed planted with mucky fingers deep into the soil — to make something beautiful appear. And yet only the most intransigent heart will not be helped by the delicate pink poppy, or sky blue morning glory, produced by the positive act of planting a seed. January is a little early for sowing, of course — but it's never too early, or too late, just to be outside. And to breathe.

15 January Everyone knows you are supposed to have a plan: in the garden, as in life. Planning something — anything — however, is not my strong point. I tend to stumble along blindly, trusting intuition to take me the right way. It works most of the time — though it caused some strife in my marriage when we had to drive somewhere new: I as the driver, Tim the superb but exacting map reader. He always had a Plan: I would simply point the car in a particular direction and drive. We usually got there, but not always in good humour. So today, though I have spent a considerable amount of time drawing a diagram of the allotment, and writing a sowing diary, I am not taking it very seriously. I know I will disobey.

My father, like Tim, would probably shake his head sadly. David is a logical, orderly man, a former engineer and lecturer in technical drawing, whose vegetable patch at the bottom of our long Essex garden was always meticulously kept, with a neat line of bamboo wigwams for runner beans, and a beautifully dug soil, edged by a long lawn, cut in military stripes. His keen eye for detail meant that there was always a right way to do things, and he would set about it quietly, cutting no corners. He has no time for that these days. At eighty-one, he is caring full-time for my mother, whose health — after a robust and active long life — has completely broken down. Dad is frail too — he has a sinister, persistent cough, and is losing weight when he has none to spare. But my mother's multiple needs take precedence. How sharply I understand their situation; how little support I can offer from the other end of the country, and, in the aftermath of Tim's death, with my own energy spent.

It is my mother's gardening style I have inherited, I think. When I was young, Dad grew lovely vegetables, but Kathleen was queen of the flowers. She presided over long and reckless herbaceous borders, her approach to her plants brutally pragmatic. She never fed them or cosseted them in any way; she simply "bunged them in", and if they grew — fine; if not — tough. Just put something else in. They flourished, of course. Often she forgot what was planted where, and in the fallow season, with all flowers and foliage gone to nothing, she regularly dug up roots and bulbs by mistake, and threw them away. Nonetheless, her stalwarts — daffodils, grape hyacinth, lilies, peonies, montbretia — have consistently survived and multiplied, and even little delicacies, such as snake's head fritillary, her special favourite, would pop up to surprise her every year.

In her prime, Kathleen was always sturdy, even cavalier, in her gardening style. "What's that called?" I would ask, once my own passion for gardening began to emerge. She would peer impatiently at the flower I was pointing to, and shrug dismissively, "Oh, I can't remember." I am the exact opposite of my mother in so many ways — vulnerable where she was tough, emotional and dreamy while she soldiered on, rational and determined, in her own particular straight line — but in the garden, I am her duplicate.

So, according to my Plan, on the allotment this year I shall grow leeks, onions, garlic; peas, French beans and runners; potatoes, artichoke (globe and Jerusalem); cauliflower, cabbage, calabrese; courgette and squashes; soft fruit and all manner of brash summer annuals. We shall see. This is just a map, after all, and not the territory itself. And I have a healthy disregard for maps. I am my mother's daughter.

17 January Remorselessly practical as she was, and certainly not a sucker for the hard sell, I never saw Kathleen pick up one of these in her life: seed catalogues — the soft pornography of the flower and plant world. But I love them, and their improbably perfect wares: showbiz flowers, all bright glossy colours, and profligacy. I have been poring over them all morning.

Even though I have only ordered from these catalogues once or twice, they are essential fodder for the black and white days of January, for fireside reading and reverie. They are useful too: sparking ideas for new planting schemes, for little exotic extras to the staple diet. (Who could resist a new shade of cascading petunia — the ultimate summer floozy of the hanging basket world?) This is window shopping for weary winter gardeners. My special favourites are the vegetable catalogues, which come spilling out of *Kitchen Garden* magazine, each January. Page after page of improbably huge onions; every potato variety known to humanity, cultivated by astonishingly single-minded growers (looking themselves like big hairy spuds in trousers); and wonderful peas, beans and cabbages simply bursting from the pages, in all shades of green and crisp veiny purple. This is definitely top-shelf material.

A rather more sober approach to the matter of January planning, the nitty-gritty of detail to back up those dreams, comes from the gardening books. Although there are hundreds to choose from nowadays, there are some writers I return to again and again, for ideas and advice on all things green. For vegetables large and small, in pots and on the allotment, Joy Larkcom is precise *and* encyclopedic. For the mix of flower and vegetable, the sensual fix of a garden, Monty Don has a velvety touch. And as for the shape of the whole thing — the sculptural artistry which completes a garden, its rise and fall, its depth and its texture — Dan Pearson has a wistful grace and subtlety.

Although my mother never read gardening books herself, she did watch horticultural programmes on the television, and held a lasting affection — shared by many northerners and all serious gardeners — for Geoff Hamilton, erstwhile presenter of BBC1's flagship *Gardeners' World*. If I am really stuck on some arcane piece of allotment business, I turn to him. He was, absolutely, a man of the earth.

19 January A busy day. At home I sowed some dwarf broad beans ("Aquadulce") to supplement the ones I over-wintered on the allotment which are looking a little bedraggled. I also sowed some peas ("Feltham First" — a pleasingly comical name), even though my father's voice is telling me not to bother, because they won't come to much. But I love the humble pea — the way its delicate and graceful shoots ping out of the earth with such optimism, tendrils curling around the nearest supports, like a newborn baby's fist around its mother's finger. I also think the term "twiggy pea stick" is one of the most endearing in the English language.

In the afternoon I went to the allotment and did some dreaded muck spreading. A pile of cow manure (delivered in stinking lorryloads every autumn by a local farmer) has been standing on my plot for a year now, and has metamorphosed from straw and cowpat into a crumbling mixture, silky soft, intensely dark, and mercifully odour-free. I dug it into a newly-reclaimed brassica patch, for luscious cabbages, broccoli and farty sprouts. Then I did lots of weeding and tidying. Very virtuous. It won't last.

20 January Every woman should have one. A shed. And mine is a beauty. I spent an hour or so on my plot this morning, tidying it up, and chucking away the toppling towers of plastic pots, used seed packets, straw and sticks — the detritus of the old year. In fact, I have two sheds — a tiny flat-pack, pointy-roofed number, which perches on my drive at home (it is so small that my country-dwelling, wood-turning brother, a master thatcher by trade, and used to cavernous barns and generous old buildings, laughed in my face when he first saw it, and snorted "What's *that*?"); and its royal and rustic cousin, the Allotment Shed. On our allotment there are many sheds. Each and every one is different in colour, shape, size and character: knocked together with recycled wood and metal, using the age-old genius of necessity and thrift, they are the very antithesis of flat pack.

My particular shed has been here for many years, silently keeping watch. It is no great looker, with its four battered wooden walls in peeling white paint; one recycled lattice window in front, and a beaten panel of thin metal strips (eggshell blue) below; an old door for the end wall; and a sloping roof — recently refashioned by our allotment secretary Don, king of DIY, to make it fully waterproof — complete with some plastic guttering, which leads down into a rusty old water butt. Functional, not fancy.

Inside is a table (also made from a recycled door), a couple of fold-up chairs, a jumble of old containers, some mud-caked boots and trainers for digging, a pile of forks, spades, rakes and trowels, and — festooned from the ceiling, corner to corner — a string of Nepalese Buddhist prayer flags, gift from my friend Sumi, allotment neighbour and friend, who shares the shed with me. I rarely sit in here, unless the rain beats me back. But when the weather is warm, I do often perch on the shed step — where the wood is worn comfortably soft with age and use — and watch the little world of the allotment, its bees, birds and rustling foliage, the frogs from the nearby pond, and the busy gardening people go by. It is a shambolic but happy place, this shed, containing all the promise of outside within its dusty, smelly old walls. The allotment garden simply would not be complete without its presidential gaze.

22 January It is my New Year's Resolution to become fitter. Not very original, but necessary. So this morning

I cut through the nearby Gledhow Valley Woods on my way to a Pilates class. The road snakes like a river through this striking valley, the banks of which rise steeply to either side of me, tall trees standing to attention, a fine mist of rain gathering on the car windscreen. Through the rain, the sun is shining and I feel at peace.

23 January On this day last year it was Tim's funeral. We had to wait two weeks after he died for the ceremony. Apparently there was a backlog. Even the registrar had seemed disturbed by the unusually high number of deaths over the Christmas and New Year period. "Everyone has been so upset," she said, rather sweetly, and somewhat naively, when I went in to collect Tim's death certificate.

The limbo before the funeral was ghastly. Every day dragged, in interminable tiredness, my body in a kind of suspended animation, my mind numb and stupid. The day of the funeral itself, in stark contrast, was an explosion of energy. Everywhere I looked there were people — family, friends, well-wishers, teachers and pupils from Molly's school — all gathered to celebrate, and to mourn.

There were two ceremonies: one at the Catholic church — to honour Tim's father, whose faith was devout, although Tim himself was not religious; and one at the crematorium, scripted and arranged in advance by Tim, complete with his own choice of music.

Molly held herself with dignity throughout. She told me later that the worst part of the day was arriving at the church. We drove behind the hearse, and stepped out to see a large crowd of people at the church doors, waiting to follow the coffin inside. We had quite a long walk (or so it seemed) before reaching them.

"Nobody smiled at me," said Molly. And it was true — all our friends and family were wearing funeral faces. But what Molly needed at that point, more than anything, was a twinkle in somebody's eye.

After the service, it was back into the cars — my elder brother following, rather splendidly, in his pick-up truck — and across the north side of town to Lawnswood Crematorium. There was a strict twenty-minute limit to the service, which felt brutal (and required the severe editing of Tim's favourite songs, which would have appalled him). Twenty minutes for a whole life. Apparently, it has been extended to forty minutes now.

Despite the constraints of time and the surroundings, the plain and functional chapel was filled with a sense of reverence, felt by the living for the untimely dead. Tim's coffin was decorated brightly: there was a silly Christmas hat he had loved, his worn blue slippers, a copy of the *Guardian*, which he read daily from cover to cover, and flowers, of course — yellow tulips, another pretty posy from Molly, taking pride of place. The hat and the slippers we have kept — the hat in a high place (he was a very tall man), and slippers under the bed.

A wreath was made by a friend, from raffia, entwined with greenery, dried fruits and fir cones, and hung about with pictures of Tim and some of the things and people he loved. The object is resonant with associations. I have kept it, but not for morbid reasons. Quite the opposite: it leaves a hint of spice and fruitfulness in the memory. And I can see a few small sprigs of rosemary, wound integrally into the structure of the circle. Dried now, but intact, needles still pointing to the sky.

Rare indeed, and precious, are the plants which give colour at the beginning of the year. The Chinese witch hazel, *Hamamelis mollis*, is one. I have "Pallida" in a pot, a gift from a friend. Shaped like a vase, or an open, upturned hand, it reveals flowers like yellow paper spiders, all along its branches, throughout January. Its scent — an unexpected bonus — is caressing and subtle. Both colour and perfume offer a momentary refuge from the monochrome dullness of winter.

24 January Birthdays at this time of year always catch me unawares, but I remembered to send cards to Tim's Auntie Babs, whose birthday is today, and to her sister, Tim's mother Catherine, who had her birthday two days ago. (It is strange how these rhythms run in families. I was born on my father's birthday; Molly and I are just three days apart; both Tim's sisters celebrate April birthdays — with just one week between them. We are connected by more than blood.) Babs is a kind and merry soul, who has lived for many years in Ealing.

I have affection for this part of London — Tim lived there for a year, before moving in with me, and I have recollections of sumptuous suppers in his little flat. Our relationship was still new then, in 1990, and he made every culinary effort to impress: this set a dangerous precedent, since he then became head cook in perpetuity, illness permitting. Between the two of us, he was always the domestic one.

We used to walk along the river bank on Sundays — the Thames curving out languorously in front of us — and watch the herons fishing: one-legged, sharp-beaked, stony-eyed. Kew Gardens was reasonably close, too, and we often paid a visit when the weather was warm. The green spaces and the vaulting majesty of the place suited both our height (very tall, collectively) and our mood: happy, expansive, in love. Summer thoughts, in a winter season. I struggle to recall the good times, but little by little they are coming back to me — with time, attention and determination.

25 January My daughter, at nearly thirteen, shows a complete contempt for gardening. Her preferred domain is indoors, lounging on a sofa, as she is at the moment, or crouched in front of a computer screen. She is astonished that I should venture outside at all, particularly at this time of year, unless it is absolutely necessary, i.e. to go shopping. At the start of my love affair with the allotment, I would lure her up there, with notions of picnics and blackberry picking, of aimless sunny days spent in the wholesome outdoors. Two years on, I am still fool enough to try, from time to time, to wind her into the fabric of the place, but my attempts are half-hearted now, without much expectation of success.

The truth is that, at her age, I was much the same. My need for the outdoors has only come with age. When I was at secondary school, I had two adored teachers — one taught physics, and the other taught art. I was pretty hopeless at both subjects, but these men were life coaches, not pedagogues. Their lessons were unconventional and curious — and they would run holiday events, as well as throwing the occasional party. The best of friends, they would argue incessantly about the relative merits of Bob Dylan and the Rolling Stones, throwing it open to the kids to decide who was right, and playing both contestants as loudly as they could, in among the easels and Bunsen burners. But the art teacher had a flaw. He loved gardens. He would wax lyrical about them in art lessons, and pore over fat books of garden design and horticulture. It left me cold. But not any more. He went before me — and planted the kernel of something sweet.

It was puberty which sent me scuttling indoors. Before then, I have fond memories of playing outside, and of watching adults garden with some interest (although not enough interest to join in). For a while I struck up a great friendship with our next door neighbour, Mr Kemp, a lovely old man with a broad Essex accent, who would chat away happily to me as he tended his plot, patiently explaining what he was doing, and never too busy to stop, lean on his spade, and have a good chat. I must remember the patience and kindness he showed, to a shy but inquisitive eight year old, the next time I complain, with the grumpy zeal of the too-busy gardener, about the neighbours' children and their endless desire to distract me.

As January draws to a close, I can see evidence of movement in the natural world. The birds are beginning to sing in the morning. It is light as Molly and I trudge to school at a quarter to eight, when even a week ago it was still dark. There are buds on bushes, and generous green foliage on crocus and snowdrop plants. The pale, watery sun is starting to have a hint of warmth in it. But much as I love being outside, I also crave the comfort of my central heating. Too much cold makes me panic. I was horrified recently, when the woman at my favourite plant nursery, in the neighbouring village of Shadwell — a strong, good-humoured type, no shrinking violet — told me that she actually suffered frostbite last winter, when droplets from the water hose sprayed accidentally on to her nose, and froze in the treacherous January sun. I need to remember that, whenever I imagine, fondly, that a job as a horticulturist might suit me. I am soft to my bones, really; it is my spirit which is wilful, and keeps me trotting, doggedly, onwards.

28 January It has not been a particularly cold winter — wet rather than icy, rain- and wind-lashed, but short on snow. Still, it only takes one night of plummeting temperatures and the little pond in front of my shed panics and freezes over. Although I worry for the life beneath, I do like its look when frozen: crisp, milky white, all sharp edges and definition. This is what I need in a garden, even one as loose and chaotic as my allotment: a clean structure beneath the scramble of flower and foliage. There need to be specific landmarks, signposts to hang on the skeleton of winter.

In my garden at home the signs are these. Out back, in the shared space, is a long trellis, parallel to the wall of the house, which tracks our privacy and lets the eye drift up to a line of trees beyond the garden. The space, thus enclosed, is narrow and dark. Just room for a placid stone Buddha in the corner, and a spiky tall cordyline in a pot. Round the corner, on the drive, stands the (small) garden shed; in its shelter, benches and a table. Some pots by the back door, with a twisted old branch and pebbles at their feet. Objects like these are helpful when the green has gone. Wood and stone beat with a slower, ancient pulse. At the front is an arch, twined with the bones of old jasmine, clematis and honeysuckle. Through the arch — the sumach tree, its velvety antlers winter bare. Opposite that, also spiny and unadorned, is the tall, red-ribbed *Cotinus*: a smoke bush without the summer "smoke" of its greeny-purple leaves. In the far corner sits the little weeping pear, its branches arching over in a pretty curve towards the earth. Punctuation marks matter in a garden. Be bold.

At the allotment I have perennials too — a whole patch of ornamental grass. An apple tree. Tall spines of thistle and stems of verbena around the pond. And there is an arch here, as at home — right in the middle of the plot — splendidly unnecessary, but a focal point,

and fun. I am slowly adding found objects here too —
like driftwood, shells and rocks — to give permanence,
some points of memory and association, amidst the
ephemeral green.

29 January Small pictures of winter. The bony black
seed head of an allium at the side of my pond, caught
in suspended animation like a frozen firework. A tangle
of pebbles scattered by my pots at home, along their
contours a lacing of frost. Mud at the allotment: cold,
thick, cracked mud. On the bramble bushes, a few
desiccated blackberries — the ones that missed the
birds' attention last autumn. A tripod of bamboo canes
tied up with gloops of grey string, stripped of their
crop, and quite bare. Abandoned in a fallow corner, a
chewed up silver CD — used to scare the birds off in
summer, now trodden into the earth after the autumn
stampede to clear up. It is a dreary scene.

30 January St Gemma's Hospice had a memorial
service today for patients who have died in the past
twelve months. Molly did not want to go, so I went
alone. It was gentle and touching — a light burning for
each remembered person. But I could not find Tim
here, and felt no sense of peace or solace. It was just the
mood I was in. Unquiet. I left and went back home,
and then spent some time outside, breathing sense into
myself.

Halfway down my allotment is a long, unruly strip,
which I grandly call the fruit patch. It is constantly
infested with weeds, and the ground is particularly

tough clay. The allotment slopes down from the shed at the top end, and all the rain collects in this patch. In the winter it becomes waterlogged and impenetrable. Nonetheless, I had a go at digging it today. It was like a bog garden. I hope the plants — raspberry, blackcurrant, redcurrant and gooseberry (all bare bones and prickles in winter) — manage to survive. The little apple tree in the far corner, which only comes up as far as my waist — and last year produced one solitary apple — looks fine. But generally, I must admit, this plot has a sad and abandoned feel to it. I shall be glad when January is over. It has such dark connotations for me now, far beyond foul weather and the pitiful, waterlogged ground.

Jobs for January

- Walk outside. Often.
- Think about the structure of your garden. Put a handful of really BIG colourful plants into your plan.
- Get your hands on lots of fat seed catalogues and drool.
- Make a lentil soup (see page 27) and set about growing the ingredients yourself, come spring.
- Sow a few seeds on your window sill, just to see something start to grow. Broad beans and peas (sweet and edible) should pop up soon enough.
- Sleep, often. Dream. The light is returning.

February

Do not be afraid to suffer, give your heaviness
     back to the weight of the earth;
Mountains are heavy, seas are heavy.
Even those trees you planted as children
     became too heavy long ago — you couldn't
     carry them now.
But you can carry the winds . . .
     and the open spaces.

Rainer Maria Rilke, *Sonnets to Orpheus*

1 February A mild and sunny day. I shovelled piles of manure on to black, empty beds, and then drove off to buy plants for a newly-created herb garden, cut out in a small circle just below the pond. I bought sage, rosemary, white lavender, chocolate-flavoured mint, basil-flavoured mint and flat-leaved parsley. The white lavender, perversely called "Blue Mountain", has an ineffably soft and lovely fragrance — not as medicinal as some lavenders. If rosemary is brain food, I think lavender speaks to the spirit. It has a graceful energy.

I felt a heartbeat of pleasure as I put these little plants in the ground. Although I do not have many, I love herbs more than any flower or vegetable; they are such sensual creatures — demanding to be stroked, rubbed and inhaled. I have a keen sense of smell: am repulsed easily by stale air or drains, unwashed armpits (and yesterday's garlic) but uplifted instantly by the rush of a lovely aroma. Particular favourites: uncorked red wine, the darker the better; almond flavoured croissants; damp, freshly dug earth; the inside of my dog's ears. The dog, a spaniel — collie cross, is a supremely tactile creature, with an endless need for strokes and attention. She lies directly underfoot, as close to me — or to Molly — as she can possibly get, providing endless scope for sensual gratification: the patting and smoothing of her long hair, fingers tickling her paws, nose buried in her pink ears.

I use lavender oil a lot around the house. Blended with lemon, it sings a particularly clear note. (How lovely it would be to grow a lemon tree, but living in Leeds, without the luxury of greenhouse or conservatory, this remains a Tuscan dream. My freshly-cut lemons come, not from the tree, but from Tesco.)

Smell, more than any other sense, evokes memory. For me, these memories are never precise — not dates, times or places; just hints and sad-sweet allusions. When Tim died, we kept the last bottle of aftershave he used; and smelled it, wore it, or sprinkled it around sometimes, in the weeks following his death: to carry him with us, on our skin, in our home. When Molly dreamed of Tim, she dreamed his smell: more nearly than face or voice, this was the essence of her father.

If I navigate my way around the world, guided by smell and by touch, the sense I most associate with Tim is taste. He had a gourmet's enthusiasm for good food and fine wine. Our courtship was conducted around picnics, extended lunches, suppers and late, slap-up breakfasts. So the cruellest aspect of his long drawn-out cancer was the way it attacked his appetite. Gradually, over the course of a decade, the barrage of drugs he had to take — chemotherapy, steroids, anti-emetics and powerful opiates — silted up his insides, making eating a chore, and food, latterly, an impossible burden on his system. By 2003, the advanced disease was eating him away. Muscles were wasting, tissues falling slack to the bone. But the minute he tried to reverse this attrition, to take in food, he would cough convulsively, and frequently retch or vomit. Mealtimes became a nightmare. I never knew what to cook him, and began to lose interest in food myself. It became as difficult to nourish the well people in the house — Molly and myself — as it was to sustain the invalid. We were all sucked into the vortex of decline.

Not just food, but drink let him down at the end. Wine and gin, lakes of which he had drunk throughout his life with great gusto (and seemingly hollow legs), lost their allure for him. All alcohol made him sicken and pall, with one startling exception. In the final year of his life, having never drunk it before, he developed a keen taste for whisky. This seemed perverse: turning to the most pungent spirit of all, when all the food he could manage was a succession of liquid supplements, and the occasional piece of fish or chicken, blandly poached or steamed. But the draw of whisky, I suppose, is its very potency. If it were food, it would be strong meat: it kicks you, and reminds you that you are still alive. One of his presents, that last Christmas in the hospice, was a bottle of Laphroaig, a peaty single malt Scotch: drinking it was like taking a mouthful of earth, sustaining and invigorating.

In the last few days of his life there were moments — small epiphanies — of enjoyment for Tim: the delicious Marks & Spencer chocolate muffin given him by Molly; morsels of fresh fried fish brought in by his parents from the local chippie. But this was too little, too late, as far as I was concerned. I despise the disease that gripped him, for this perhaps more than anything else — that it took away his greediness, his lust for food and for life.

2 February Another mild day. This is a luxury — up to the allotment two days in a row. In 2003, when I originally signed for my plot, the pond was one of the first places I tidied up, stealing many plants from my front garden to help it along. Today I noticed, around the pond in particular, that there is plenty of new growth, pushing up through the old, weedy remains of last year: loosestrife and sedums and cheerful chives. I spotted daffodil spikes driving through a messy, overgrown grassy patch by the shed. And I have frogspawn, masses of it! My mother, who adores frogs, would be delighted. It seems very early for spawning, to my untutored eye, but the winter has been mild. We are coming quickly to spring.

5 February I have begun to teach movement classes again, after a three-year break during the final stages of Tim's illness. Today I taught a workshop at a rather beautiful Methodist chapel in Meanwood, Leeds, converted now into a yoga centre, but retaining the magnificent church organ at one end, and some delicately coloured, leaded windows high on either wall, which flood the hall with a soft, uplifting light.

Perhaps dance is the closest we can get to the movement of the elements: to the flight of birds, the poise of animals. Nowhere is this more true than in the so-called "slow dance" of T'ai Chi and Chi Kung — an ancient Chinese technique which I have studied and taught for twenty years. It is slow, exact, subtle. Because of this, it is sometimes hard to attract students, addicted, as most westerners are, to the quick fix of the gym and "feeling the burn". Even yoga has to be action-packed and sweat inducing.

But classical T'ai Chi is very different. Its movements coalesce into a twenty-five minute sequence which takes you, symbolically, through the three stages of life — childhood, adulthood, old age — so that every time you practise it, you rehearse your whole life, and death, going round in a daily cycle of becoming and falling away. Some people love it immediately, others are afraid of the precision and slowness it demands. It is always a reflection of your own state of being. When Tim was close to death, I had no energy for T'ai Chi: it was too rigorous, too truthful. But now that I am stronger, no longer in the depths, it is calling me back.

50

7 February I tidied up the borders in my front garden, squatting on my haunches to turn the earth over with a trowel. The wind was blowing, and brought a sweetness to the air. There are crocuses coming under my little trees: the tenderest of shoots in the bleakest month. Later, I noticed a blackbird — a bright, bonny creature — bouncing along in the freshly turned soil, hunting for worms with its inquisitive yellow beak. A bunch of daffodils I bought at the weekend (as a sneak preview of spring) have just come into bloom on the window sill. They smell, deliciously, of honey.

My working life has always been somewhat erratic and anarchic. For ten years, from 1994 to 2004, I was nailed to the mast, a lot of the time, by Tim's illness and by the desire, in the early years of her life, to be with Molly a lot, because her father often could not be (either mentally or physically). In the days when he was working, he was out till the evening. She would sometimes be in bed by the time he had grappled with the commute home (from north to south London, when we lived in Stockwell; and from Bradford, across town to the north of Leeds, once we had moved to Yorkshire). When, in 2000, he stopped going out to work, and was based at home, they had more time together. He was still well enough to play with her — she, at six, loved make-believe games and dressing up, and they both shared a tremendous capacity for silliness.

Things got a lot harder as his health deteriorated. She was frustrated sometimes. Why would he not wake

51

up and play? But she adjusted to his rhythms. Close to the end of his life, when she was eleven, they shared a lot of mute companionship, just cuddled up watching children's television. Tim adored television. His daughter inherited his passion.

Yet, despite the love they shared, I was the physical and emotional glue in the household. Tim never felt able to discuss his illness with Molly — he could not find the words and left the painful conversations, the fielding of difficult questions, to me; and his energy was so low, as the disease progressed, that I had to run the house for both of them, shielding Molly from the worst episodes of Tim's illness, and shielding Tim from the tireless efforts of his daughter to engage him, when all he could do was surrender to his disease and sleep. There was no room in my life for paid work: if I had a full-time job, any job, the family would have fallen apart.

But even without the cancer to cope with, I was never really nine-to-five office material. I started off respectably enough. In 1979, when I left university with a reasonable degree in languages, I made a beeline for London and worked as a trade journalist for a year, in a conglomerate just off Fleet Street — back in the days when that address still had significance, just. It was the only nine-to-five job I have ever done, and I learned my trade assiduously, but loathed being tied down in time and place. In 1981 I left and became a freelancer: a crazy, penniless existence, but with an emphasis on the word "free".

For the next decade I ran from deadline to deadline, reviewing and writing background pieces about the arts, and in particular theatre, oblivious to the glamour of the actors, writers and directors I was meeting daily. It was just the air I breathed.

But somewhere along the way, in my late twenties, I became ill and disillusioned. Writing about other people's art — seeing rather than doing, criticizing and analysing rather than being immersed in the medium myself — began to pall. And I was living in the fast lane, working all day, reviewing theatre — and partying — well into the night. I did not take care of myself.

In my late twenties I had surgery on a long-undiagnosed ovarian cyst. It took me a while to recover, and in the journey back to health, via yoga, and especially T'ai Chi, I discovered a particular passion for contemporary dance. Already thirty, I started a postgraduate training at the Laban Centre for Movement and Dance in London; performed, directed and worked with actors and drama students: not writing about them now, but training them. Throughout it all, T'ai Chi was burning, like a slow fossil fuel. It was my link to the earth, before ever I dreamed of the garden.

One of the final movements in the T'ai Chi sequence, "Pick up the Lotus Flower", is described thus by one of the medium's greatest western exponents, Gerda Geddes:

The lotus represents everything that is (lovely), so before you depart from this world, you pick up the lotus as if to say, "Thank you for everything that was beautiful in this life."

People — myself included — are often frightened to visit the dying. They see their own death before them — and, in a society where success is predicated on youth, good looks and the perfect body, it is challenging to witness a body ravaged by illness, transformed from its previous, healthy incarnation. But beauty comes in unexpected guises. In 1990, when the first of my contemporaries — Patrick — became ill, and was dying of AIDs, I was struck, one day, by his enormous grace. Often he struggled, with panic and horror, at the deep and difficult process his body endured, but sometimes — and on this day in particular — he was calm and quiet. When I went in to visit, he was sitting half-propped up by pillows, resting his emaciated body. When he turned his face — one which had turned so many heads in his dancing days — towards me, I felt a sense of transcendence.

"You're beautiful," I said, and meant it.

"So are you," he replied, and smiled. The dying are generous, too.

Tim, in his turn, had a haunting loveliness about him, as his body wasted and he was on the verge of death. Beyond the ugly symptoms he had to endure was something far deeper and more lasting. It was there after his death too, when I visited his body, the morning he died. It has to do with the spirit of a person, their undiluted essence. This is the gift the dying offer to the living, if we can bear to take it.

54

* * *

I have always struggled with a great opposition: the life of the mind and the life of the body. Writing; dancing — with a great gulf in between. Only now, at nearly fifty years old, are the two drives softening and uniting within me. I wonder how long a person needs in their life to become properly focused? To their dying breath, I suspect. That was certainly what I noticed in Tim. The nearer the end, the clearer he got. (There's nothing like a deadline, for sharpening the senses.) Being a gardener — thinking about and shaping the physical world whilst ankle-deep in dirt and experiencing it — is certainly helpful: a natural lesson in balance.

The garden in February has a downward pull. The soil is heavy: it lures you towards it. Then, when you succumb and kneel right down (making lovely mud patches in the fronts of your jeans), a different energy emerges. The bulbs defy gravity better than we can. The shoots are there, of the early spring flowers — hundreds and hundreds of them, sparking into growth. Dig around, with fork or fingers, in a patch which isn't busy with bulbs. Loosen the surface, and pick up a handful of earth, on a dry enough day for it to let you. It may look sad and old from above, but get really close, and it smells full of promise and zest; enjoy the feel of it — it's ready for action.

8 February I have been reading old journals. When Tim became ill with cancer in 1994, I started to document the tortuous progress of his illness, as a way to make sense of something chaotic and overwhelming. Writing is useful: it contains, clarifies, creates a useful distance and perspective. That, at least, is the theory. In practice, the writing process — the diary of this dreadful disease — was arduous and debilitating. I picked up, and put down, my pen over and over again in a ten-year dance with death and dying. The resulting notes are patchy, often overwrought, and wholly incomplete.

And if writing were hard, reading the entries, even now, long after the journey's end, fills me with a deep and pervasive nausea. Not just because the story was never going to have a happy outcome, but because the suffering Tim's cancer caused — to him and those around him — remains undiminished by time or distance.

I often felt, as we went through different stages of treatment, remission, recurrence, that this was some kind of private war, fought on the battleground of Tim's body, its repercussions played out in the minds of the onlookers. My diaries, usually written in times of acute distress, have the tone of raw news: dispatches from the front. I realize now that this is not enough. Hope has to be found: a brightness in anyone's dark. I had to walk into the garden to find mine. Whenever the tension in the house — or even just in my head — became too much, I would fling open the front door and walk around the borders. Before long, the chatter in my brain would start to ebb, and the pressing need to weed, prune, or tidy some wayward shrub or ailing plant, would inevitably take over. The balance returned.

But some facts are unalterable. My diary gives me 8 February 1999 as the date a course of chemotherapy started for Tim, at St James's Hospital, Leeds. He had been told, at the end of 1998, that his disease, five years on from diagnosis, was now terminal. Tumours were multiplying along his spine, in his chest and on the lymph nodes. Old tumours, reduced by surgery and radiotherapy in the early years, were also steadily regrowing. Palliative care remained the only way forward. Except for one thing. Chemotherapy is almost never successful for this type of cancer, but they wanted to try it in the vain hope of success. Dacarbazine was the drug they chose. (Chemotherapies always have hideous, dettol-flavoured names, like laboratory rat poison. On initial diagnosis, in 1994, Tim was given huge doses of a drug combination with this charming acronym: CHOP. It succeeded only in making him deadeningly sick.)

There were no immediate side effects this time around: just a sinister lull. Then, one week after treatment, he began to withdraw, mentally and physically. Catatonia set in. Soon he developed a raging temperature, was rushed into hospital with a urine infection (possibly triggered by the treatment), and given high doses of intravenous antibiotics. The chemotherapy had no curative — and certainly no palliative — effect. It simply caused another alarm, a further complication.

It is easy to be angry about the many times the treatment offered to Tim made him ill — seemingly worse than he had been before. And yet in 1994 surgery saved him; in 1997 radiotherapy gave him time. The many drugs he swallowed, over ten years, certainly caused terrible side effects, but this was the price he paid for wanting to live. And at the root of it all was kindness. Kindness in the male nurse, who calmly and efficiently administered the chemotherapy drugs on that February morning in 1999. Kindness in the doctors who prescribed the regime, knowing that the chances of it doing any good were slender, but risking it, for their stoical patient — at forty-one, a contemporary of many of them — and for the sake of a "maybe". In the name of hope.

Many were the hospitals and clinics, doctors' surgeries and outpatients departments where Tim and I sat and stared, as we waited for him to be seen. The ones I remember most clearly were the ones where nature and art were present, to soften the deadening wait, the awful tedium, the anxious consultations and threatening clinical procedures. The presence of a picture to divert the eye — like a beautiful mandala on the wall of the radiotherapy unit in Cookridge, Leeds, which I spent at least an hour staring at once while Tim saw his consultant, letting it lead me into a soothed and almost meditative state — or, more importantly, a green garden outside, to watch or walk in, makes a world of difference, both to patient and companion, in difficult times.

I remember the woods near Cookridge in winter, cold but beautiful — it was an old isolation hospital, surrounded by trees. Tim and I walked there sometimes, stamping over bracken, getting the smell of illness out of our nostrils, and enjoying the sweet

58

dampness of moss and lichen; the stillness of the old stones. I remember a beautiful water garden at the Royal Brompton Hospital in London — where Tim had major chest surgery in 1994 — which brought a sense of smoothness, depth, fluidity, with its pebbles and green planting, to a situation fraught with the jagged edges of shock. I remember the tranquil walled grounds of St Gemma's Hospice in Leeds: the flowers so colourful and serene.

But I try to forget the ugly blunt corridors and brutal entrances of St James's; the hard surfaces of the local doctors' surgery, with not one intact magazine to read, but with bars at the window and plain concrete outside; Accident & Emergency — forget, forget, forget; the midnight chemist's at the station, surrounded by junkies and vomit . . . I have a lot of forgetting to do. The quality of the experience ensures the quality of recovery — whether physical or emotional. With green in the equation, everything cools and clears, and the worst of times can be sustained.

I used to hate February, and wrote about it once as "the deadest month", dreary and dull. I feel different now. I look with a keener eye for signs of growth, and there are many. February 2005 has been mild so far, and the earth is pulsing with life. Beauty is all in the becoming. The clumps of snowdrops massing at the fringes of our little local wood and in people's front gardens — their small, grey-green stems huddled together for support, soft white flower buds swelling within the ranks — are far more exciting to me than the fully-bloomed specimens which will emerge as February progresses. Just like Christmas, much of the gardener's joy lies in dreams and anticipation.

In the winter months outside, I am forced to be busy, to keep moving. Even mild Februaries in Yorkshire are hard on the extremities. I miss the languid pleasure of being in the open air and warm enough to settle into quiet. I have always craved solitude and silence. This drives my over-occupied friends crazy, and it was a luxury I could rarely indulge during ten years of caring for Tim day and night; but being alone — sweetly drifting — remains a strong need.

Before I could read, before I could even walk, I would sit on a blanket in the garden, so my mother later told me, and hold a little Victorian hardback, called *Progress and Poverty*, in my hands. Perfectly still. Not reading — but escaping?

I certainly discovered the use of books early — to avoid confrontation and argument in a noisy family — and loved them passionately. Once I could read, each book became a separate world. I would reinvent myself — have a different life, entirely — each time I started a new story. And the greatest beauty of the book was that it could be closed whenever I grew tired of my new territory. In this way I had power and control, when really I was helpless; a child.

Like the child on the blanket that I once was, Tim sought solace in reading — but towards the end of his life rather than at its beginning. He would sit for hours in the front garden, in summer, consuming acres of newsprint, and book after book, putting one down only to pick up another. Fiction became his playground and his travel pass, his escape from a painfully constricted situation into an unfettered fantasy world, where he could enjoy a life that life itself now denied him: space, and time, and freedom.

Here is a hymn to the humble broad bean. Like onions, these beans are winter survivors. Although they can be planted in spring, I try to sow a few in toilet-roll tubes (very classy) in the autumn, to start a good strong root run, and then plant them — tubes included — in the ground, to take their chances. Hope always triumphs over experience, because they do get horribly bashed about by winter's meanness — chewed by mice, pecked by birds, buffeted by winds and icy rain. But one or two plants always survive.

Come February, they nestle next to the onion patch, vying with their neighbours for a badge of courage — and they gladden my heart. The flowers, when they arrive in spring, are rather pretty — white clusters with a black-eyed blob at their centre — and the beans themselves are so glamorous, resting in their grey leather jackets in fat, fur-lined pods. It is worth growing them just for the fun of podding, but of course they taste delicious too (and are packed with protein), an odd, humming smoothness coming on the tongue and lingering at the back of the throat, once your teeth have pierced those tough little skins.

★ ★ ★

61

10 February It is my daughter's half-term holiday, traditionally time to take a breather and get outside, but for now the garden and the allotment must fend for themselves. I am spending much of my free time travelling up and down the A1, visiting my parents — who are both very poorly — in Essex. My father has discovered the reason for his persistent cough — some kind of growth obstructing the lung — and my mother has just had an operation for a fractured hip. This fracture went undiagnosed for many months, a signal to me not only of Kathleen's indomitable toughness (she was crawling around in constant pain for many weeks), but also of a certain disregard for the pains of the elderly, which is both saddening and insulting.

It took the persuasion of my elder brother, and an alert doctor in Accident & Emergency, finally to diagnose the break. After this, in January, things moved swiftly. Quick admission; effective surgery; equally speedy discharge home. But post-operative complications have set in at home, and her wound is infected. We push to get her readmitted. Kathleen is outraged: the last place she wants to be is back in hospital, but there is no alternative. Indomitable no longer, my mother grows weaker by the day.

When I go in to visit her today, I take some fat bunches of shop-bought daffodils, which cheer her a little. My mother's spring garden is always glorious. Every autumn for many years she has planted more bulbs, and the resulting mass of blooms make a feast for tired eyes. Now, as the garden prepares to launch itself into another spring parade, Kathleen, for the first time in forty years, will not be there to see it. The shop daffodils, in a vase by her hospital bed, are poor consolation.

12 February Back to Leeds, and my own little garden, so much smaller than my parents' and very different in style. What started out, in 1996, as a bald grassy patch with narrow, empty beds, bordered by a privet hedge along two sides and a wide, plain concrete drive along the third, has become, through the years, a wild and whimsical jungle of foliage, with trees, shrubs and bamboo all crowding each other out, and vying for attention — brushing your face and body with their wayward branches as you enter the tiny central space.

There are no opulent herbaceous borders, and I am bad at bulbs, so in winter and spring there is precious little to see. Come May, and the copper and bright green foliage emerges, branches shoot up from the ground almost overnight, and nature's alchemy sets to work.

Right now, apart from an occasional snowdrop and the striped stems of crocus, it looks a little threadbare — which is entirely how I feel. To make matters worse, there are craters and bare roots here and there (thrown into stark relief by the ruthless exfoliation of winter), where I have plundered the borders for tasty-looking specimens to populate the allotment pond and, as usual, have failed to clear up after myself. All my energy — like a new love — is being diverted into this other piece of land. The demanding mistress.

I put my feet up in the evening with a copy of the trusty *Kitchen Garden*, full of useful tips and advice (as well as fat seed catalogues in January), and beautifully illustrated throughout with gleaming vegetables and leafy growth, framed by impossibly manicured plots. (How times change. When I was a child it was *Look and Learn*. With puberty came *Jackie*, then *Cosmopolitan*, then the heady militant days of *The Leveller*, *Spare Rib*, *Marxism Today* and *Tribune*, most of which I both read and wrote for. Now it has all bedded down to *Kitchen Garden*.)

I read today that allotment people are either Farmers or Gardeners. This rings true. When I look around at the other plots on my site, there are some which resemble quaint and lovely Elizabethan potagers, with forget-me-nots and cherry blossom, and even a tiny lawn. Others are set in gulag mode, stripped to the bare essentials, with brown efficient earth producing row upon row of fat, splendid crops, and never a single flower to disrupt the yield. I am definitely a gardener. I insist on beauty and diversion at every turn, which makes me a ridiculous under-achiever in the cropping stakes.

In February, I would be hard pushed to prove my aesthetic credentials — my land is as bare and bleak as the Russian steppes. But spring and summer will change all that. I must force myself to remember the loveliness that has disappeared, like Persephone, into the underworld — ornamental rhubarb, plume poppy, allium, daffodil and tulip — and be confident that it will fully return. If it can stay in the mind — this is my hope and belief — then nothing, no memory, no person, no deep, enriching experience, is ever truly lost. February is a bit of a lost month. But March is already on the horizon.

16 February As we go into the last two weeks of February, we have been smitten with snow and cold. The allotment is abandoned in favour of blankets and books and fortifying red wine. Outdoors cannot be entirely abandoned, however. There is always Muffin the dog to walk, and, unlike her grumpy owner, Muffin loves the winter. She is now eight, and has come a long way since we rescued her, via the RSPCA, in 1999. Then her coat was sparse, flesh meagre, and tail a thin long droopy string. Now, she is plump, with thick fur, plume-like tail, and a gleam in her eye. She has so much hair these days that summers can be a trial, leaving her hot, limp and exhausted. But brisk winter mornings put a bounce in her step, and snow delights her. At the slightest dusting, she runs in ever-decreasing circles, snout down, snuffling and sneezing with joy.

Muffin is my chief gardening companion. She enjoys the allotment — so much more space to roam than at home — and, when the weather is warmer, quickly settles down in some grassy corner to snooze, lifting her muzzle from time to time to sniff the air. Peace is only disturbed by the passing of an occasional cat, since where cats are concerned, Muffin obeys only one internal command. CHASE. She invariably ends up in the wild bramble hedge at the far end of the allotment, and has a devil of a time disentangling herself.

Invariably, a twig or brown crinkled leaf breaks free with her, hanging from her ear like some wild gipsy jewel.

We had a dog throughout my childhood — another crazy mongrel called Tess — who was a powerful ally of mine. Always an anxious little individual, I often had some inexplicable ache, whether physical or existential, which I could never quite share with another human being. So I gained great comfort from lying on the floor, stroking and playing with the dog, whispering long streams of nonsense words into her hairy, understanding ear.

Tim did not grow up with animals, although he had a natural affinity with them, and dogs were his particular favourite. Quite late in his illness, I suggested getting one, for company and diversion.

For a while I had wanted a pet for Molly, too. I thought it would be nice for her, as an only child, to have another creature around; instead of rolling on the floor with a brother or sister, she could at least have play fights with a dog. The problem was, in those days, she loved cats more than dogs, and the neighbours were scared of cats, so that was out. But when she met Muffin, at the RSPCA rescue centre, she immediately liked her. Muffin's jumpiness unnerved her a little — though she soon found a way of calming the dog, climbing into her basket, carefully grooming and crooning to her, with a patience the adults could not muster. Their bond has been steadfast since then.

Tim was wary of her, too, at first. Being a clean and tidy man, he found it hard to adjust to having an animal in the house — muddy paws, fur balls on the carpet, and the occasional disgusting pile left in the hall for us to tread on in the morning — but he grew to love Muffin deeply, and she took care of him to the end, lying quietly at his feet or under his bed, always close by, silent. On our last visit to the hospice, Muffin came along. Tim barely realized she was there, but I took his hand and placed it on her head. She gave him one gentle lick. For weeks after he died she looked for him everywhere.

There is nothing like a dog for getting you out and about. I have walked in woods and fields where I would never have dared go alone. The dog is my direct link to nature — she makes me leave the house, makes me walk. On my travels with her I meet other dog walkers — some chatty, some lost in their own inner worlds, but all there treading the old paths, retracing old steps, continuing the ancient ritual, one foot in front of the other — under the trees, by the lakes in the park, under the sky (even in the pouring rain).

When, at the end of life, the time for walking is over, a dog can still be an invaluable companion. Touch — that fundamental sensory stimulus — remains a primary need, even when the other senses start to fail. The softness of a dog's fur under your hand can be an immeasurable comfort, and it is no wonder that dogs are used in hospices as therapeutic aids. Someone I teach told me that one dog, who was a regular visitor to the wards at a local hospice, was so loved by a patient that, when this patient died, the dog was invited as guest of honour at her wake.

28 February Time to chit some potatoes. An arcane gardening word — "chitting" — and inherently comic, almost scatological. I once had a marvellous crop of potatoes, grown in a double-layered dustbin liner outside our back door. The method was simple: roll down the liner to a few inches high; fill it with a mix of soil and manure; place four or five "chitted" potatoes on the surface; cover with another layer of soil, then wait for foliage to appear. Keep adding soil/manure, and rolling up the sides of the bag, as the haulms (stems and foliage to you and me) get taller. Only the leaves need the sun — the rest of the plant needs dirt and dark, for the tubers to develop and not to go green. When you get to the top of the liner, just water and wait.

This was the same year that *Gardeners' Question Time* on Radio 4 came to Shadwell in Leeds, and I asked Bob Flowerdew when to harvest my crop. He threw me completely when he asked if they were Early or Maincrop potatoes. I had chucked away the sack label weeks before, and had no idea. Oops.

In the end, I waited until I could bear it no longer, and the sack was groaning with leafy growth, then, in midsummer, cut back the tops and plunged my hands in, foraging for gold . . . My reward was rich: a tightly packed treasure trove of lovely, tasty potatoes. I could not believe my luck. I have never dared try it again.

How could I follow that? But this year I must. I cannot have an allotment without growing potatoes.

Chitting is easy. Buy a bag of seed potatoes from a garden centre, place them in egg boxes, "eyes" upward, on a cool window ledge, and let them catch the light. After a few weeks some healthy green sprouts should emerge (not the white worms of neglected eating spuds) which, once it is planted, will kick-start the potato into growth. Earlies in mid-spring (to beat the potato blight), and maincrop in late spring. It is not an exact art. As to how to plant them — that is as varied as the individual gardener who does it. I simply intend to dig a trench, put the potatoes in, shoots up, and cover them with a foot of earth, and hope for the best. For now, simple chitting is the task.

I was sheltered from death all through my early life and well into adulthood. When relatives died, even important ones like my grandfather and uncle, I was kept away from the funerals. That was the custom then. Protect the children. It was a convention I cannot quite reconcile myself to, even now. So the first death to have a proper impact was that of my beloved grandmother, when I was thirty. Although she was in her nineties, although the death was natural, peaceful, to be expected, I howled with disbelief when the call came. It was as if I had been punched in the stomach, leaving me winded for months. At last, I was growing up.

After this, death began to stalk me with increasing regularity. This was the early nineties, when AIDs cut a swathe through the young gay community in England

and America. There was no cure, no prophylaxis then, and the treatment was blunt and brutal. Superstition and fear stalked the hospital wards. I knew a number of gay men in London; some were very close friends. In February 1990, the first of them succumbed to the disease.

Patrick and I had lost contact for a while. I had not realized how badly his health had deteriorated. So it came as a shock when he rang me one evening, quite out of the blue, from his hospital ward. His voice, once brazenly sexy, deep and strong, was now unrecognizably feeble. I struggled to identify who it was from the rasping tones, the gasps and silences, even suspecting a hoax. Then he spoke his name.

"It's Patrick. Will you come and see me? And bring some quiet tapes, some flower remedies and oils?"

I acquiesced at once, but with some trepidation. I was unused, then, to hospitals, and had no idea what I would find when I got there. But there had always been a gentle, humorous bond between Patrick and me, a shared interest in alternative therapies, a love of quiet classical music, Chopin and Brahms, a certain tenderness. I could not refuse him now.

I felt faintly sick, and very nervous, as I made my way up to the ward of the Middlesex Hospital. He was in a small room on his own, and when I went in, I smelt the smell of disintegration. Patrick lay, crumpled, on his high hospital bed. Once muscular and toned — a trained dancer — he now looked entirely wasted. Around him was the litter of well-wishers — half-eaten bits of fruit, cards, flowers — all with the stain of putrefaction. To this day, I cannot look at a star fruit without remembering Patrick, and I never buy them.

Here was a man reduced to nothing. Barely thirty, he was frightened and dying. His death took several days, amidst volatile scenes and desperate struggles. It is different these days. The nursing is kinder; the drugs are more sophisticated; the terrible prejudice is reduced. But the shock of his death has never left me: such a brutal counterpoint to the elegance and style of the man, cut down in his prime.

I like to think Patrick would have become a gardener. Of all my male city friends from that time, he is the most likely to have gone green. He had a natural talent for making his surroundings look lovely. Even the tiny ground-floor council flat he rented in Stockwell, south London — on an estate so broken down, both physically and morally, that he once sat and watched as two guys brazenly pushed a neighbour's stolen fridge-freezer past his back door in broad daylight — was swathed in soft colours, glittering crystals and quiet grace. There was no garden outside his window, but there should have been.

We ended January this year in the cold, dark and wet; but February has come to a close in bright, sharp frost and snow.

Seven years ago, in 1998 — a transitional time in Tim's life, before his condition became terminal, and a year I seemed to document more closely than others — I recorded a mild end to February. Smell and colour dominated my diary then, as it does now. February makes me hunger for stimulus, for the wake-up call of spring.

In 1998, as a recent refugee from the brick and concrete of a south London estate, all things outside — even gardens themselves — seemed novel and exciting. The simplest things delighted me. They still do. Like the pungent smell of a flowering currant bush, brushed past in a neighbour's garden one morning on the way to school, releasing its heady aroma, so similar to the blackcurrant fruit itself. (How clever of plants to mimic the taste of the fruit within the smell of the leaf — rub a strawberry plant, and you will see what I mean. Smell the growing bush of the tomato long before its flowers form, and the promise of its fruit is already there in your waiting nostrils.)

One tiny forget-me-not, pale blue, popped out on the last day of February 1998. I was so desperate to see it bloom, I wrote a detailed note describing it. And I noticed a blue flower coming through the dark geometrical leaves of the periwinkle plant near my front door. (Both these flowers have long since left my garden. I don't know where they went — probably to a neighbour's garden down the road, via the wind or a bird's beak. Nature manages these changes with a careless shrug of the shoulders. Easy come, easy go. I am trying for the same insouciance.)

Colour and scent: the offer of both mystery and pleasure. Why do yellow (witch hazel, daffodil) and blue (rosemary, crocus) seem to dominate the early months of flowering (after the winter white purity of the snowdrop)? There will be a reason, scientific and sound. But to me those colours are clear symbols of hope and promise: canary sunshine in a cloudless blue sky.

I don't mind the frost of this year's February — it wakes up my brain. And I still like the taste of fresh snow on my tongue, just as I did when a child. There is vigour and clarity in the cold air. But let's get this done with quickly now. A bit more light, please, and the stealing in of warmth from the weary old sun. Roll on spring.

Jobs for February

- Pile on the manure, if you have an allotment, and then dig, dig, dig. (I used to get a delivery to my front door from a farmer in North Yorkshire, to mulch the front garden. But it doesn't half pong. The neighbours will hate you.) Or pray for snow, in which case, you'll just have to stay inside, won't you?
- Plant a dogwood, *Cornus alba*. Their gorgeous, glossy red stems will add some fire to a dead garden.
- Buy some seed potatoes and put them in egg boxes, eye side up, to "chit" some green shoots for planting in spring.
- French marigolds can be sown in February. Great for cheerful colour in your borders later in the year, and to control pests in your garden.
- Cress can be grown at any time of the year. Easy peasy, and lovely in an egg sandwich.

March

The temple bell stops
but the sound keeps coming
out of the flowers.

Zen Master Matsuo Basho

It does not matter what the weather is doing. As soon
as March begins, then — for me — spring has arrived.
I love the seasons of change, autumn and spring, best
of all. You never quite know what will happen next.
Spring, as its bouncy name suggests, is particularly full
of mischief, and I find myself very stirred by its arrival.

March was always the month when Tim began to
have more energy, even in his sickliest times. Like a
hibernating dormouse, he would start to blink his eyes
at the world outside and find some extra strength as the
sap began to rise. Housework — always a chore —
came very low on my list of priorities at the height of
my role as nurse-cum-carer, but even I would be
shamed into action in March: the vernal light shining
into every mucky corner. Spring cleaning. It's true, I do
start to polish my little world more when the new year
— and this is the real new year to me — kicks in. Early
spring is rarely gentle. The earth has to crank

everything into growth, and the weather is whipping up storms, blowing in ears, and nipping relentlessly at fingers, noses and toes. This is not the time for sloths. Every impulse is to action. Stand by your spades.

4 March Four days in, and the weather has already stopped play. We have snow, quite a lot of it. All plans for digging and mulching have had to be halted for the time being. I have returned to the drawing board, to think about my peas. At present, they are neat and tidy, shoots an inch or so high, in little pots sown early on my kitchen window sill. This is the good bit: they look so keen, green and hopeful. But the worst thing about growing vegetables is the intricate aftercare. Often they need supporting, with complicated constructions of wigwams, sticks and canes, and nearly always have to be netted against the onslaught of birds and vermin; those mighty predators. Peas, in particular, have delicate shoots which need something to grab hold of in their pursuit of height, light and air. It's a tricky business.

As usual, there is a wealth of conflicting information in the gardening books: should it be a double row, or single? What kind of support? How wide or narrow should the spacing be between plants? I settle on the simplest scheme possible — a single, jaunty diagonal row, on the patch down by the apple tree, plants four inches apart, set about with leggy branches for support and a net thrown over for good measure. As yet, of course, it is totally theoretical, since we are ankle deep in snow. I must content myself with daft little diagrams and dreaming. Am I becoming a pea-obsessive?

Clematis montana alba. For an early show of bright, white flowers, on vigorous climbing stems, with abundant fronded leaves and foliage, this plant is superb. I have one growing up the arch in my front garden. I planted it one autumn. It streaked up the support in a single season, and then abseiled across to the apple tree, waving its arms towards the road and clothing the whole top corner in beautiful wedding-bell finery, from March to June. It has repeated its show every spring since then, and is a cheerful and pretty performer, so early in the season. It should be welcome in any garden happy to accommodate its tendency to show off and sprawl.

7 March I bought ten new raspberry canes, a pound a piece. Bare, dead-looking sticks, with short straggly tails for roots, it takes a hefty imagination to see fat ruby fruits ever growing on these prickly individuals. But they will. "Autumn Bliss" is the variety, chosen for their lovely name (I am an autumn baby) and the fact that they are modest growers, height-wise, and do not need supporting. One job less to do. The metal pole and wire barricades I have seen at the allotment, supporting the taller, more top-heavy raspberry breeds, are entirely daunting and rather ugly. Not a hope in hell that I might build something like that. No, I praise the self-supporters of the fruit and veg world, and carry on my search for the easy way out.

I planted all ten canes down by the compost bin, in my raggedy, boggy, beleaguered fruit patch, spacing them about twelve inches apart. And there they now sit, valiant foot soldiers of mud, drizzle and filthy greyness. May they bear dazzling jewels, come September, and may the birds not pilfer them first.

8 March At home, I have a little plastic greenhouse. It cost all of £5 from B & Q and is perfect for outside the back door, perched on the concrete drive by the old coal shed. It works beautifully, as this is a south-facing wall and catches what minimal sun we have, all year round: everything I sow in it pushes through happily, on somewhat haphazard trays, under a pale plastic sky.

I planted some more peas and broad beans out here, because my narrow window sill is full of the ones I started off in January and my broad bean population needs a boost after the winter's depredations. Also, I sowed an early summer cabbage with a pointy, pale green head, called "Hispi" — delicious, apparently, with lots of melted butter. Something about this pretend greenhouse, and the pots of seeds tucked inside, made me very hopeful for spring.

9 March Today, I planted a small sumach tree, *Rhus laciniata* — just like the one in my front garden — at the top corner of my allotment, by the shed, in honour of Tim. It came from my friend Sumi's garden, whose voluptuous borders shimmer with abundance all summer. I have high hopes for any plant which starts life with her.

I first fell in love with the sumach in 1995, when I watched one week by week in a south London park, as it went through a particularly beautiful autumnal metamorphosis — its lacy leaves turning from soft green to burnt orange, to glowing yellow, to incinerator red, before dropping, suddenly, to nothing: all bare sticks, after a spectacular funeral pyre. What a way to go! Since then I have wanted one with me in every garden, it is such a graceful, dainty little tree. And tough as old boots.

It rained relentlessly as I dug the hole for planting. Correction: it poured — stair rods from heaven. Cutting through the thick, matted grass with my spade into the heavy, water- and weed-logged clay beneath was an act not of faith, but of pure unadulterated folly. But the wetter and more isolated I became (not another soul in sight — human, bird or animal — in such appalling conditions), the more cussed I felt. This damn tree was going to be planted, come what may.

The spot I chose was one that Tim had gravitated to, on his rare visits to Oakwood Lane in the summer of 2003, just before he was admitted to the hospice. He would totter up to our plot at the far, wild corner of the allotments, in his thin, wavery way (it was climbing Everest for him, just to get there without falling), and then sit for a long time to recover.

At the side of the shed was an old water butt, a rusty metal chair and a layer of rubble, stones and bricks, which someone must have used to build with, once upon a time. Not the most attractive spot on the plot. But Tim still spent one whole oblivious afternoon there, sitting on an old wooden board on the ground in the hot sun, picking out stones meticulously: attempting, in his painstaking way, to make order in this one small, barren place.

How different we were in life, he and I: me rushing around breathlessly, trying to take in the WHOLE of it, sorting out the big vision; him honing in on some small detail and working at it doggedly, diligently. It made sense that this particular area should be in memory of him — made sense that I, too, had to struggle as he had done, had to be determined, in order to get the little tree into its rightful place. One small corner of wet unwelcoming ground. I did it in the end, no ducking out, but was absolutely sodden by the time it was done. And thoroughly bad-tempered.

It is hard to remember Tim as he was before he became ill. We were together for fifteen years: ten of those years were consumed by his cancer, and the four years prior to that taken up with the illness and death of several close friends.

"All our time together has been dominated by sickness," he said sadly, towards the end of his life. And it is true — except for 1989, the year we met, a year in which the summer, in my memory, was exceptionally long, hot and lovely, the autumn particularly mellow. How we bend time and memory to fit our own needs.

Still, I cannot make one year count for ten. For a long time after his death, my sleep was blank. Then the dreams came, and they were very bleak — Molly's even more so. Tim kept appearing, alone in his hospital bed, nobody there beside him; no way of reaching him or helping. Desolation for the dreamer, and for the one dreamed of. Slowly the repeated nightmare, the knife of grief stuck in the chest, started to recede. The second year of bereavement has been different: much of the raw anguish of loss has been assimilated. But still Tim feels lost to me: the well and happy Tim, the young man before he was kidnapped by his illness, is still hiding in the shadows. I will keep on digging — in the garden, in my mind — until I find him.

11 March I went down to Essex to see Mum and Dad. My mother is still in hospital, still in a room on her own because of her infection, and bored out of her mind. The word "extrovert" might have been invented for Kathleen, such is her constant need, her compulsion even, to be with other people. The solitary confinement she now suffers is a form of torture for her.

My dad is sweet and faithful, to the point of exhaustion, visiting her every day despite the rigours of the drive there and his own continuing ill-health. On his visits, he urges her constantly to eat, but she has no interest in food. Television bores her; she is too deaf for radio; books from well-wishers pile up on the window ledge, unread. She is slowly switching off. A blazing fire is going out in front of us. I feel helpless to improve her lot. I try to talk to the hospital staff, but they seem remote, and always very busy. My mother's loneliness is not their concern.

Often, these days, I try to think of an appropriate way to die — halfway through digging a hole for my cabbages, maybe, keeling over my spade in a dramatic final flourish, ending up face down, splattered in the mud. (There is a man on our allotments who has gardened there since the war. In his nineties, he has stalwartly refused to relinquish his plot. I think maybe he, too, would choose to die at the spade, close to the soil which has been beneath his feet for so many years.) Second scenario: smashed on champagne — giggling inanely, then suddenly gone. Lights out. Finish. To end, enjoying something that was so relished in life. Gardens. Champagne. That would do nicely. Anything, but these endless, faceless, sour-smelling hospital wards: places where I have had to watch some of my favourite people end their days disconsolate and lonely.

There are lighter moments. I engage in subterfuge with my father. Mum's mouth is so infected that nothing tastes good any more, but she thinks she might like a Bailey's, with plenty of ice. We take in a few mini bottles, and she gulps them down with lipsmacking satisfaction. It is definitely not what the doctor ordered, but gives her a few seconds of greedy relish, as the thick, creamy liquor slides down her throat. That's more like it. Dad buys a stock, and takes in the illicit booze each time he visits.

Last summer I bought some baby cardoon plants from a walled garden in Helmsley, North Yorkshire, and they have thrived — turning into architectural specimens of striking beauty. They boast broad silver leaves, deeply serrated, fanning out from a bold central stem, which grows tall and proud, producing spiky flower heads, with a purplish tinge, to grace the hot summer months. Already, in March, the new leaves are large and lovely, after the old ones died away to a shrivel in the winter cold.

The cardoon belongs to the thistle family, and has no culinary value (although some hardy souls claim the leaves can be cooked — yeuch!): it is on my plot because it adds an unusual majesty, and will act as a companion to the globe artichokes I want to grow later this year.

Globe artichokes look rather similar to cardoons, although they are less spiky in appearance and do not grow quite so tall. But they offer a far greater treasure for the kitchen, in the shape of fat juicy hearts surrounded by thick fleshy leaf layers, which taste delicious when cooked. Flowers — purple thistles, like the cardoon — come later, but cut some buds early for an exotic supper, and beware the bristly choke, which will do the same to you!

I have been reading about the artichoke, and realize it likes everything my plot cannot provide: maritime climate, good drainage, fertile soil, no wind, full sun. Well, in the summer we do get some sun — otherwise, it must take its chances.

A Mediterranean relative of the sunflower — hence its bonny and robust nature — the globe artichoke smacks of real glamour to me. (Nearly all the artichokes grown in the USA are found in California, and in 1949 Marilyn Monroe was the first California Artichoke Queen! There's pedigree.) I was deeply impressed when I visited the sunny summer allotment of a teacher friend in Otley, when we first moved to Leeds, and saw his abundant rows of artichokes. (I had certainly never seen such things in the Essex gardens of my childhood.) I vowed there and then to grow my own some day.

I will always remember the first artichoke I ate, not from a tin, but in the traditional manner — peeling off the fleshy leaves of the freshly-cooked bud, one by one, dipping them in melted butter and sucking out their marrow with a slurping, messy greed; then fighting over the real prize, the heart. I was with Tim and Molly — who was still quite small — on a visit to two great friends Tim had known since his theatre days, Mike and Nina.

One of Tim's first jobs after college was as an administrator for the British Theatre Association (now sadly defunct) in London. This is where he became friendly with Mike — an actor/teacher/director — who worked on the summer schools Tim ran for the BTA in the mid-1980s. I first saw Tim here too, in my incarnation as theatre journalist, though it was still a couple of years before we met properly. Nina came into the picture a little later — she, like Tim, worked backstage.

Both Mike and Nina loved Tim deeply, and always brought laughter and fun to him, however ill he was feeling. Mike is a trained chef: food matters to him, and he is always meticulous in its preparation, a quality he and Tim shared. On this particular occasion, we were sitting around their table simply eating artichokes. I do not remember the exact year — though it was summer.

But I remember the pleasure of the company, and I especially remember that curious and succulent vegetable: the ritual of eating it, slowly, messily, binding us all together in some way, through time and space.

17 March It is much warmer now, and is turning into a mild and pleasant spring. But there has been an almighty wind blowing. Up on our Yorkshire hill, we are very exposed. Unfortunately, my little greenhouse was an early casualty, and all those hopeful little pots have gone for a burton. Undaunted, I planted them again.

I am used to retracing my steps, over and over, though I still resent it, still struggle. Tim's illness took us down the same track many times, in a constant dance of remission, recurrence, hope and despair. I am an impatient person — cool on the outside, fire within — and I spent ten years wanting a solution to the deep and difficult problems caused by Tim's complicated cancer. But there was no solution, I can see that now, it was just life: messy and chaotic, often disappointing, and certainly painful, yet always remarkable.

Sometimes I look at websites and books to do with grief and loss, and the ways people seek to overcome them, particularly by growing things, by making gardens, wondering if I will find the process I am going through reflected in the experiences of others. But I am often appalled by the material written on death and bereavement. The professionals talk of pathology, that's their job. The bereaved, in their search for meaning, often err too far in the other direction, coating their sentiments in sugar and soft pastels, eulogizing the beautiful, blameless lives that are now over. Nobody seems to talk about the long, dark journey involved, the loneliness of the survivor, which is shot through with a great furious push towards the light. Nothing pretty about it.

There are honourable exceptions. Actress and writer Sheila Hancock was interviewed for Radio 4's *Woman's Hour* after the death of her husband John Thaw. "You have to be practical about grief," she said, a sentiment which has sustained me more in the months since I heard it than any amount of glorious sanctimony. You *do* have to be sturdy, to withstand all this dying. So sturdiness drives me on, tired and irritable, and makes me repot my scattered seeds when part of me, the bigger part, longs to hurl them from this side of the universe to the other, with a mighty stream of invective hurled after.

Wild garlic is a wonderful plant. It is springing up now — with bright green, glossy fanned leaves — from the damp earth in our little local wood, and on the steeply sloping banks which lead down to the river at the forest fringe of Roundhay Park. I first came across wild garlic, en masse, on a visit to friends who live in an old farmhouse in North Yorkshire. Their land leads down to a narrow valley covered in woodland. In the spring the valley's slopes are carpeted with thick green garlic from top to toe: the lacy white flowers, which come later, an added bonus to the glorious, pungent foliage. You can rip up the leaves and chuck them into soups or stews to give them an earthy kick, but I have never managed it successfully. Extracting the promise of that piercing aroma, and distilling it into taste, is a skill I lack. The leaves look limp and sad as soon as the juice is ripped from them.

Still I am delighted to be surrounded by the stuff. It is an exotic Yorkshire treat to me — I never encountered wild garlic in the South, although I never looked for it. I do now. It comes as a perfect companion to the emerging bluebells in our local wood. The bluebells boast a similar waxy sheen on leaves and stems as they push through the undergrowth in March, under the still bare oaks and beeches, looking quite different to the soft foliage — a more reticent grey — of their earlier cousins, the snowdrops.

19 March Easter is early this year. We travelled down to London to see friends in Muswell Hill. My father is due to have a tissue biopsy, to see what is causing his ghastly cough, the obstruction on his lung, and the persistent problems with his breathing. He will be in the same hospital as my mum, so I plan to visit them both while we are down south. I have a dreadful foreboding. As usual, with me, the deep worries of my unconscious convert conveniently into physical symptoms. I develop a raging sore throat and high temperature, and have no choice but to lie down for several days, leaving my friend to field the children — hers and mine — whilst I remain semi-conscious, and literally speechless. Some things are beyond words, as I am about to find out.

★ ★ ★

21 March It is the day of Dad's operation. Both my brothers are on hand to ferry him, visit Mum, and take care of both. These splendid big brothers — and their wives — are stepping into the breach. They have borne the brunt of care for Mum and Dad over the last couple of years, while I have been taken up with Tim's dying — the children becoming the parents, in a strange but somehow balancing reversal of roles. I love them for this. I cannot do it: geographically, physically or emotionally. I am spent.

I fear, when the result of the biopsy comes back, it will confirm the worst; but for now, it is a waiting game.

"He's worried, I know he is," says my mum, during one of our increasingly rare phone conversations from the hospital. This is an understatement that is totally uncharacteristic of my mother, since she is someone who has made an unpaid career out of exaggerated story-telling and hyperbole. It is an indication, both of her withdrawal from life — a damping down of her vital signs, her unique vivacity — and of her reluctant, grudging, yet bone-deep concern for the husband she has sparred with, and cleaved to, for fifty-eight long years of marriage.

22 March We travelled back to Leeds. As usual, the first thing I did after parking the car on the driveway was to leap out and check the garden — and the "greenhouse". The winds had been busy again, so some of my pesky peas are up-ended in the borders. Molly says she always feels sorry, seeing me arrive after a long journey and immediately rushing to my pots to check for casualties, shaking my head sadly at the damage. But I don't mind. As I said, it is my territory: beginning again.

Some gardens from my childhood have an almost magical significance in my memory. My grandmother's garden is one. I realize now that it was probably rather small, but to a little girl of six or seven, it seemed full of delights. My paternal grandmother (my mother's parents died long before I was born) was a kind, intelligent, gentle person. We share the same first name: Elizabeth. She had a gruelling early life in the Lancashire cotton mills — her schooling cut brutally short, in the interests of child labour, leaving her barely able to read and write. She came into her stride in her fifties, however, when she worked for a number of happy years in the same mill factories, but this time as a cook, running her own kitchens with strength and economy, whilst ensuring that the workers were always very well fed. She made mouth-watering pastry, and the smells which came from the tiny kitchen of her corporation house in Ashton-under-Lyne — of cheese and onion pie, roast chicken, Lancashire hotpot — still make me hungry, forty years later.

Her kitchen opened out on to a small lawn, beyond which was a winding path, with busy, overgrown beds on either side, leading down to a shady shed. There was an air of mystery and seclusion in this stony path, taking me down and away from the world. Grandfather had tended the garden, but by the time I knew him, he was a stroke invalid, tongue-tied and housebound. His emotions — frequent tears of frustration and outright anger — were volatile and erratic, and he could be scary to a timid child, so I was pleased to take refuge in his garden, and swing from the green wooden gate, pretending I was on a horse, galloping away.

It is ironic that this grandfather, dead by the time I was eleven and, as a result of his catastrophic illness, a virtual stranger to me all my life, left me a bigger legacy than I would ever have imagined. I discovered only when I was in my late twenties that he loved the theatre (I had already been writing on theatre for several years), and had written plays, dozens of them, for the local church.

At the church door, we part company, since God is not a reality in my life. But he was a prolific writer, the only one in the family I am aware of. And a keen gardener. He was also gone before I had a chance to say hello, let alone attend his funeral and say goodbye. Yet something of him remains, deep in my DNA. Although I long for the serenity of my grandmother, I suspect I have more than a streak of Grandad's irascibility, leaking out as the years roll by.

I was eight when my parents bought their own house in Braintree, Essex, moving us all from the rather jolly council estate near Meadowside at the other end of town (where they roasted an ox every carnival day, and I, in my feverish fancy, thought I could hear the beast wailing in the preceding days, as it awaited its own slaughter) to a semi-detached house in more secluded surroundings.

Here we inherited a long and lovely garden. At the far end was a big orchard of apple trees, owned by a nasty man with an airgun. This did not stop my two brothers scrumping, or prevent our wilful mongrel Tess from romping among the long grass for regular diversion. She was shot at, at least once, but she didn't seem to care. There were fields beyond the orchard running all the way down to the railway line. It was great for kids, and we roamed free. Now there is a fast and furious dual carriageway running through the lot, a housing estate, and a massive out-of-town shopping complex. Oh, and a McDonald's. They paved paradise, all right.

23 March It is just under a week since I replanted my "Hispi" cabbage seeds, and already sprightly shoots and baby leaves are poking through. This is impressive: there is always a second chance in the garden.

I have wrestled with the winter of people's lives for the past fifteen years. No wonder I yearn for spring, and feel my heart leap when a new baby is born. No wonder I dig. The beauty of the garden to me is not a surface distraction in my life, but a deep-rooted need for nourishment and renewal. When Patrick died of AIDs in 1990, John, closest friend and ally for nearly two decades, became ill simultaneously, and died in 1993. Later the same year, another friend, Stewart, succumbed to the same wretched disease. All three young men plundered huge resources of energy in their surviving friends. They held on tight to life, even as it was being ripped, untimely, from their grasp. It was exhausting for everyone. And yet, for me, it was just the beginning.

When I came home from Stewart's funeral in the autumn of 1993, Tim was out of sorts. Molly, then a year old, had cried and cried, and he had been unable to soothe her. He felt weak and tired, and as the autumn changed into winter the tiredness became persistent, all-pervasive. He joined a gym to try and build his strength, but this made matters worse. He caught flu and could not shake it off. He worked, and came home shattered. In 1994 came the cancer diagnosis: not an "easy" cancer, either, but one that had top-flight NHS doctors in London and Leeds scratching their heads at its complex presentations, and which was to twist and turn in him for so many years.

I would like to record an incremental growth in wisdom and strength, as I coped with my years as a carer. But I cannot. I still feel consistently at a loss. When Patrick lay dying, the first time I had witnessed such a profound and terrible process, I felt sick and sorry and sad. What he needed, I thought, was strength, calm, love, but I sat like a bewildered puppy at his bedside. The bewilderment has never left me.

Now I am a veteran carer, a chronic holder-of-hands, an emotional sponge for the deep and trenchant needs of the dying — best friend, husband, mother — but in no way the wiser, in no way sure that I have been helpful at all. This is not humility. It is the truth. But one thing I do know — I have borne witness. I never closed my eyes to the pain of those people I loved, and now it is in my bones until the day I let go and die myself. I am left with a tough and troubled heart. Maybe this is simply what it means to be human?

Strength comes to me in consistent measure, however, from the swell of new growth in the garden; the sturdy push from the earth's core, particularly in March, enters through my filthy boots, and the soles of my feet, right into the marrow of my bones. Green shoots in the spring are nothing short of miraculous. They are truly my life support machine.

26 March I am digging over the last bed on my allotment — up near the big grasses (pampas and *Stipa gigantea*) and Tim's little tree. This is where my eager cabbages will go when they grow up, so I had better get a move on.

28 March I sowed some tomato seeds, "Gardener's Delight", Brussels sprouts and carrots, "Early Nantes", in my greenhouse. I always grow tomatoes outside my back door, because the summer sun is strongest here. Whether in large pots or growbags, on the unceremonious concrete slab of a drive, they usually thrive. This year, in the chaos of imminent events, none of today's sowings — except the carrots — will survive. Never mind, my neighbour usually gives me tomato plants at some point; I'm not proud.

It is a week since I was in London, when all the worry was for my father. But over the past couple of days the focus has switched again to Mum. There have been confused family messages going back and forth about her condition. It is clear she has entered a critical stage. My mind disappears into a familiar fog.

At nine o'clock in the evening, Dad himself phones, to say that the infection in Mum's wounded hip has spread rapidly to her liver and kidneys. She is being given oxygen to help her breathe. The implications are deadly. There is no way she can survive this: she has had enough. My senses are reeling. I had not expected such a sudden and brutal end.

29 March My father has been in touch during the night, with short, grim bulletins. He phones again at 5.20a.m. to tell me that Mum has died. I have lain all night in a sore, semi-conscious state, with the phone under the pillow to stop Molly being jolted awake by the dreaded early morning call. When it comes, the talk is brief. Tender and solicitous to the last, Dad wears his suffering with an almost unbearable grace. Already I am packing a bag. Molly is not with me this time — she has seen enough trouble in her life for now — as I set off down the trusty A1 once more, to join a quiet gathering of the clan at the family house, and to start a familiar round of registering the death, arranging the funeral, and phoning a huge cohort of friends and well-wishers. Time once again to say goodbye.

Flowers can be genuinely healing at times like this, and sometimes startlingly symbolic. I bought a red camellia in 1996, the year we moved to Leeds, and kept it in a pot in our back yard. It grew and grew, with its waxy green foliage throwing an elegant shadow on to the brick and trellis surrounds. But it never produced a single bloom in eight years. Then, in 2004, two months after Tim died, it threw out a canopy of deep and vibrant red flowers, as if in his honour — as if it had something to offer now, a colourful part to play in a world turned grey. When my father phoned to tell me Mum had died, he mentioned a pink camellia that she had loved and fussed over in the back garden. It had ailed somewhat in recent years, and failed to flower, but now had come suddenly into bloom with the approach of spring, after several fallow years. He placed one pink flower on her body in the hospital, close to her heart, after she gave her last breath.

I know little of the literary language of flowers, preferring the direct, sensual communication of their colour, scent and texture. So I did not properly realize until now that the camellia, the Chinese rose, is an ancient symbol of love. Of course, I went through the usual pseudo-tragic adolescent languors, gaining most of my early emotional experience from books: sighing dutifully over Dumas' *La Dame aux camélias*, and revelling in the fate of his fallen, redeemed heroine. But it was all academic to me. Now, many years later, with word very definitely made flesh by my many losses, I am struck by the following: in flower language, the pink camellia is said to mean "Longing for you"; and the red one, "You are a flame in my heart."

My mother was born in the spring, and has died in the spring too. This was her season: she had the vigour and energy of a young lamb, a capacity to love children — and to be like a child herself, bouncing around from one thing to the next, with huge enthusiasm — right

94

into her eighties. I cannot begin to imagine the gap she leaves in my life. This is too much, too soon, after losing Tim. With each person who dies, there is a long break, before they return to me, integrated in memory and thought. Sometimes this takes years. With my mother, it will be the work of a lifetime. She was, of course, at my life's core. It is like having the umbilical cord cut all over again, and I am adrift.

My parents' Essex garden — Kathleen's beloved spring display — looks wonderful at the moment. In the front there are vibrant, fronded peonies, pushing towards fruition in thick sturdy clumps; daffodils and tall yellow tulips are coming to flower; grape hyacinths give a gentle hint of blue skies ahead; the sword-sharp leaves of the day lily offer sculpture, definition; and the tiny crocuses, so recently jaunty, are creeping away in deference to their clamorous late-March neighbours. This is a teeming mass of activity: appropriately matching the vitality of its creator.

In the back garden, the *Clematis montana* "Elizabeth", a birthday present one year from me to my mother, is vigorous, and about to bloom. Beyond the low wall, where the birds flock to feed, hides the gentle pink camellia. Under the tamarisk tree beyond that, pretty fritillaries nod their heads. Everywhere you look, the foliage is a lush bright green. As the spring season takes hold, life pushes forth urgently, from soil and stem. Newness is in everything. Buds and flowers are fat to bursting, and the garden is in full song. How can my mother be dead?

Jobs for March

- If you have the space, plant some autumn-growing raspberry canes. They produce really tasty fruits, and the bushes grow quite neatly.
- If you don't have a greenhouse, buy a little plastic one. They work. Sow some vegetable seeds, like peas, broad beans, tomatoes and carrots.
- Plant some good value climbers and bushes, like the butterfly bush, or a spring-flowering clematis.
- Architectural value in a plant — such as the artichoke and cardoon — is always good. It's fun to grow these in a garden, as well as on the allotment. They are striking, and produce foliage and structure most of the year round.
- Camellias can be a little demanding. They must have ericaceous compost, or acid soil, and may take several years to produce flowers. But when they do, it is a marvel. And the glossy green leaves are decorative too.
- Snake's head fritillary. These delicate little flowers pop out early in spring. Very, very exotic. Plant the bulbs in autumn for a spring show.

April

[When] the ghost of loss
gets into you,
may a flock of colours,
indigo, red, green
and azure blue
come to awaken in you
a meadow of delight . . .

John O'Donohue, "Beannacht/Blessing"

2 April This month begins with the shout of daffodils, and ends with the silky seduction of tulips. Everything is later in the North than in Essex, so our daffodils are still tightly budded for now. It will only take a few warm days, and they will be off. I have never seen so many daffodils as there are in our neighbourhood. The big elegant roads that lead up to Roundhay Park are flocked with them, and although they are not a favourite of mine, it is impossible not to be cheered by their strong, sunny faces, beaming down in their thousands from the grassy banks by Soldiers Fields and Canal Gardens. This was once, at the turn of the last century, the route of a proposed tram line (so that the city's masses could visit their favourite park in style), and the daffodils seem to be waiting, like cheering crowds, for the miraculous new contraption to appear! It never has, unfortunately.

I disagree with T. S. Eliot that "April is the cruellest month". It *is* wild and sometimes destructive, and it does, as he continues, mix "memory and desire". The weather is a crazy switchback, the ground teeming with confusion and growth. But I love this. The birth pangs of the earth are so physical, so full of energy and hope. Maybe it's a woman's thing?

3 April Fiddly details today. I planted my little pea plugs outside, at a jaunty diagonal, as planned back in February. I used biodegradable pots, for ease. They went straight into the ground, without the fuss of replanting, so the tender roots can remain protected against the heavy sludge of my soil. They had looked splendid in their individual pots at home. But now they are outside, they seem small, straggly, over-pampered individuals. It's all a question of scale. Last autumn I pruned the two apple trees in my overcrowded front garden. (Is this the right time to do it? I have no idea.) The result was a big, unwieldy bunch of knobbly brown offcuts, which I used today — in a satisfying fit of recycling — as a column of support either side of the pea plants. Beware the pigeons! Netting to follow.

Jerusalem artichokes — unprepossessing, shrivelled brown tubers, used mainly in soups, and notorious for making you fart. They don't hold a huge allure, I must admit, but I planted some, none the less, next to my raspberry patch. They do have their uses: the foliage growing high, green and bushy, to bring some drama to an otherwise flat terrain, and acting as a bit of a windbreak on our exposed piece of land. They also, unexpectedly, produce yellow flowers at the top of their huge stalks — whose tininess is preposterous and totally out of proportion to the rest of the plant. I like that. As usual with me, it is the gardener (with sculpture and design in mind) rather than the farmer (looking to his belly) who wins out. But I will eat some of these things when they ripen, I promise. Just stay downwind.

4 April Exactly three months after starting "the great dig", I finished turning over my last patch of unreclaimed earth on the allotment, next to the newly-planted artichokes. This will be for potatoes. The ground here is very heavy clay, waterlogged and grass-infested. It should have plenty of muck dug in or the potatoes will be unhappy. I did as much as I could. Really, I feel like the little Dutch boy with his finger in the dyke. Floods and weed infestations, and the constant, quiet determination of the land to revert to wild: these things can turn a woman's brain.

When I first moved to Leeds and started to garden, I became obsessed with slugs. They even invaded my dreams, in their many shades of black, yellow and grey slime, and I had to invent ever more cunning and cruel plans to annihilate them. These days, slugs are the least of my problems. No self-respecting invertebrates, with their love of shiny shoots and smooth surfaces, would bother crossing these barren prairies of clay. When it rains in April — and *of course* it rains in April — this allotment defies me to remember it's spring. My boots are permanently mud-caked. All the allotment flowers are taking their time. I have to struggle to hold on to the promising breezes of March: to the memory of Mother's vibrant spring garden, and the reality of the daffodils as I drive back home down Princes Avenue, where the crowds are waving.

5 April It was Mum's birthday today. Strange. Haunting. How different to two years ago, when she was eighty, and all her children — together with *their* children — piled down to Essex to cook her a celebration meal. She sat in the middle of the mess, beaming and scolding, great-granddaughter Summer on her lap, noise and chaos all around her. In her element. The silence and stillness she leaves is deafening.

6 April A visit to the reclaimed wall garden in Helmsley, North Yorkshire. It nestles beneath a ruined castle and is a wide, open space, given over to brambles and bracken for years, but now lovingly cultivated with flowers and vegetables in the style of an old-fashioned kitchen garden. Friends in the nearby village of Ampleforth introduced me to the place. Now I go every year, and today allotment neighbour and friend Sumi came along with me. We ferreted around happily outside, and then wandered through the pavilion (an ornate white building with exotics growing behind broad glass panes, and serried ranks of seedlings and

100

offshoots being groomed for selling: a kind of northern Kew Gardens). Of course, at this time of year, the plants give little clue as to their potential. Your imagination has to work hard, among the green and brown stubby shoots, to conjure up a picture of what they may become in a few weeks' or months' time. It is always a risk. I bought a red clematis — Helmsley is the official show garden for the British Clematis Society, so this felt like a safe choice.

Red is the most wonderful colour for a flower: intense, passionate, life-affirming. My mother, bright poppy that she was, would pick out red clothes without hesitation — red coats, scarlet dresses, bright scarves. It is mainly in the garden that I am drawn to red, although my wardrobe is getting brighter too. Slowly I step into my mother's shoes.

I was pleased to see that the allotment bird-scaring technique of suspending old CDs from sticks was being employed to good effect throughout the vegetable beds in Helmsley. But they placed their sticks at a 45-degree angle, I noticed, whilst I have been pushing mine in bolt upright. Result: their CDs swing freely, and rather elegantly, to and fro on their string, whereas mine get choked and tangled around their parent sticks at the slightest gust of wind. These finer points matter. I shall improve my technique.

7 *April* It has been reasonably mild so far this spring, apart from some maverick winds, and despite my grumbles about the rain. But the return of very cold weather is forecast. Although this is entirely integral to

April, I am outraged at the news. As soon as March is over, I expect a few blue skies, and *some* warmth, at least.

I took a look at my broad bean plants, which I have tried to over-winter for the second year running. Only two have survived, which is disheartening. The mighty onions, however, Japanese red and white, are going from strength to strength. I have a little Toyota Yaris, and am well aware of Japan's engineering skills. It seems they can engineer onions too.

Today is Thursday. Singing day. I have always loved to sing, and have a strong but untutored (and somewhat unpredictable) voice. I never found the right group for me. Then, one morning, four years ago, in 2001, when Tim was at a particularly difficult stage of his illness and the strain was telling on us all, I met a fellow parent and dog walker while I was out on a gloomy solitary ramble. Maggie immediately caught my mood, and sensed its dark undertones, having nursed both parents through terminal illness herself. She told me about a local singing group — no experience necessary — with a cheerful and encouraging teacher, working in the oral tradition (no sheet music, just listening and learning by ear).

I was nervous at the very thought of meeting new people, let alone singing in front of them. But all the same, I was desperate for some release from my anxiety, and managed to pluck up the courage to go.

At first, my voice was thin and wavery, my throat aching with the effort — and probably with suppressed emotion — but, week by week, it got stronger and deeper. The experience of singing in harmony with others — sometimes sweetly, sometimes raucously — set my spirit free. And it made me laugh. I recommend it above pills or booze. In the stealthy and all-engulfing silence of cancer, singing gave me a powerful voice. It made me new friends, too.

10 April Once again, I am robbing my little garden at home to populate the allotment. I took *Rheum palmatum* — a giant rhubarb-type leaf, but ornamental, which strikes forth dramatically from a single red point in the soil every spring (having reduced itself to nothing over winter); globe thistle — bristled, spiky, with a dreamy blue hum of colour in summer; and a pillar-box red poppy. I planted the poppy under Tim's tiny sumach tree, because he bought me the plant one Mother's Day. Poppies — with all their remembrance associations — fill me with a particular pang of delight, they are so fragile and yet so determined to come through. I have an opium poppy in a difficult side border at home. Every year it paints itself scarlet, blossoms bursting forth in May and June, and every year, invariably, a gust of wind takes it within a couple of days, scattering its doomed petals across the drive.

We try to recover our dead in some unexpected ways. When Tim was alive, we definitely had a His 'n' Hers book and video collection, even to the extent of separate shelves. He had a penchant for the weird, even macabre end of the spectrum: writers like Jim Crace, Jonathan Coe, Glen David Gold; films by

David Lynch, and dark psychological twisters, with the singular Kevin Spacey. But now that Tim is dead, I find myself watching the films he loved, and reading the authors he collected so compulsively. I suppose I am looking for him, am seeking repair, and it has certainly educated me, made me understand him a little better, even if it has not brought him back.

Similarly, today, I find myself flicking through cookery books, trying to find the ingredients and instructions for pea and ham soup (with dumplings), a particular staple of my mother's cuisine. She was an excellent, hearty cook, but lousy at handing on recipes. I never once saw her weigh or measure her ingredients, and she became irritated when asked for the details of any dish. In the kitchen, as in the garden, she worked entirely by instinct. Who knows, I may even plant spring-flowering bulbs for her in the autumn — a chore I detest, but with a different vibration for me now, when I remember how much pleasure it gave her.

It is these simple, constructive acts which heal in the end, perhaps more completely than any counselling. As soon as Tim died, I went to see the clinical psychologist who, together with her redoubtable predecessor, had been so invaluable during the five years when his cancer was terminal. I told her it was time for me to stop the sessions now.

"What will you do to help yourself recover?" she asked.

"I shall dig and I shall write," I said. And I have.

★   ★   ★

11 April I planted some maincrop potatoes in the ground today, after chitting them for a few weeks, making a humble short ridge in the granite-hard earth at the far end of my plot. (I should have rotovated, but I hate machines, and they chop up the worms like a mincer, so I relied on clumsy digging instead.) I think they are King Edward — a suitably regal crop — but of course I long ago lost the net in which they were bought. How absurdly lackadaisical I am with seed labels and packets. It's a wonder anything grows for me at all. Anyway, I am deeply excited by this: it's the first time I have grown potatoes in open ground, and it's rather like learning to drive (which I finally managed, at the age of forty-four) in terms of being a proper "grown-up" gardener.

12 April The trouble with digging and weeding is that it creates more and more space, hungry for crops. I have such cramped conditions at home, with only one narrow kitchen window sill, and my beloved mini-greenhouse full to bursting point (and also liable to keel over in the slightest wind), that I am anxious about sowing enough seed to be productive. So I have sent off for a batch of back-up plug plants — French and runner bean, brussel sprout, broccoli and cauliflower. What a cheat.

Proust, famously, had his Madeleine cakes — and there is nothing quite like fresh baking to set our memory juices running — but for me it is a certain warm sweet breeze, the first true fragrance of spring, which takes me back to the past more quickly than anything else. And the place it takes me back to, always, is Hungary. I spent a good few months there in 1988 and 1989, not long after leaving my work in journalism to qualify as a dancer and movement teacher.

I had a dear, though volatile Hungarian friend, who edited a drama magazine I wrote for in London, and who then moved back to her native country to take up a post as dramaturg to one of the leading national companies: the Csiky Gergely Theatre. She invited me over, first as a guest, and then as a movement coach to the company. Interesting — since the actors spoke little English, and I spoke no word of Hungarian. The power of body language, semaphor, wine and good will got us all through.

The first time I went was in the depths of January 1988. It was snowy, bleak, and very beautiful. The second visit was in spring. The theatre was in Kaposvar, a country town two hundred miles south of Budapest. The theatre building, in accordance with the status of its director and leading players, was brand new and expensive, but built in the grand old Austro-Hungarian manner: a great gorgeous wedding cake of a place, set among a canopy of trees in a park in the town centre.

When I arrived in April 1988, the blossom was just out, the leaves on the big old trees were fresh and green, and the scent in the air was sweet and intoxicating. I fell in love, unsuccessfully, with a black-eyed, raven-haired actor, but also with the entire company, and its ramshackle, bohemian lifestyle, played out in the charismatic hum and buzz of the theatre and its immediate surroundings.

The company had lived and worked together for twenty years, with fresh-faced newcomers joining every season to swell the repertory ranks. Most of them lived in actors' flats a hundred yards from the stage door; they ate, drank, loved, and fought out their off-stage lives in the dark subterranean bar and green room of the theatre — coming out into the fragrant Kaposvar air infrequently, to trudge home at some ungodly hour for some much-needed sleep. (Even they gardened, however, with most of them having access to little family houses by Lake Balaton, where fruit, vegetables and herbs were cultivated, as they had been down the generations. Hungarians come from powerful peasant stock.) I was delighted to be among them for a short while — an honorary member of the troupe — and the experience was sweet.

Now, fifteen years later, the heartache, the memories, even the personalities, have faded to sepia. When the Socialist regimes in Eastern Europe imploded in the 1990s, traditional Hungarian theatre, including its generous state subsidy, broke apart too. The actors are now dispersed, taking what work they can in a new, aggressive, commercial scene. Andrew Lloyd Webber has usurped Gogol and Chekhov. Ria, my friend and former editor, died of breast cancer in 1994. She (the person who first introduced me to Tim in 1989) was a vital link with Hungary. Now that link is long gone. But each time spring comes around, every year for the past sixteen, I smell that particular heady fragrance as if for the first time — of new blossom and hopeful breezes — and I am back, for an instant, under those graceful trees, in front of that beautiful theatre, in the heart of old Europe, and I am in love.

With spring warmth comes a second association: gin and tonic, the perfect drink for fine weather — another reason to grow a lemon tree. Tim made the best gin and tonic on earth. He would take a tall, slim tumbler, pour a hefty slug of gin into the bottom (preferably Bombay Sapphire — fabulously, decadently blue), along with enough ice to sink the *Titanic*, and then fill it to the brim with tonic, completing his work with a thick juicy slice of lemon. You were drunk on the first inhalation. I still pour myself a gin very occasionally, but it always tastes sad, somehow. For me, that particular drink died with Tim.

14 April We have travelled down to Essex, for the worst of reasons. It was Mum's funeral. Yesterday I went to see her body in the Co-op mortuary. This was a mistake. When I went in to be with Tim at the hospice, barely an hour after he had died, his spirit was still in the room. I felt peaceful sitting there. I felt *his* peace. He seemed very present, and when I entered the room, I could almost sense a movement in his chest — a stirring in his heart — that was comforting, and not in the least strange.

But Mum has been dead for two weeks now. She is utterly gone. The mortuary room was cold and dark, lifelessness its only defining feature, and I felt breathless with the weight of it. Her funeral, by contrast, was calm and lovely, with a rather jolly wake afterwards in a familiar local pub, booze and chat flowing freely (Mother didn't like half measures of anything). But I am sick of doing this now. I have placed an embargo on anyone else dying — ever.

18 April Molly is back at school, after special leave for her grandmother's funeral, and I am back in my Yorkshire garden. The cold weather we were promised has not materialized, but rain certainly has. Again. The earth is sodden after repeated torrential downpours. This does not bode well for delicate seedlings such as my peas, and I am not sure the potatoes, freshly planted, will enjoy sitting in a bog, but at least this water will soften up the ground, which is still rock-hard. Because of the rain, I stayed away from the allotment and sowed seeds at home instead: specifically, cucumber "Marketmore", to scramble up two tripods of pea sticks; and red chilli peppers to keep as ornaments for the window sill.

It still astonishes me that seeds — those dried little specks of nothing — can produce such a startling and incandescent array of flowers and fruits, such variation in colour, shape and size. I don't have the reverence for each individual seed that some gardeners do — am rather more wasteful and scattergun in my approach. But, oh, how I marvel at what pops up. Every time, I am lost in wonder. Peppers, in particular, look delightful when they appear: the thin sly scarlet of the ripened chillies, and the waxy blunt green of the sweet variety, emerging from stems and leaves that are elegant, cinched in at the waist, *and* tough. They are a real enhancement to a dull little corner in the house: no need to eat them. Just look at them, and they will cheer you up.

19 April I dug over the second potato bed and planted seven more seed potatoes. Not ideal conditions, but I have to get up here when I can. One modest little row of potatoes — I am working at such a micro-level — and yet it still tires me out. Farmers, livestock and arable, must be so tough. I bow to them (stiffly).

20 April This would have been the birthday of my cheeky friend John, who died in 1993. I knew him for eighteen years. We stuck together from the moment we met, at an introductory lecture at university. We were both eighteen. John was a real hell-raiser: the devil to my Dr Faustus. He loved to party, and was always the centre of attention. If he did not get the adulation he felt he deserved, he would dance, sing, make a scene, until everyone's eyes were on him once again.

On his thirty-sixth birthday, in 1993, he was in a west London hospital, dying messily and painfully. But still, there was a party. People began arriving in the early evening, bearing bottles and cards. The word spread. Soon, a spontaneous happening was in progress. Someone sat with him, reading from the growing stack of written messages. By now, John was barely conscious, but working on the assumption that hearing is the last sense to fail, we continued to talk and read to him.

Outside the darkness of his single room, friends and relatives sat in the bright, clean ward, in small groups, raising a glass (well, plastic cup) to a much loved and well-known figure from a particular south London scene. The reminiscing went on for some hours, and became quite drunken — it is remarkable that such an anarchic gathering was permitted on a ward where the patients were so ill, and is a testimony both to the wonderful ward staff (who recognized the ritual importance of the occasion) and to the spirit of John himself, party animal to the end.

I grieve for all those young men who died in the first swathe of the AIDs epidemic, in the 1980s and early 1990s: it was a catastrophe. Rules were broken, as on that hospital ward, and then the rule book itself was thrown away. New and colourful ways were invented to celebrate unorthodox lives cut down, so brutally, in full swing; new ways were found to mourn and to survive such multiple losses. But the pain of it was appalling. It knocked a whole generation for six.

21 April John died the day after his birthday, in 1993. He stuck around for the celebration, and then let go. Stylish. It was John who took me to the west coast of Ireland, when we were both in our mid-twenties. It was the first truly wild place I had been to — and we travelled on his clapped out old motorbike, from the heart of Brixton right to the end of the Beara peninsula, furthest finger of land in west County Cork:

next stop America. With its high, vertiginous cliffs, crashing seas, jagged rocks and glittering bays, it felt like the end of the world.

This trip sowed the seeds of something "other" in me: a deep desire to be outside, and close to the earth and its secrets. The mercurial weather, and the dramatic, uncompromising landscape, blew my head open, emptying it of words and city thoughts, and filling it with dreams of falling into the seductive embrace of sea and sky.

I do not think the gardener in me was born then — what use a garden in that wind-blown wilderness? — but the desire to be outside, the ability to be only truly contented outside, certainly was. Thank you, John. The irony is that he was rather frightened of the wide open spaces, and longed to return to the safety of the city. He never went back to Beara after that initial trip, but I did. And, in my head, I have never really been away.

22 April Yorkshire weather is definitely not as volatile as that of Ireland's south-west coastline, but this year it's certainly very changeable. It seems to be one day hot, one day cold, with no sense of stability or continuity. Today was very sunny and warm. I decided to dig up a clump of bamboo from my front garden, and split the clump in two, to sit either side of my allotment arch. A reasonable enough intention — but it proved sheer hell to execute.

I was under the mistaken impression that bamboo would be easy to shift, because of its shallow roots. But I did not reckon with the intricate web of tiny fibres that bind these roots in place, and which make digging them out a struggle to the death. I sweated and cursed, and pushed and pulled for over two hours. My spade could scarcely penetrate the impacted soil. In the end I resorted to using a kitchen knife to rip and tear through the fibrous tangle. Halfway through I gave up, and went indoors to lie down. Then I went back outside and faced the same ordeal all over again. It is the toughest job I have ever faced in the garden. It felt as if I were hacking an enormous, stubborn beast to pieces, which, in a way, I suppose I was. The clump finally came free, but it was a hollow victory: ever since it has been transplanted, it looks dry and bleached and deeply unhappy. Moral: never move established bamboo; it clearly has a deeply ingrained sense of place.

The biopsy results are back. They confirm what we all suspected: that my father has cancer on his right lung.

24 April I planted a *Viburnum davidii* in a corner bed on the allotment. It is a good-value plant, although not terribly exciting — producing berries and flowers for much of the year, and boasting dark green, shiny foliage. It does look a little suburban amongst the wild grasses and vegetables, but I shall give it a chance.

I put a few strawberries around the base of the arch. The rest of the strawberry plants are scattered amongst the *Miscanthus* and *Stipa* grasses next to the pond. In a rash moment, I promised the children next door the pick of the crop. So far, hardly a flower has emerged, let alone any fruit — although it is still early in the season.

113

Lacking faith in my ability to produce, I can always fall back on the supermarket strategy: shop-bought punnet, transplanted into wicker basket, and sprinkled with authentic allotment soil.

25 April It was hot and sunny today on my plot, and not a soul in sight. The only sound was birds, and a distant rumble of traffic — as if the city were miles away, and not just beyond the allotment gates. I felt privileged to have such a big stretch of land all to myself, even if the jobs I had to do were fiddly. First, I improved my pea net — placing tiny upturned clay pots on top of four long bamboo canes, two at each end of the planting, and then draping fine netting over the lot, weighing it down with stones.

Nets ruin the aesthetic, of course, and I hate covering up my bonny pea sticks with camouflage, but if I didn't, it would only take a five-minute dive-bombing raid from the local pigeons (an evil bunch), and my meagre little crop would be decimated. So nets it is. It looks reasonably neat. I am ludicrously proud of completing even the simplest DIY job. This is the result of my sticking my head in a book when I was about eight years old, and not taking it out again until I was thirty. I am insanely impractical, but somehow things work around me — and when they don't, I simply pretend they do.

I cleared the grass and weeds around the pink lavatera I have planted at the side of the shed. This ordinary, though tough and flower-abundant plant was put in to complement another lavatera down by my rather unsightly compost bin, with the wish that it would grow high, fast and furious, and act as a billowing punctuation mark at the top end of my site. Unfortunately the other mallow rotted clean away during the great rains of mid-April, leaving nothing but a withered brown stump. The one that remains, by the shed, is currently five inches high and showing no signs of growing any taller. Gardening in my head and gardening in reality: there is a whole world between the two. I suppose I just never reckon with things dying on me. I make that mistake with people too.

I cleared the dry, dusty border in front of the shed. Then I planted nasturtium seeds here, and around the base of the arch. I love their high summer colours of yellow, orange and red, and the hexagonal, marbled leaves, with a white point at the centre, geometric lines running out to the scalloped edges. Most of all, however, I love their sheer profligacy. People eat these leaves in summer salads, but I draw the line at that. You can take this back-to-the-earth business too far.

The eggshell blue of the painted metal panelling, which runs down from my shed window to ground level, shimmers discreetly in the brilliant sunshine, and makes the old shack look like a sea-side chalet — quite lovely. Brightness transforms everything. Late April shines like a jewel, after rain.

As I was leaving, I found Charlie, allotment chairman, by the front gates, gloved up and gathering nettles for a liquid fertilizer. He says it smells nasty, but the vegetables love it. I vow to try this later in the year.

★ ★ ★

27 April I am lucky with the days I choose to be outside. Yesterday was wet, but today is sunny again. Just the dog and me on the allotment. Bliss. The tadpoles in my pond are thriving — the smaller ones wriggling like crazy at the water's edge, the fatter ones sunbathing on a stone in the shallows.

I dug over the bed near my "rockery" (there is one rock in it, at present, plus plenty of overgrown grasses and weeds), ready for the brassica plug plants — broccoli and the like — due to arrive by post in May. I am trying to establish some kind of simple crop rotation, with brassicas following legumes (peas and beans), and roots following brassicas, so that the plants get the right amount of minerals from the soil; but this is a complex art, and luckily I don't know enough to be too rigid about it.

There are four flower heads on my cardoon. They look splendidly exotic. The architecture of the plant itself is beautiful: silver-grey, deeply serrated leaves, rising from a strong central column. Like a Roman emperor, haughty and merciless.

How things echo and repeat in my history. At the end of April 1994, a year to the day after best friend John's death, the biopsy on Tim's chest tissue confirmed it as cancer. The way we were told felt laughably shambolic, especially considering this was a leading London cancer hospital. First, they lost his notes, and kept us waiting for an hour while the paperwork was chased up in another building. Then we were forgotten completely

— until a shy inquiry of a nurse jolted their memory. Finally, we faced a young, nervous and not very friendly doctor (deputizing for the consultant), who sat a million miles away from us on the other side of his desk and muttered something about a "malignant Thymoma". Tim was silent. I was bewildered.

"Does that mean he has cancer?" I asked — the first time the "C" word had been uttered by anyone, during weeks of investigation.

"Yes," he said, not looking up from his notes, not looking us in the eye once. I hated him for that. Now I just feel sorry, for all of us — it must be possible to do this better.

A desultory conversation ensued, about "follow-up treatment . . . yet to be decided . . . chemotherapy, surgery, blah, blah, blah . . ." Then we found ourselves back on the street, walking in a daze to the underground station, and waiting for our District line train home.

"Does this mean I'm going to die?" Tim said, his voice disappearing faintly down dark tunnels of panic.

"No," I replied, my own voice equally distant, my heart sharp with pain. And indeed he did not. For a whole decade to come — a decade in which he watched his baby become a child, and his child become a beautiful young girl — he did not die. Bravo, Tim. So, in this month of bleak diagnoses and funerals, set against such hope, abundance and colour in the growing garden, I know: my father will not die either.

29 April Today I had to strim the wayward grass paths which wiggle haphazardly between the beds, and are putting on vast amounts of growth in the current climate of liberal rains and warm sunshine. Strimming is a ghastly job. Both petrol-fired machines in the communal allotment shed are big beasts, requiring goggles and harness and all the strength you can muster. They put strain on the back, the arms, hands and fingers, not to mention ears. By the time I had finished — and for many days after — I felt a disturbing buzzing ache right through my body from the vibrations. But the serious haircut has transformed my plot, which has gone from overgrown jungle sprawl to a way-ward, but rather bright and pretty jumble of a garden.

30 April Allotment barbecue — the first of the year. As usual, it was a friendly, though slightly disjointed affair, with people who are used to digging in parallel, and pausing only for the odd chat about marrows and the like, suddenly faced with the need to make proper adult conversation. My dad was staying, so he came along. Always the more reticent partner of his marriage, he sat quietly on the sidelines.

"If your mother were here, she'd know everybody's life histories by now," he remarked ruefully, about an hour after we arrived. We went home early.

The tulips are softly stealing the daffodils' thunder, as April sings its dying notes. The gaudy forsythia spreads its sparkling yellow fizz throughout the neighbourhood. There is a hint of mauve azalea; creamy-red oozes from a local pieris; grape hyacinth are massing under my apple tree; and even the occasional bluebell, in our wood, declaims its celestial prologue to May. Spring has landed.

Jobs for April

- If you have sown peas indoors, now is the time to plant them out. Give them plenty of twiggy support.
- Plant Jerusalem artichoke, if you feel sturdy, and if you have space.
- Poppies. Every member of this vivid species has beauty and charm. If you buy some plants now, they will flower in a month or two, and multiply year on year.
- Plant your seed potatoes.
- Send off for plug plants to augment any failures of seeds.
- Do *not* split bamboo!
- Sow some nasturtium seeds for low summer cover.
- Strim, mow, dig. Reshape the borders. It's time to get spruce as the growing season gathers pace.

May

Now, and I muse for why and never find the reason,
  I pace the earth, and drink the air, and feel the sun.
Be still, be still, my soul; it is but for a season . . .

A. E. Housman, *A Shropshire Lad*

1 May Today was wet but warm, a dewy May day, fresh with promise. Spring often makes me restless — as if searching for answers to non-existent questions — but a mild May morning such as this has the power to appease. I visited a local garden centre — places I generally regard with a rather snobbish contempt, but which sometimes yield treasure, amidst the ornamental kitsch. Unexpectedly, I found some trays of leek and Cos lettuce plug plants, which delighted me, since I fail abjectly to grow these from seed. I went straight to the allotment and planted them, despite the boggy conditions. The lettuce are sitting among the herbs; the leeks tucked in next to my onions and garlic.

Slowly my contentment with this plot is growing. It is such a different space to my tiny front garden, which is deliberately discreet, shady, and overgrown with soft purples and greens: a place to hide in and brood. The wide open space of the allotment shouts

120

out its bright and gaudy opposition. Amid the hollyhocks and nasturtiums and pointy, perky vegetables, there is nowhere to hide. You are exposed to the big sky, and the cheerful diggers on every side. The openness makes *me* feel more open — tougher and more amused by the world. It's too easy to take things seriously at home; the walls press in, and the garden is too close to the house, where Jobs Are Always Waiting. The allotment unscrews my head, and lets the demons fly away.

2 May The morning brought brilliant sunshine, and a considerable breeze. I moved some of the strawberries on my fruit patch (a particularly juicy variety, called "Sophie") up to the rockery. Their feet were getting very wet, and the fruit would certainly rot as soon as it appeared. Such a pretty plant, the strawberry — sprightly green leaves and a delicate white flower in May, followed by the erotic red charge of its fruit, come June. Everything takes a bite out of my little berries before I get to them, snails and birds in particular, but I don't mind. It is enough just to smell their heady fragrance when the sun is warm, and the dew has been upon them.

At home, I potted on my summer "Hispi" cabbages and put them, together with a few lettuces, into my mini-greenhouse. Just in time. There was a deluge in the afternoon, with water cascading down the drive in torrents, which sent me scurrying back into the house. So much for that sunny start.

★ ★ ★

3 May Thunder, lightning and hailstones the size of gobstoppers. This is Old Testament territory. I had fondly imagined May to be fecund, mellow and still: a youthful ripening of the gardener's year, fulfilling spring and heralding summer. But the first three days of the month so far have brought weather fit for autumn and winter, as well as mellow May. Nature confounds me. I sowed some sunflower seeds at home: "Fiorenza", which, judging by the picture on the packet, promise to be a deep rusty red, with yellow tips, and will grow to about five feet tall (much more petite than the classic giant variety, which grow stems the size of small tree trunks, and are a devil to cut down in winter).

After lunch I took a cautious look at the allotment. The whole site is under water. Soon we shall have a canal system where the paths used to be, and will be getting around by gondola. But when all gardening grinds to a halt, conversation can begin, and I had a fascinating talk with our resident bee-keeper, who has taken over the furthest, wildest corner of the allotment, and colonized it with hives, protected by a living willow screen. Moira is the bee equivalent of the SAS, complete with white helmet and padded protective suit, and is often called up on a bee hotline to rescue neighbourhood gardens from errant swarms. Her own bees, she assures me, are perfectly well behaved, and they certainly produce an intense, intoxicating honey. (A spoonful a day, of the most local brew you can find, is said to allay hay fever symptoms. This makes sense, as a way of treating like with like, since bees feast on

122

exactly the same pollen that triggers allergies in so many humans. And as medicine goes, it's sweeter than most.)

4 *May* Dry and cool today. This weather is like a switchback ride. I sowed some lettuce leaves at home — the purple ones seem to repel slugs more successfully than the green, although I generally get a limp crop from lettuce, whatever I do.

I also put in some beetroot, which has fat, easy-to-sow seeds, and, unlike the lettuce, always comes true. I do love this root vegetable. It has glossy good looks, with robust, red-veined leaves and fat crimson bulbs, and is full of iron and hearty minerals; but what a pain they are to cook! The pan turns indelibly purple, and the bubbling and boiling takes hours. It's a bit of a chore to eat too, although rather thrilling — like consuming your own congealed blood. It is none the less essential for any allotment, being such a willing vegetable. Beetroot is a particularly good neighbouring crop for onion and carrots, since carrot fly, which operate by scent, are put off by the pungency of the onions, and beetroot is friendly towards both.

Companion planting — the putting together of particular flowers and vegetables, which grow healthily side by side and ensure optimal crops — is a fascinating and esoteric art, about which I know little. But I pick up snippets of information here and there, and as the years go by, I hope my gardening will become more subtle, more quietly informed by this old wisdom. I do know that French marigold, *Tagetes patula*, is a

123

particularly powerful ally in the vegetable garden. Every year I plant some, but cannot quite manage to keep it going through the periods of drought and inevitable summer holiday neglect. It is nowhere near as tough as nasturtium (which is a wonderful decoy for greenfly) but it's certainly useful. Marigold will help beat your bindweed; grown with potatoes it deters eelworm, thanks to its powerful secretions, and it helps tomato plants stay healthy. Garlic, another customer with a pungent aroma, is a useful companion too: planted next to lavender, it increases the oil content of the herb. It is also kind to raspberries, improving the health of the plant and the quality of its fruit. I have only tested one of these hypotheses so far, by putting some garlic next to the white lavender in my herb patch. Call it my imagination, but the scent of that little lavender bush is particularly exquisite.

5 May A good bright day for walking. Buddhist monks extol the virtue of this basic form of exercise, believing that "mindful walking" is a powerful meditation in itself. I can see their point. When I focus fully on the contact of my foot with the ground, and the rhythmic swing of arms and legs backwards and forwards through the air, I do begin to feel complete. My monkey mind subsides.

Early, at eight, I went up to Roundhay Park, a big open space for roaming in (one of the largest public parks in Europe, or is that just my Yorkshire boast?) and less than a mile up the road. Then, after lunch, I took a turn with Muffin through our local wood. The weather had become windy and showery by now, but it did not matter. At this time of year Gipton Wood is at its most beautiful: carpeted with bluebells, and dotted with delicate white and yellow wild flowers, which make use of the warm sunlight before the oaks and beeches put on their dark summer green, and everything is plunged into shadow. Today the trees looked gorgeous too: bright and sappy, in their new light covering of leaves. There is one place — the furthest, quietest corner of the wood, otherwise surrounded by roads and an urban population — where the bluebells flower most densely. There is such beauty here, when the sunlight slants through the branches, the blue of the flowers softly mirroring the blue of the sky — like a miniature heaven fallen to earth — that it becomes almost melancholy: a fleeting loveliness. The bluebell season is all too short, two or three weeks maybe, from the first shy pop of blue buds to the final crash of extravagant foliage under its own deep, wet weight.

I have two associations with these flowers, both linked to Tim. A few years before his own death, Linda McCartney died of breast cancer. As a hard-core John Lennon fan, the McCartney clan holds little interest for me, and Tim was positively derisory about their easy-listening brand of music. But Linda was brave, I think, especially in the way she went. On the day she died, one of the tabloid newspapers ran a picture of her and Paul, happy on horseback, and printed the last words he spoke to her, as she lay dying, about riding on her favourite horse through the woods, among the bluebells, under a sunny sky. Now Tim never rode a horse in his life, but he loved our little wood, and walked the dog there several times a day, in the years when he was well enough to do so. The bluebells held a special magic for him. He always said we should take a picture, but we never did. Now I am left forever with an imprint of Tim, and bluebells, and Linda McCartney, all mixed up in my head — a curious and unlikely combination.

All sadness has its own unique history. But sometimes it links, unwittingly, to a deeper, shared ancestry. "The bluebell, *Hyacinthus nonscriptus*, is the hyacinth of the ancients, the flower of grief and mourning," so Derek Jarman tells us in his wonderful gardening diary, *Modern Nature*. Hyacinth, the king of Sparta's son, was beloved of the wind god Zephyr, but preferred to give his favours to the sun god Apollo. One day Apollo and Hyacinth were playing quoits when, in a fit of jealousy, Zephyr caused a sudden wind to catch up the quoit, and it crashed into the boy's face, killing him. According to Greek myth, Apollo, consumed with sorrow, created the purple-blue flower from the drops of blood which fell from the dying boy. So, as Derek Jarman says, do not ever pick the wild plant, since it will only wilt and die, and besides, "the blue-eyed flower with its heavy fragrance belongs only to the sun."

6 *May* A dry day, bright and breezy. I spent the morning up at the allotment, weeding. The bindweed is curling its treacherous fingers around some of my plants. I am constantly at war with this nasty individual — its spidery, invasive roots and cheerful, murderous

126

tendencies. I used to dream of eradication, now I realize that it is a case of uneasy cohabitation. My hope is that cultivating the land, year on year, may at least curb its worst excesses. Nature's biggest impulse is to revert to wild. For all our efforts with spade, trowel, strimmer, and above all, patient, bony fingers, we can hope, at best, for a temporary truce. And that will do.

I do not live as other people live: with a job, pension and mortgage; something saved in the bank for a rainy day. Circumstances (and, if I am honest, temperament) have denied me all that — Tim's long illness made it rain till it poured, exhausting all the negligible securities we had. Friends and family have been enormously generous — people generally are — but the daily struggle continues. Life is a little hand-to-mouth, to put it mildly. When I feel well, this seems like freedom — a quiet, joyful collision with a fast, noisy, material culture; a true alternative. But when I feel sick, alone or afraid, it is an unmanageable strain. Where am I now, between those two extremes? Sometimes there is joy, sometimes panic, but I feel uneasy, even when I seem calm. I know how much I have been through, and how pitiless the world can be. I wonder if I can sustain the different space I inhabit, and keep it vibrant; safe.

The tadpoles in my pond are less wriggly — they have gone deeper into the water, and are growing and changing shape. Evolution before my eyes. I wonder if they get impatient to be bigger, older, the way I did when I was a child, and my own daughter does now?

127

Actually, most of the impatience in my garden is a projection from the gardener on to her placid domain. I long for my potatoes and Jerusalem artichokes to appear, for example, but not a squeak: they just don't care.

My shoulder hurts from pulling and tugging at intransigent taproots. On this heavy, impacted clay, weeding is tough work. It is too easy to wreak damage on the body when you garden — too easy to keep going, for just another few precious minutes, beyond tolerance level. Steady on. The weeds will just have to wait.

There is a remarkable organization in London, called the Medical Foundation for the Care of Victims of Torture, and part of their work, which is the psychotherapeutic treatment of traumatized refugees, takes place on allotments. People from different countries and cultures are given pieces of land to work, the aim being slowly to heal their troubled minds and bodies as they tend their plots, with the help of a psychotherapist and gardener who work alongside them. I was particularly struck by the story of Farouk, told in *The Healing Fields* (a book about the Foundation's allotment project by Jenny Grut and Sonja Linden), in a chapter called "The Weeds of the Mind". Farouk, an Iraqi Kurd, set about purging his plot of all weeds, making an ugly mountain of earth and invasive roots and stems. Compulsively he dug and dug, much to the annoyance of his fellow allotmenteers. Nothing was planted. The place looked more and more like a wasteland. It took the skill of the psychotherapist to interpret his strange and seemingly unfulfilling approach. "You need to bring the weeds up to the surface . . . That's the only way. If you leave any trace, they will grow back again. Like your memories . . . That's what all these weeds are, aren't they? Bad memories, bad feelings, bad thoughts."

When I become oppressed by the invasion of unwanted growth on my own allotment, I think of Farouk — who slowly learned patience, with his memories, as with his weeds, and eventually made a beautiful, productive garden.

There is, of course, no comparison between his experience and mine. Torture, exile: these are unimaginable extremes. But I, too, use the garden for more than just growing. It is hard to quantify what exactly happens when I work outside. There is the obvious desire to create something tangible and lovely. But there is something darker too: a compulsion to tame — both the ground, and the wildness I have within me. Sometimes I want to dig until I drop, and often I push the boundaries of what my back, my body, can endure. Why? I cannot put into words what this process might mean, but it feels like some kind of purging. A making good of lost time, missed opportunities. Usually I feel healthier, happier, calmer, when I have spent time gardening. But there is a kind of fury in the mix, as well. Sometimes I hurt myself, am too hard on myself, and on the world around me, in the deep and desperate wish to be well, to make the uncomfortable past go away.

★　★　★

10 May For the past three years I have been writing a novel. Today it was turned down flat by an agent — the second to say it has no value in the commercial marketplace. I know what I should do — blow the dust off another copy and send it somewhere else. But I feel too crushed to do anything with it now. All through Tim's long illness I wrote — as prolifically as I did when I was a journalist. But the writing, just like my role as carer, remained hidden, unrewarded. The publishing world now seems a nightmare of ruthless certainties, and I am so long out of the game. I had better stick to the garden for a while. At least I shan't get refused entry there.

The fruit patch needs weeding — again! There is a heavy grass infestation. But still, small fruits are forming behind the flowers on the gooseberry and currant bushes. I sowed some basil seeds at home — they usually come true (although the purple variety is more temperamental), but grow small and very slowly. The tomatoes got potted on. I generally have happy experiences with them: always a crop, even if they have to be put in a bag (plastic, not brown paper, as you might imagine) in a dark drawer to ripen properly. Green tomato chutney? Haven't the patience, although my mother-in-law produced jars of the stuff for years, and it was delicious. I worry about some outdoor greenhouse seedlings — sunflower, pea and lettuce — as it is very cold at night. They must simply take their chances.

The first leaves on my potatoes are emerging, four weeks after planting. But I don't have a good feeling:

the leaves are too dark, unprepossessing. Is something wrong?

My dad begins treatment for his lung cancer this month. They wanted to give him both chemo and radiotherapy. I stuck my neck out and said, "Don't have the chemo." He is eighty-two. He likes his food and drink — there is a quality to his life, even though arthritis and diabetes set inevitable limitations. Chemotherapy, at least as I have experienced it at second hand (given in extremely high and toxic doses, admittedly), can impair life's quality to a deadening and sickening degree. It can certainly save lives; it did not — could not — save Tim. Could it save my father? Instinctively I have doubts.

To my astonishment, Dad's Macmillan nurse backs him unstintingly in his decision to opt out: she goes with him to the consultant to speak up for him. The consultant agrees. There will be radiotherapy only. This ease of communication, this open dialogue about health, is not what I remember from the years I spent with Tim in cancer hospitals in London and Leeds. It was all so muddy then, so compromised by the severity of Tim's cancer, his youth, his complicated presentations of difficult symptoms. I never felt powerful and suffered from my lack of agency. But maybe one gift from that time remains — the ability to send a clearer message to my father? Who knows. I just feel quietly glad.

★   ★   ★

11 May I was up at my allotment by eight in the morning, feeling very smug. There was warm sunshine, and a ground heavy with dew. My CDs are twinkling in the light, swinging free from fishing lines over the lettuce and herbs. Nothing but birdsong in the air. There is lush vegetation around the pond now: purple-headed chives, and their taller cousins, the alliums; rampant yellow loosestrife — almost Chaucerian in its old English vulgarity; beautiful deadly foxgloves; and the fleshy leaves of *Bergenia* and juicy sedums. In the pond itself is a rather invasive bulrush, which will have to be evicted before too long, and an elegant purple iris. Closer to the shed, along its dusty perimeter, a white Jacob's ladder is unfurling. Nothing lasts long here, however, it is so dry.

I notice that something has been burrowing in the earth beside the little white flower. A fox? They occasionally play hopscotch with stones around the pond. Who knows what they are up to now? Edwin, a new plot holder to my right, often comes here at night, since he works shifts, and is a nocturnal creature anyway. He says he sees all sorts of animals roaming about, under blood red moons and sharp shiny stars. If he sits very quietly, which he is naturally inclined to do (can of lager in one hand, fag in the other), they cavort around in front of him, unbothered by his presence. During the day the allotment may belong to the plants and human endeavour: at night it is the domain of the wild things. And Edwin.

The purple lilac is in bloom, down in the far hedge. Beyond that is a perimeter fence and a special needs school, which lets its children out for long extended sessions of play and sport. By ten o'clock today the kids were hard at it outside, shrieking with joy at being liberated from class. Someone on the neighbouring estate was doing DIY — the tyranny of power tools rearing up like warfare across the still space. The early morning peace was shattered. I filled a dustbin with water, and cut nettles into it to make a liquid manure. I felt very pleased with myself for this simple act of husbandry. Then I went home.

Some May mornings seem to hold the whole world in their breath. The tranquillity amazes. I remember a perfect day spent once on Ilkley Moor, with Tim, when he was reasonably well, and Molly — still small enough to enjoy a pointless ramble among the rocks. It was in the days before we had a car, or a dog, so we travelled to Ilkley by train, and wandered up the steep hill to the Moor, not quite knowing where we were going, or why. Apart from its posh tea shops, Ilkley Moor is most famous for the Cow and Calf rocks, huge slabs of stone jutting high above the valley below, casting a severe and ancient shadow. But we did not go there; we simply ambled aimlessly among the curving moorland paths, and settled for a while by a big old stone, basking in the sunshine and the unusually still air. Molly trotted about, doing small-girl, make-believe things with sticks and grass, and finding secret hideaway places in which to delight herself. Tim dozed. I just sat. And a great sense of peace stole inside me. In any process of repair —

when something inside you has shattered into pieces — those small, intact moments are the ones that must be found in your memory, and polished until they shine.

14 May I went with friends to Lotherton Hall Show — Lotherton being one of the many beautiful Yorkshire estates, complete with grand house and garden and rolling acres beyond, given over now to the visiting public: an essential source of revenue. The country show is something Yorkshire does brilliantly well. I grew up in Essex, which had carnivals and fetes in every little local town, plus the big and commercial annual Essex Show. But these all pale into insignificance compared to Yorkshire events.

The season invariably opens with the Otley Show, which I find fascinating. First, there are the livestock pens, with all the big beasts — Aberdeen Angus breathing damp fire down soft wide nostrils, a smell of wet straw and fresh dung rising up from underneath them; then come the horse and dog events; the plants and produce tents; rows and rows of colourful stalls; sheep shearing stands; stoat and weasel races . . . and, in the middle of it all, and best by far, the competition marquee. This is full of paintings and pictures, home-made jams and cakes, and — my favourite — hens' eggs, grouped in threes, and assessed on colour, size of shell and the yellow of their yolks: all presented by local people, and scrutinized by sombre judges in an atmosphere of intense, not to say ferocious, rivalry. This tent is always packed, and I could stay there for ever, gazing at the shiny eggs and listening to local gossip, as spicy as anything Alan Bennett might conjure in fiction.

15 May I cannot deny it. My mood is low. There is a huge sense of loss in my life: Mum dying so soon after Tim; the rejection of my book (which had been a labour of love in difficult times); and the constant worry about money, which is in alarmingly short supply at present. I don't require much to keep me happy — enough to eat, a drop of wine to drink, something to cover the rent and the running of a small car, small dog and growing daughter. Never mind the South of France, the means to get beyond south Leeds are hard enough to conjure!

Anyway, it's Sunday morning, traditionally a time for the allotment. Sunday is always very busy, because all the jobbing nine-to-fivers get up there then. There are plenty of cheery souls to lift me out of my gloom. Some more of my potatoes are through, and, at last, some shoots of Jerusalem artichoke. But something has been nibbling them, so they looked a little frayed at the edges. I know how they feel. I am confident they will recover. Am I so confident about myself?

The earth is cracked wide open in places by the recent dry winds. It looks alarming — like the bottom of a river bed in drought — but heavy clay always does this. It will soften soon enough.

I dug over a patch I have reserved for brassica plugs, when they eventually arrive (a cold, wet spring has checked their growth, the suppliers say, so delivery will be late). Cabbage, broccoli, cauliflower. There is enough muck on this bed to make digging possible, even in the dry conditions. (I remember once watching a neighbour attack his back garden with a great pick-axe. I was astonished, and somewhat alarmed, but having encountered the granite earth myself since then, and feeling the jolt of a metal spade bouncing back into my hands as if from solid concrete, I understand his draconian approach.)

I watered the bamboo by the arch, but it is still sulking, and does not look at all happy. Deep purple is a favourite colour of mine in flowers, and I indulged my passion today by planting a purple *Penstemon*: it is reminiscent of the foxglove, tall and graceful, with a wistful and pendulous hang of the head. I grew one at home once, called "Blackbird". This one is a slightly lighter one — "Magpie" — harbinger of doom, but only if it produces just one bloom.

The seeds sown at home — peas, sunflower, beetroot — have all been failing miserably, much to my disgust. I have no idea why. But when I looked today, two sunflower seeds have popped up, and a few little lettuce. Suddenly I feel rich again.

I went for an evening walk with the dog, and cried all the way through the wood. I find solitary woodland walks ideal for profligate and wanton weeping. The dog did not care, she just skipped and ran amidst the dappled shade of the young trees, the masses of bluebells, and the swathes of waist-high cow parsley. I did not care either. The trees can take it.

In the night I had a nightmare and woke up in a terrible panic. It was as if I were looking into the face of fear and sorrow itself, naked, undisguised, and ugly.

16 May My hands are very stiff after a recent bout of strimming. This won't do. I need my hands for writing, teaching (my movement work is very tactile) and planting. I did not realize how much I use them until they seized up like this.

I bought some ready-made French marigolds (easy bedding plants are a bit like buying frozen meals: very bad for the soul, but entirely necessary from time to time), plus some miniature sunflowers to help pollinate my beans. I also sowed some squash and dark green courgettes — seeds to be placed on their edges in the pot. (What's *that* about?) I slept during the day, a favourite pastime, and dreamed about purple sprouting broccoli. Very healthy, after that horrible nightmare. But everywhere I go, I see a single magpie.

17 May Another dream. Of beautiful and vast expanses of perfectly tilled, brown, bare earth.

18 May Peas and beans. They do not grow well for me. I think I will have to pay them more attention: watering, feeding, mulching — that kind of thing. It is this aftercare which gets tedious (and difficult, when you do not live on site). I took the net off the peas: pests have eaten most of them, so the birds might as well have the rest. On the outside of my diagonal of pea sticks I put the miniature sunflowers, and when the French beans arrive, I'll plant them alongside too.

A few more leaves are appearing on the potatoes. I put some French marigold in with them, to beat the eelworm: careful now — not too neat a row. This is not a municipal planting scheme. I was happy in the sunshine, listening to the birdsong. There was a cool serenity in the air. Thank goodness the recent high winds have dropped — everything is sighing with relief.

21 May Otley Show. As sublime as ever. The eggs were golden and gleaming.

22 May There was a big rainstorm in the morning. After lunch I took some blue and yellow daisies (bought at the show yesterday) to the allotment rockery. I tidied up the leek patch, took the nets off the broad beans, and planted runner and French beans. I was the only person around: always a treat. Even so, there's usually some dead friend or relative whispering unfinished business in my ear. Who was it today? No one at all, just myself. How refreshing.

23 May The dog has a new red neckerchief. She is very pleased, and we head off for the woods to show it off. May really is the month for this little wood. It is positively gleaming, with its bluebells, celandine, Jack-by-the-wood (lacy white) and pink honesty. A lovely old man who walks his dog here every day, and feeds two robins by the north gate, tells me this wood was once part of a vast swathe of woodland which made up the ancient Sherwood Forest. Can this be true? I like to think so. It gives Gipton Wood a more romantic air.

25 May I am rather in awe of the clematis family — so vast and beautiful, and, in my experience, tricky to get the hang of. I never feel I dig deep enough, or master the arcane art of when to prune ("If it flowers before June, don't prune" apparently). All that business of not cutting into old wood, and sorting out the early, mid and main season flowering — it worries my brain. Everything that can go wrong with clematis, usually does for me. Anyway, I have had some successes. I think the earlier, more robust varieties are a safer bet. The *Clematis montana alba* looks fantastic in spring, dripping like white honey all over my arch. And now, *Clematis* "Nelly Moser" is in flower in the front garden, with its voluptuous blooms, white stripes sashaying through the middle of big pointed pink petals. It is a Barbara Windsor of a flower — huge bosoms on a tiny spindly body — and far too extravagant for the modest pergola it leans on in my garden. I bought it in honour of Mother, really. It's a bit over the top for my liking, but she took delight in its excesses — and particularly its jaunty appellation. Any name remotely silly to an English ear had her seal of approval. *Sisyrinchium* in the garden; in the kitchen, Chicken Cacciatore. She had a daft, sometimes scatological sense of humour, and words came galloping out of her mouth before her (considerable) brain could catch up. She once floored a friend, at the height of sanctions against South Africa, by solemnly criticizing her friend's choice of bank, and declaring that "I would *never* bark at Banclays." Whenever I pass a branch of the notorious sanctions buster, I still snigger. Mother had principles, as well as humour. I don't bark there either.

I planted some giant sunflower seeds, and tidied up my little terrace at the back of the house. I have an old stone Buddha in the corner, and placed three slate-grey rocks and a twisted gnarl of wood beside him. Plus some of my favourite pebbles in an earthenware bowl of water. I love stones. They have their own language, somehow, and you have to be very still, and very patient, to hear it.

26 May I drove to a local nursery for three red-hot pokers (*so* vulgar) to cheer up my gloomy potato patch, and two copper *Heuchera micrantha* (tasteful) for the front garden.

The grass is knee high at the allotment — it is a lesson in persistence — but I can't face using the strimmer again. I planted out some Scarlet Emperor runners, as much for their vivid red flowers as for the beans they produce, and a couple of sweetcorn for the edge of the potato patch. Who would have thought sweetcorn would flourish in these northern climes? But it does.

We are nearly at the end of May. My father has been having radiotherapy, and I call him often.

"How are you, Dad?"

"I'm feeling fine."

Since Tim never disclosed exactly how awful he felt — except in extremis, when all barriers came crashing down — I should perhaps feel uneasy now, or excluded, as I used to do. But I do not. I believe my father. He is surviving. At eighty-two, another chance is offered. How remarkable this life is.

28/29 May When Tim nearly died, in 2001. I looked into an abyss. Three things happened. One, an old dance injury in my lower back returned, and flattened me out. I could do nothing, except lie on my back on the floor, and suffer. Two, after flirting with Buddhist philosophy throughout my thirties in a bashful and slightly surprised way (my family are diehard rationalists), I began to meditate daily. The Buddhists are not afraid to look death in the face, without a god to hide behind: that taught me courage. Three, I discovered a teacher of the Alexander Technique, which trains you to pause, and challenge habitual patterns of thought and physical behaviour. Slowly, I unravelled the chronic muscular tensions caused by being stuck in "fight or flight" mode for many years, which finally made my back go "ping". Sometimes, to come to our senses, we have to be landed, like a fish out of water: gasping for breath, for life itself. Then the change comes. This weekend, I travelled to Kendal, in Cumbria, for an intensive weekend at the Fellside Training School in Alexander Technique. This stuff works. My back is safe. I am still working on my brain.

★ ★ ★

30 May Well, that is typical. I have been waiting all month for some plants to arrive by post. The weekend we go away, the globe artichokes arrive. They have been sweltering in their padded plastic pouches in the outhouse for two hot days — and more, in transit — and they look decidedly sickly. The leaves are long, attenuated, and there are black blotches on them. A sort of mould of despair! I ripped the packets open immediately, and could almost hear them gasping for breath. Straight up to the allotment, to plant them out. Who knows if they will make it? Still, better for them to have known the earth, even for a few days, than just to have been hurled in the bin. I should start a plant sanctuary for all the lost and hopeless green things of the world.

31 May Insult to injury: the pigeons have dive-bombed all my artichokes and upended them contemptuously on the bare earth. Bloody cheek. I replanted and netted each one. You don't get me that easily. On the potato front there is gloom, however. I think my little crop has failed. Bob Flowerdew would be sadly shaking his head. Obviously, I should have stuck to black bin liners.

Some spring onion and kale seedlings are through. And I planted some outdoor cucumbers up a tripod of canes.

Today is the last day of Dad's radiotherapy. I ring in the evening, and he says he still feels fine. Well, I never! May is a beautiful month. No heartbreak here.

142

Jobs for May

- Raid your garden centres or plant nurseries for plug plants to augment vegetable plots — lettuce, leeks and onions are usually available in trays of six or so. If your seeds fail, plug plants are a marvellous second chance. (Don't hesitate to grow veg in your back garden. They are decorative as well as productive.)
- Make a liquid nettle manure. Take an old plastic dustbin and fill it with water. Cut down a big clump of stinging nettles (gloves must be worn — and long sleeves!) Plunge the nettles into the water, put a lid on top and leave it to stew for a week or two. It will make a great liquid feed for hungry vegetables, but it stinks to high heaven, so is probably not something for a tiny city garden.
- Sow sunflower seeds. There is a beautiful range of size and colour available now, you don't need to go for the giant yellow beasts. (But, let's face it, they are FUN, and never fail to gladden the eye — so easy to grow, too.)
- May is a fantastically fecund month. Grass and weeds grow a mile a minute — so much more vigorously than our tenderly cultivated flowers. But do not be faint-hearted. Strim, mow, weed, as often as you can, and never once imagine you will be able to keep up with the growth.
- French marigolds: sow them, or buy them readymade, but do find a place for them somewhere. They seem to be a most helpful and powerful little flower. The insects love them — and their strange

scent is a potent fix for many vegetables. Also, how orange can you be? Little madams.

- Sow runner beans. They grow fast and well, and since they climb, rather than spread, they will fit in a small space.
- Sunny day? Sit outside (or by an open window) and sit *still*. Enjoy what you already have. Isn't it lovely?

June

Summer is coming. Maximum light. Sunshine, a big shiny sky, and a bewildering hum of colour and life. Down on the ground, the soft fruit season is upon us. This can only mean one thing. Summer Pudding. The true taste of the sun — raspberries, blackcurrants, redcurrants. The intense colour of these little fruits — lollipop red, purple and black — shines off the bushes and brambles on which they grow, with all the voluptuous promise of a summer still young, still singing from a fresh throat. I grow all three ingredients, though my raspberries come later, so for those I rely on the generosity of summer-fruiting friends, or the greengrocer.

My blackcurrant bush is a veteran, since I planted it in my new garden in 1996, and it has survived transplantation to the allotment with no complaints. It never fails to crop heavily. I have happy memories of sitting cross-legged on the lawn with Molly, when she

145

was only five or six, and picking the hundreds of fat currants which dripped like jewels off this one small bush. She was amazed at the treasure it yielded: I was too. We got a belly-ache from eating too many uncooked berries, and faces and fingers were stained with purple dye — but it didn't matter, we were happy. My redcurrant bush is very new, but just as willing — I am ready for off.

Tim was a superb cook, and he had a few signature dishes that marked the ritual of the passing seasons: a rich, alcoholic chocolate cake for autumn; chicken (with crumbly roast potatoes and glazed carrots) for winter; creamy, broad bean risotto for spring; and for summer — Summer Pudding. I have never dared make it until now. The arcane, almost mystical attention he paid to the mixing of the fruits; the weighing down of the layered pudding with heavy objects; the presentation of the finished article, upturned — thrillingly fast — from basin to plate; all these aspects made me tremble to try it myself. But this is my moment.

As always, I choose the simplest, most straightforward route to my belly. Whilst Tim had complex, regal tastes in food, I think I must have been a peasant in another life — there's nothing nicer to me than rough chunks of bread and cheese, hearty stews and spicy soups, crisp salads tossed in lemon; and for afters, slices of apple, segments of orange. Berries from the bush, raw. Food writer Nigel Slater is my ally in this: not only does he write with an almost obscene sensuality about his recipes — he keeps them beautiful, short, direct.

He has a fast version of Summer Pudding, featured in his book *Real Fast Puddings*, which works straight from the bowl. I adapt it for myself, putting slices of white bread at the bottom of an oval dish. Then spooning of soft fruits — in my case, blackcurrants, raspberries and some bought blueberries — that have been cooked together in honey and water to produce a gorgeous mass of split berries in a thick, dark syrup. More slices of bread, then fruit; ending with a top cover of bread, the remaining berry juice poured on top, everything pushed down neatly. After half an hour, I eat it, scooped directly from the dish, with a dollop of crème fraiche. A perfect combination, which makes the mouth explode with pleasure. Food from the sun god. I am initiated.

2 June I love the summers in Leeds. We live in a part of the city — the north-east — which is close to green in every direction. But choose how you look with care, because we are right on the edge. One way — grimy, inner-city streets; the other — leafy outlands. To get to us from town is an unpromising journey, along a busy and bad-tempered Roundhay Road, through the run-down back-to-backs and ramshackle shops of Harehills. If you look left from our house, that is what you will find. But look right, and there are riches: the ancient and glacial Gledhow Valley Woods; the rolling hills and pastures of Roundhay Park; and our own neat little Gipton Wood — all within easy distance. Climb in a car, and the roads to Wetherby and Harrogate open up in corridors of green, with tiny villages to either side, set in the middle of abundant, long-established fields and tangled hedgerows.

All of this is a walker's dream, especially when the weather is warm and the colour is back in the world. But there is joy for me, as ever, in not moving at all, but just basking in the sun at the allotment, watching the butterflies start their summer dance, between the buddleia and the ornamental grasses; and reclining on my blue, stripey deckchair in the front garden, where the foliage of shrubs and trees — inordinately huge — is now in full shout, curving competitively over my head to make a private, outdoor chamber.

June 1994 was so different. We still lived in Stockwell, south London then, locked in by buildings on every side and sweltering in a heatwave, in our tiny upstairs flat. Tim was newly diagnosed. During June he was gripped by a course of chemotherapy, both punishing and toxic, which robbed him of all his hair, and most of his life force. He sat like a stone, poisoned to his core. Any anguish he felt was held down so deep, even he could not find access to it, and he became pale, ashen — unrecognizable as the sunny, smiling young man I had met five years before.

Molly, meanwhile, was just under two. Inside her was a strong ego; outside, a dry, raging eczema. Her little arms, legs and face were flushed with red: her angry skin seemed to reflect the outrage she felt at what was happening to her dad. I played piggy-in-the-middle,

148

ministering to the two of them as best I could, the heat of the sweltering, treeless streets only adding fuel to the fire of our predicament. The move to Leeds, two years later, in 1996, was a soul-saver.

We had been talking about leaving London for some time. Where we lived had become a nightmare: we were forced to move from Stockwell by the arrival of a — seriously disturbed — nuisance neighbour, and were rehoused by Lambeth Council, to a sink estate in Clapham North, only to find that the local dope dealers used the corridor outside our ground-floor flat, day and night, to congregate and settle scores between themselves. Meanwhile, Tim was unhappy in his job. His illness was in remission now, but he was vulnerable to stress — and there was conflict at work. Motherhood had made me vulnerable too. The streets on the mean side of south London — a happy enough playground when I was in my twenties — now seemed fraught with potential strife, particularly with a two year old in my care. We had no plan, except one: to escape. And we did just that. Tim handed in his notice, we gave back the keys to the flat, and fled.

We knew we wanted to head north — it was in our blood, with parents from Lancashire and Yorkshire — and decided on Leeds, Tim's home town, where we stayed with Tim's parents and friends during the summer of 1996, while we looked for somewhere to live, and for work. Somehow it all fell into place.

At the back of our minds, maybe, when we ran from London, was the fact that we were running away from Tim's cancer, too — his remission (though only temporary) a signal for a new start, a clean break. Although a risk, and a great leap of faith, it was the right thing to do. The only thing.

The streets here can be mean enough, like Stockwell, but at least we found our little patch of earth — a house with a garden — to cushion the blows, and access to green spaces, and freedoms undreamed of in inner-city London.

3 June My friend Melissa and her family came to stay for a few days. We know each other from way back, since working together in our twenties as journalists. Melissa is a talented and experienced writer. When I went off, waywardly, at thirty, into the world of dance and theatre, she stayed with her writing, honing her craft to a high degree. Now, she listens to my complaints at having the novel rejected. Her advice is refreshing, non-conciliatory and robust: keep writing, she says, just don't stop. Even in my current mental fog, I realize the power and clarity of her advice. It is odd how we can avoid, sometimes for years, the very thing which may be our greatest strength. But I know this: although I may have left my writing from time to time, it never left me.

One of the best things my mother taught me was the gift of a good companion. She cultivated many loyal and vibrant women friends in her life, who were a rich source of mutual support through the years. Melissa is a good friend in that mould — and my mother loved her too.

★　★　★

The carrots, "Early Nantes", which I sowed at home in March and then planted in pots outside the back door, have produced fine green feathery tops. They might be ready. I pull a few but am disappointed. The roots are small, and several have "forked", or divided into two, making a poor, pale little crop. This happens when the soil is too rich, with added manure or compost — and, frankly, the pot was too small. I planted them above the ground like this to avoid carrot fly — which doesn't like high altitudes — but I should have sorted out a bigger container. There's not even enough here for one measly bowl of lentil soup. So much for growing all my own ingredients. I have failed potatoes and forking carrots! At least the onions have fulfilled their promise.

4 *June* I ran a T'ai Chi workshop today, and made the grand profit of £3. I do love teaching — there is an idea that "you teach what you need to learn", and my work is all about balance, flow, internal quiet, and being steady on your own two feet. But £3 for two hours' effort? Really!

Something happens to people as soon as June is here. I notice it, particularly in my teaching. My classes have become an accurate barometer of the weather, a signal of the changing seasons and concomitant human moods. In autumn, a rush of new adult students turn up, eager to "go back to school". By winter, there are the regulars, only deterred by heavy snow or illness. Spring brings a fresh batch — like juicy saplings, keen, bendy and alert. But in June, it all falls apart: the most

151

reliable attender is suddenly nowhere to be seen. It's as if the sun takes the lid off people's heads, spills all their sensible beans out, and leads their itchy feet off on some other adventure. Halfway through the second pint, at a riverside pub maybe, they might remember that they were meant to be elsewhere . . . But who the hell knows or cares?

5 June The sunshine is suddenly in retreat. The birds, the wind, the rain, have all inflicted damage on my globe artichokes. They have had a rough start, and I love them all the more for it. I am acutely aware of how random life is on this allotment. It is not always the most plump and promising plants that come through, and not always the ones I most fervently want to succeed. I simply have to do the best I can, and then trust to chance — and nature — because my interventions do not often count for much. In Samuel Beckett's wonderful words: "Ever tried. Ever failed. No matter. Try again. Fail again. Fail better."

In the past three days, vegetable plug plants, ordered earlier in the year but held up by poor growing conditions, have arrived by post, thick and fast. Sprouts, broccoli, runner beans and cauliflower — they are like demanding baby birds, beaks wide open for nourishment. Plant me! Feed me! Water me! I am a new mother, all over again.

I planted runner beans, "Enorma", right away, next to the Scarlet Emperors I put in last month. I always enjoy watching these climbers hurtle ambitiously up their bamboo tripods: thick twining stems boasting handsome foliage and bright tiny flowers. They are such good value. (The other day, a dog walker stopped me as I was unlocking the allotment gates, and asked me the name of a beautiful climbing plant she had spotted on someone's plot. Rather than the usual clematis, she wanted to grow one of these round an arch in her own garden. She was amazed when I told her it was no rare exotic species — just a humble runner bean.) They are supposed to be voracious feeders, and some gardeners dig deep trenches of rich compost for their roots, but I find them quite accommodating. The changeable weather of the last few weeks, however, has been trying, even for these giants. I hope they settle in OK.

Sorrow catches me unawares, even on the sunniest day. I sit, and tears come. Then they stop, and I rise back to the surface. This is the rhythm of recovery — haphazard, unpredictable, much like life itself.

6 June A dry, clear day. Although the recent rain has wrought havoc among new seedlings, it has also brought an intense and luscious green to established shrubs and trees. This green makes me greedy: my eyes grow fat with looking. And when the clouds drift away, the sky's face, washed clean by frequent showers, is a perfect, complementary blue.

Although surrounded by buildings, both behind and beyond its perimeters, the placing of my allotment is cunning. It allows the sky to unfold fully above the gardeners' lucky heads, and a wide horizon of green to emerge beneath. Shame it is that we spend so much of our time bent over in attitudes of toil, bums up, heads and hands in the dirt. I tried hard to avoid this today, but did scramble around planting sprouts on the bed closest to the wild grasses.

How is it that my fingers become instantly encrusted with filth, even though I wear thick gardening gloves? And that stinking juices from the compost pail, which I bring from home every week full of vegetable peelings and old fruit, always end up down my front, even though the bucket has a close-fitting lid and gets decanted very carefully into my open allotment heap? For years, in London, I believed I was oh-so-urban. It's a lie. I am a born-again crusty.

But consider the rewards: a sharp-leaved yellow iris, fluttering like a Mediterranean bird on the little pond. Geraniums, pink and blue, cheap, cheerful and chatty, to either side. And, by the shed, the tall purple verbenas and globe-headed alliums. Paradise comes in small packages; a single flower, a flash of colour, and early summer sun. The bee lady walked past with her honey-comb box, bringing in a new swarm. She is like a bright flower herself (when the bee helmet is off), with blonde hair and a wide, shiny smile. I instantly feel better when I see her.

At home, a scarlet poppy burst into flower today. This consoles me, since one of the local children (too young to know not to) has systematically decapitated all the others, an act of insouciant vandalism which inspires in

154

me a deep, unreasoning rage. I could not smile at him for days when I realized what was happening.

The seeds of discontent are being scattered, like those of the squandered poppy. Is it time to move from this house, where we have lived cheek by jowl with neighbours for nine years, seven of them with Tim, two without? I can feel a wind of change beginning to blow.

In the front garden, the *Cotinus* (smoke bush) is a deep, dark, satisfying mass of plum foliage; it is set off in the rest of the garden by flower head dots of white, on the lace-cap hydrangea, the cotoneaster, and the ever-faithful viburnum. White is a welcome colour, a necessary simplicity, amidst the growing summer profusion.

7 June I did some work on the brassica patch today. I planted out some broccoli — or rather calabrese (the fat green little trees which ripen in summer, not the skinnier purple sprouting variety, which doesn't appear until spring), cauliflower "Astral", and summer cabbage "Hispi". The early bird would probably have put them in sooner, but things have been late this year, due to a cool, wet spring. And anyway, I seem to be slow in most things. It's just my way.

Here is my confession for today: I put slug pellets around the new plants. Gone is my truce with the great slimy brigade. The true organic gardener would be horrified with me. I hate those pellets, too: even the type that are "kind to birds and animals" surely contain some nasty chemicals. What to do? The slugs have arrived in force now I have added compost and manure to my soil. The more I cultivate, the more they love it. Were I to put these little plants in today, without pellets, chances are they would be chewed to bare stalks by tomorrow. Sometimes even the stalks go too, and there is just a hole, a memory, where the plant once was.

Nematodes — a type of flatworm, which offers biological slug control — are the real answer. But they don't last long, are limited in the area they control, and have to be applied much earlier in the season to be fully effective. Again, I am late for the school bell. I put a big net over the entire bed to finish with, to ward off air and ground attack. The little rows of green look lovely.

When I came home, I chatted to a neighbour, who said she had been thinking of Tim, now that it was sunny again — and of how he used to sit in the garden and read.

"Sad, isn't it?" she remarked. I agreed. Then she startled me with her next aside.

"You often look as if you are in a dream these days, you know."

What does she mean? Eighteen months after Tim's death, am I still in shock? And I thought I was doing so well. I remember listening to food writer Nigella Lawson on the radio, a few months after the high-profile death of her husband, journalist John Diamond, in 2001. He had written extensively about his throat cancer in a *Times* newspaper column, and there was big media coverage of his funeral, including photographs of his widow, looking glazed and pale.

Nigella Lawson herself says she thought she had appeared calm, normal, composed — then she caught sight of the pictures, and was horrified at how far from the truth that was. My neighbour's comment, similarly, jolts me into a new awareness. I *have* been coping well; nonetheless, I have travelled a long way from the person I used to be — and the journey back to my own centre will take some time.

8 *June* BIG SUNSHINE. My local nursery, the Polish-owned Wolinski's, was teeming with produce. I bought some *Crocosmia* "Lucifer" for the allotment. This flower, which I know as montbretia, always reminds me of Ireland, where it grows, orange on sword-sharp leaves, with lush abundance, in hedgerow and garden. "Lucifer" is the bigger, fire-engine red variety. Also, I scooped up some hollyhocks — pink and white — and fennel — green and bronze — to brighten up my (failed) potato patch.

The fennel plant is enchanting. It grows to a fair height, romping up to my shoulders and beyond within a year, and looks both architectural and graceful, delicate flower heads floating on strong, upright stems. The flower seeds prolifically, and the dried seeds make a bracing tea: good for the digestion, like peppermint, but less abrasive. I grow fennel in both my gardens. It is domestic, with a bit of a wild streak, and looks lovely in vases as well as in the ground. Apparently it is not a great companion for vegetables, but I don't care. I like it.

I went straight from the nursery to the allotment to plant out my new purchases. Lee, who has gardened here for years, sauntered past, to give his verdict on my poor potatoes.

"I reckon they've rotted," he says, a brutally simple explanation. The days after planting them, in April, were a deluge of rain. "They had the worst kind of weather," he explains. "Loads of rain, then lots of wind to dry and crack the surface of the ground, leaving all the water sealed inside." So my potatoes just sat and festered in their tomb. I felt strangely consoled by Lee's explanation, even though it's clear I could have helped the situation by conditioning the soil more before planting. Let's just blame the weather.

Today I had enough time to take a proper break, and walked down to the special picnic spot by the main storehouse for my lunch. It is lovely here. Don, the secretary, has worked his magic, creating little seats and bird tables, cutting back into the wild growth to make a sheltered green space, complete with friendly notice: FEEL FREE TO SIT OR SNOOZE. I lay on my back on the grass after eating fresh French rolls and ham.

Memories were sparked, as I lay, of childhood picnics long ago. Every summer we would take day trips to Clacton or Frinton. On the way, just before arriving, we always stopped at the same bread shop for crusty rolls, and when we got to the beach, Mum made them up with cold meats and salad. They tasted delicious. It was worth being the runt in the middle, on the back seat of the car, squashed between two noisy brothers and a yelping dog; worth fighting car sickness, for the first whiff of sea air and freedom — when nausea converted to healthy hunger, and I wolfed down my rolls with gusto. The past. That strange other country — with a passport to visit, every now and again. Today, just by chance, it was crusty fresh bread that took me back over the frontier.

After lunch it was hot — 24 degrees Celsius and steadily climbing. Time to wear my floppy straw hat: eccentric Englishwoman on the loose. The sun can be merciless up here, where shade is minimal. I do look extraordinary sometimes when I am working outside — grass in my hair, sweat and mud streaks on my face and fingers, and a distracted, almost wild gleam in the eye. Now and again, I catch a glimpse of myself in the shed window. It's an unedifying sight. On my doomed potato patch I planted out two types of squash — "Delicata", with white and green stripes, and "Tablegold", which has small, acorn-shaped yellow fruit. Then I watered and netted them all, and fringed the whole patch with my new *Crocosmia*.

9 June Oh no. All my new little seedlings are in, the weather is dry, and the water supply is off! The pipes — old and rusty — have sprung a leak on the ridge above my plot. Lee and Don have been digging heroically to pinpoint where the trouble is, so the verges are piled high with thick yellow clay from the subsoil, and there are deep gaping trenches down to the pipes — just when it was all beginning to look so pretty! I scraped the barrel of my old water butt (also starting to leak) for something to pour on my parched new plants.

In the evening I managed to sneak back for an hour, while my daughter was at Guides. I walked the top way to my plot, pushing through the bramble hedge to get there. As I stumbled along I passed two guys sitting out by their shed, supping cans of Stella Artois, which they raised, rather sheepishly, in a toast, as I went past. I think they half expected a rebuke, but they certainly weren't going to get it from me. "How civilized," I said, and they grinned. On the way home I stopped at the Co-op for a can of my own to drink on the doorstep. Gardening gives you APPETITE.

14 June Suddenly it's cold again. And wet. So far, the new seedlings have survived. But the outdoor cucumbers I planted a little while ago have shrivelled to nothing. There is dismay among the gardeners — so many of the vegetables are still so small. Maria, on the double plot behind mine, which is always hugely productive, says her sweetcorn is normally a foot higher by now, but it's still by her ankles. It has not been a good growing year.

15 June I took a friend up to the allotment for lunch. It really is the best place for eating out: fresh, natural decor, and it could not be cheaper. (Exclusive too — members only.) However, guests are expected to work their passage, so I thrust a hoe in Kath's hands and followed her along the row, picking up the decapitated weeds and slinging them out for compost. (I don't recycle the more pernicious perennial weeds, especially not bindweed, which needs no encouragement whatsoever. Even the smallest segment of root or stem will send out its tiny suckers, like underground guerrilla fighters, in an instant. Burn or bin the stuff on sight!) Some miniature sunflowers, bought ready-started to give some early summer colour, have popped their petals open today: three smiling faces, making the pea patch look jolly.

Something is happening. It's here. Summer has definitely landed. There is a stirring, a fizzing in my blood. I urgently need a haircut. Suddenly my clothes are getting colourful again. The sloppy grey jumper is chucked in the back of the cupboard. Skirts, dresses and flip-flops come out. The rhythm of life. A hopeful beat. Yes.

17 June Today was hot, humid and overcast; the weather is so changeable this year, confusing plants and humans alike. It is very difficult, working in humidity. My legs tend to ache easily anyway — the accumulated stress and shock of the past few years seems to have weighed them down with lead — but damp heat makes everything inside slow down, and I am covered in a nasty film of sweat even before I begin to dig.

In my mid-twenties, I spent three months in Bahrain, helping look after a friend's young family. They invited me partly to convalesce after a bout of glandular fever, and I seemed to spend most of my time hand in hand with a tiny tot, flopped around the compound swimming pool, turning an astonishing and dangerous shade of mahogany and overwhelmed by torpor. However, it did the trick, and I returned to London with all the old fevers burned away.

There was no cool pool to distract me today, so holding lethargy at bay, I managed to plant some courgettes in the middle of the last empty vegetable bed, on an awkward sloping corner by the compost bin. Courgettes are greedy for food, warmth and water, but they repay their debt of toil with a beautiful, bold display — giant, palm-shaped leaves springing from stems which creep along thickly at ground level. Later, they throw out canary yellow flowers, star-shaped and prolific. The baby courgettes which form from the flowers are tasty and tender. But leave them too long and they will grow into huge impenetrable marrows, the like of which my mother — a splendid cook in all but this — used to serve up, valiantly stuffed with mince and onions, as an economical and nutritious supper, the memory of which makes my culinary heart sink.

I have a young rhubarb plant on this corner patch too, gift from a neighbour, and not by a long way my first choice of fruit. Although I should be ashamed to admit it, living in the famed "rhubarb triangle" of Leeds, Wakefield and Bradford, I really don't like it much; it leaves an acid film on my teeth. But the plant itself is magnificent, with whacking great crinkled leaves on top of flushed ruby and yellow stalks. And it grows with a vengeance on this soil. The man on the plot above mine has a jungle of the stuff and spent an hour or so hacking it down today. He came across to give me some. My heart sank. "Add lots of sugar," he said. It looks as tough as old boots.

Although I hate using slug pellets, I notice that all my little cabbage and broccoli plants have survived and are surrounded by the slime of a thousand slaughtered slugs . . .

18 June I taught T'ai Chi today, in the middle of a heatwave. (Some people *did* turn up.) Later there were intense thunderstorms. Everyone in the class felt peculiar, including me. We did a lot of lying down.

19 June I do not come from a family which devotes much attention to graves and memorial plots. Although I loved visiting churchyards when I was young, it was less from spiritual need than curiosity about the old names and dates on headstones — a child's glimpse into times gone by. Now that I have lost so many people I loved, the question arises: how to remember them formally? A place to visit, an object to view, might bring clarity to a confused inner landscape of emotion, thought and memory.

Whitby will always be the place I associate most keenly with Tim. It was somewhere he wanted to show me, right at the start of our relationship: a Yorkshire initiation for this Essex/London girl. And we spent some happy, carefree times there together. The high south cliff, where his ashes are scattered, symbolizes both beginning and end of our particular journey, in one wild and beautiful place. But Whitby is not easy to get to quickly.

Adel Woods, which I walked in today, is just a mile or two up the road, and not far from where Tim grew up, and went to school. St Gemma's Hospice has a piece of land in Adel Woods, dedicated to the memory of hospice patients. Baby trees have been planted, and a beautiful, rough-edged granite stone, carved in commemoration, marks the entrance to the site. Last summer my brother Nigel gave money towards a tree-trunk bench, which will be placed, with others, along the woodland pathways for people to sit on and reflect. There are no names or plaques here; it is a discreet corner, suited to Tim's unassuming manner. A quiet man in life, and quiet in memory.

But things did not look so good today, as I walked around. In a year, the saplings have grown, but so has the undergrowth, and the paths have temporarily disappeared under bushes and brambles. This place is meant to be semi-wild, but still requires managing. I felt disturbed, and rang the hospice to let them know. They promised to contact the council whose job it is to keep the wood healthy. The experience made me realize that I should have something in my own garden for Tim — bring him back home where I can keep an eye on him.

It is a messy process, assimilating loss; finding ways to settle down with the one who has disappeared for ever. The different, often incomplete attempts I make to memorialize Tim — whether in writing, photos, scattered ashes, benches, belongings (what to keep, what to throw out?) — show me one thing. I am still far from moving on. This grieving is a long and complex work.

20 June Melissa's recent visit put a boot up my bum. I am writing again.

21 June Summer Solstice. The longest day. It's odd to think that the dark will start creeping back, just as the summer finally seems to be revving up. Everything changes. A hippy at Stonehenge (filmed for the early news) put it rather neatly: "One breath in, one breath out. That's all we have."

June is juicy. It's all that sap, rising up through stem, into leaf, into fruit. There is a ripening in the air. When I walk through the woods, if the wind is in the right direction, I swear I can smell the sea. June is also a time of wishes. And I wish my toes were dipping in the ocean. Right now.

22 June I showed willing, and made a rhubarb crumble. It was surprisingly tasty.

The wind and rain in early June battered my runner beans. Such promise, come to nothing. But Lee came past yesterday, while I was away, and, unbidden, planted some healthy new ones for me. He also gave me some of his strawberries, which grow with abandon on his well-established plot. Casual, unexpected acts of kindness like this happen all the time at the allotment.

It is why I feel so at home here, so soothed and welcome.

My friend Laurie is over from the States for a flying visit. We first met when she came to London in 1986 to train in choreography and dance technique at the Laban Centre. I was there too — but as a beginner, whilst she was in the advanced group. Some classes we shared, however, and soon became close.

Now, as a performance artist, Laurie divides her time between New York and New England, and travels to all sorts of far-off places for her work, and for fun. When I listen to her schedule I feel more than ever that I have feet of clay. Life goes much more slowly for me, but still we happily chime. I took her to the allotment and we wandered about, picking a few peas and broad beans for supper. I showed her the sweetcorn which has been causing such consternation.

"In America we have a saying," she tells me. "The sweetcorn should be 'knee high by the fourth of July'. And actually, I don't think it'll be far off target." I hire her as my motivational gardening coach on the spot.

When we were back at the house, my neighbour came round to give us the first picking of cherries from their tree. The tree, which now stands as high as the house and is always full of leaves, blossom and fruit, was grown from a cherry stone forty years ago. Laurie and I sat outside in the front garden, eating the cherries, spitting out the stones with some gusto, and podding my beans. It was the first time I have sat out at home all year. Can that really be true?

★　★　★

24 June "It is your mind that creates this world." This is a quote attributed to the Buddha. I have it printed on a postcard, which depicts a dark room with a window looking out on to the towering mountains of the Himalayas, and a clear blue sky. I know about that dark room, and even though I remember to look through my window, it is sometimes still a struggle to see the view. Grief plays such strange tricks on the sufferer — and I began my grieving even before Tim died. I feel I lost him, at some level, a long time ago, in the endless hospital corridors of his chronic and debilitating illness. Now the garden gives me ground for my feet — and a Yorkshire version of a Himalayan landscape for my eyes. But the weeds of worry grow, in the second I stop looking, and then it's back to the dark room, alone.

Still, this week has been a kind of turning point for me, just as the year is revolving on its axis. Since Laurie visited, I have started to sit out every day, and have eaten out regularly too. I am coming out of my shell. And it's nice to meet the garden again, like a dear old friend. The allotment takes up so much of my attention these days, but this little space at home has been quietly waiting for me to return.

The little tree I planted nine years ago, in memory of my friend John, is quite tall now, its laced foliage forming a graceful canopy over the grass, providing shade for a panting dog, and for hot human toes. Opposite is Mother's purple smoke bush — and the two plants almost touch across the space between, as if talking to each other or trying to hold hands. John and my mother were very alike — great-hearted extroverts who loved and competed with each other in equal, noisy measure. Somehow, they still communicate, through colour and light, and in the movement of the leaves.

27 June I was up on the allotment before nine o'clock. I love this early slot, when I am organized enough to get here. It is hot, bright and dry. Summer has exploded into action since mid-June, and everything is growing wildly. I worked for a while on the fruit patch, which is always covered in weeds, and as I wandered around the rest of the plot, I noticed that the beleaguered globe artichokes have all survived. Bravo! Then I picked some gooseberries, onions, peas and broad beans. The onions are fat and lovely — it is definitely worth planting Japanese autumn sets for over-wintering. It's still officially too early to harvest them, but they are ripe and ready.

I sat on the shed step for a long time: it's a much better view from low down. The teasels and alliums, plume poppy and buddleia waved gently over my head: I felt like a ladybird peeping into the overgrowth.

30 June There were tropical downpours today, and I dashed up to Oakwood Lane in between the raindrops. The heat and wet have triggered astonishing bursts of growth — grass and weeds, chiefly, but there are crops too. The runner beans are romping up their poles and over the arch (Lee's gifts being the winners in that particular race); the leaves on the squash and courgette are a deep, healthy green; the spiky new shoots from the artichokes are growing silver-fresh.

Dad had a check-up at the hospital, following his treatment last month. They are pleased with him. I am too.

So we are halfway through the year. This always happens too soon for me, the light expanding to its fullest before my brain has a chance to let it in; but time has its own logic, the seasons their own natural imperative. Tucked between the dreamy promise of May and the blowsiness of July, June, I find, is an enigmatic, gentle month. There are not many birthdays among my friends and family — most of them fall in spring or autumn — and death keeps its nose out too.

I am left with the loveliness of the garden, which takes over now, and is growing, growing, growing. The colours are filling and ripening in the sun, but are not yet too gaudy. There is room for pink — on the mallow, in a rosebud — before the big-hitting primary colours of July smash us between the eyes. June has a soft feeling, even though it can switch between hot and cold, between dry and wet. It has not quite relinquished the capriciousness of spring: but it has a subtlety, a quiet charm.

For some reason — with its cheerful optimism, its hint of early summer and celebration — June reminds me of my father's sister, Ella. She was a tender and graceful woman, with a soft Lancashire accent, a maternal warmth, sparkling, mischievous eyes, and a full-throated chuckle when amused — which was often.

Right to the end of her long life she was deeply religious, but remained totally open-minded. Inquisitive about other philosophies, beliefs, even scepticisms, she welcomed everyone, and always had time to listen and reflect. She was one of the few people I have met who seemed entirely at ease with themselves.

It was often summer when I visited her, to enjoy the reliable provision of sandwiches, cakes and tea; the careful, listening ear, and ready, reassuring smile. She was a soothing presence in my life, as a child and young adult. She is dead now, and I look for her spirit inside myself, as I carry on seeking ways to heal and repair. The summer sun, especially at this stage in the season, before it has become too relentless and fierce, is a powerful tool in my medicine cabinet. The knot between my eyebrows is softening. I am smiling more often. The warmth lulls my mind.

Jobs for June

- Plant lettuce leaves, rocket, radish. Grow your own summer salad. I have more luck with pots and window boxes than the open ground, where the slugs can be merciless.
- Make a Summer Pudding (see page 147).
- Mow the lawn. And again! Tedious. Leave one patch — under a tree, maybe — a bit curved and wild. The longer grass looks lovely next to a cropped lawn. Definition is important now — the cleaner the edge of the turf, the more voluptuous the border will look.

- Play with pruning. I cut back ruthlessly all the time. You can make interesting shapes by taking branches out below, as well as above and to the sides of big shrubs. I also cut right into the centre, so that I can look through the middle of a plant to the other end of the garden. Look at forms, at the third dimension: plants are like living sculptures. (If you make a mistake, as I do frequently, it will normally grow back, like a bad haircut.)
- Can of lager on your doorstep — or any scenic spot you can find. It's a sign of summer.

July

Imagine that any mind ever thought a red geranium!
As if the redness of a red geranium could be anything
but a sensual experience . . .

D. H. Lawrence, "Red Geranium and
Godly Mignonette"

1 July Today I weeded the cabbage patch. I lead a
glamorous life. And I have high hopes for these
cabbages. They will be the most succulent in the land.
My magnificent cardoon — giant relative of the thistle,
six foot six and counting — has produced a crop of
handsome blue flowers. It makes a stark focal point on
the edge of the plot, a silver-grey skeleton, topped with
blue, against a translucent sky. The light behind it is
piercingly lovely.

July 1989 was when I first met Tim. I was back barely a
month from my working trip to Hungary, and was still
homesick for that beautiful, chaotic country, and its
charming, chaotic people. It was not so easy, in any
case, to shake them off. The Kaposvar company came
over in July, to perform Gogol and Chekhov at the Old
Vic, for the London International Festival of Theatre.
My friend Ria, their dramaturg, came too, to act as

172

interpreter and chaperone to the company's two maverick artistic directors. She invited me for dinner at the flat where they were staying in Primrose Hill. It was her ex-husband's place, she said, and he had a lodger called Tim, whom I would probably meet too. (In fact she put him in charge of the cooking, which was a smart move.) When I saw him, my first impressions were pleasing and calm. "What a kind-looking man," I thought, "and what a lovely smile he has." His smile did not let me down.

For me, July belongs to the geranium. Or to be specific, the variegated pelargonium. Scarlet red is my favourite colour. When we lived in Stockwell, the flat next door had window boxes stacked with these red-headed temptresses. From their window to ours, beneath the window boxes, stretched a washing line on a pulley. When the sun shone, it felt more like a cheerful slum in Naples than a council flat in south London. Since then, I have grown pelargoniums in pots and boxes every July. They are bright and cheerful, thrive on neglect, and last all summer long. The season feels incomplete without them.

It is eighteen months since Tim died. People say the first year, the first anniversary, is the worst. I am not so sure. There was a thick cocoon around me throughout the whole of 2004. Although there were things to do — the flood of bureaucracy which follows a death is insanely misplaced — I felt strangely protected. Shock and exhaustion enveloped me like a blanket, and people stepped in with cushions to soften the falls.

A week after Tim's death, his Motability hire vehicle, as regulations insist, was driven away. Friends and family clubbed together immediately to buy us another car, an act of generosity which I will never get over. Then Tim's father Leslie, and Catherine, his mother — always a tower of strength despite her own tremendous loss — paid for Molly and me to fly to Spain for a week's holiday with their cousin Rose. Financial agencies made allowances, as I struggled to get my affairs in order. There was protection, from known and unknown sources, steering Molly and me through strange days and amnesiac nights.

Molly developed a passion for the American series *Friends*, using endless reruns as comfort on the day her father died, and for a long time after. I will always be grateful to Ross, Chandler, Joey, Phoebe, Rachel and Monica — fictional ciphers with hearts of gold — for holding my daughter's hand in the darkest times.

So, although my fatigue was extreme to the point of worry — was I actually ill? Might this be M.E. or worse? — I passed through the first four seasons anaesthetized at some deep level.

The second year has been very different. There are pressures both internal and social. Mother must find work. Daughter must go to school — her first year at a large comprehensive. It is a painful awakening. My anxiety levels have risen exponentially: I am very aware of how far I was left behind during my long years looking after Tim. It seems a little late to start catching up with the world now, at nearly forty-nine.

In her memoir on the death of her husband, *The Year of Magical Thinking*, writer Joan Didion makes a distinction between grief and mourning. For her, a transition happened six months or so after her loss: "Until now I had been able only to grieve, not mourn. Grief was passive. Grief happened. Mourning, the act of dealing with grief, required attention." For me, mourning proper began on the first anniversary of Tim's death. Like sensation returning to frostbitten toes, this process, this "attention", is acute and electric. Sometimes it has a hopeful clarity, with well-remembered times of togetherness and affection. Sometimes it is bleak and broken, an endless repetition of absence. The days have acquired a rhythm of sorts — I have created some work, and there is always Molly, the dog, and the allotment to hold me fast. But an awareness of Tim lingers in the back of my brain like a constant, cracked refrain. He is gone, and the manner of his going was brutally hard.

Mourning is like a deep black hole: I tiptoe around the edges of this hole, peering in, always on the brink of falling, always pulling back just in time — holding on barely to solid ground, to the living, breathing world.

These days, I notice, Molly and I both respond with a particular alertness to the deaths of those around us, both in the community, and in the world at large. At the end of June this year, a young PE teacher at Molly's school was killed in an early morning car crash. Neither

175

of us knew him personally but the event had a visceral impact. In the same month, a teenager went swimming in Waterloo Lake in Roundhay Park, emboldened by soaring temperatures and adolescent chutzpah. He became trapped in the thick weeds under water, and drowned. The glaring heat of summer makes these random losses more cruel somehow. The sun can have a pitiless sheen.

On my allotment, where there is no shade to soften its hues, colour takes on a particular intensity at this time of year. In the unbroken beams of summer light, green has a thousand layers: it shimmers from tree top to hedgerow; from shrub right down to the tufted grasses and foliage at ground level, all framed brightly against the dark brown soil. Red pierces with its clarity, on montbretia, nasturtium, strawberry and runner bean. Flower heads of purple, pink, yellow, orange, and even pure white, wipe the eye clean with an undiluted and pristine palette. Just to look becomes a banquet. Walking past the evening primrose, its tall, strong stems ringing like bells with a succession of yellow flowers, I bend down and bury my nose in a bloom: it smells warm, subtle, and very womanly, somehow. Is the garden essentially female? Or am I unashamedly biased?

2 July This Saturday marks the beginning of a tumultuous week on the world stage, kicking off with the huge Live8 concert in Hyde Park (prelude to the G8 conference on Third World poverty and debt).

176

Although I would rather be gardening, even I can see that all this is pretty special, and I hang up my old boots, to go into town with Molly and see the proceedings on a big screen in Millennium Square. Later we watch it on television for hours. A succession of rock dinosaurs belt out old hits, to an enthusiastic and undiscriminating international audience, as the clock ticks towards twelve.

Pink Floyd, playing "Wish You Were Here" for Syd Barrett, that beautiful lost boy of the psychedelic era, flashed me back to my early teenage years, when Syd (along with Che Guevara) was one of the poster boys for my rebellious youthful posturing. I had imagined Syd as long-since dead, and thus eternally glamorous. The truth — always more mundane — was that he was living with his mother in Cambridge: ill, reclusive, burnt out.

Towards the end of Tim's life, he revisited old loves, in music and in books. It was as if he were rewinding his own tape, taking himself back to the beginning, to the happy madness of being young. Pink Floyd was one of the many nostalgic CDs he made me buy in the last few months of his life. At the time I mocked his more tendentious prog rock choices. How I would like to play them all for him now!

4 July Laurie, it's really true. The sweetcorn *is* knee high.

5 July The basil I have grown from seed on the window ledge at home has not come to much. So I cheat, as

177

usual, and nip down to the local shop to buy some. Even though it's in a growing pot, the shop-bought specimen looks as tired as my home-grown ones. But beggars can't be choosers. The Indian woman at the check-out plunges her nose into the leaves before she hands me the pot. I can tell she is not impressed.

"The basil we grow in India has a far stronger scent," she says. "The leaves are smaller, dark and serrated. Basil is a holy plant in the Hindu faith. Every house will have pots of it growing, and pray to it regularly."

After this, it feels almost sacrilegious to rip the leaves and scatter them, along with balsamic vinegar, over a mozzarella and tomato salad I make for lunch. I do it, all the same. This is an inferior English-grown basil, after all. Fit only for the belly.

6 July The G8 summit took place at Gleneagles in Scotland today. A commitment was made to ending Third World debt and increasing international aid, and Bob Geldof remained upbeat. But thanks to George W. Bush, global warming stayed far too low on the list of priorities. Our weather has already been changing, and this year in particular has seen unusual seasonal swings and shifts. Heat and drought will have a huge impact on the garden. Most vegetables are naturally thirsty beasts. How will they cope? What will we grow? What does Mr Bush know, or care, looking through the opaque windows of the White House at the manicured grounds outside? (I bet they don't get bindweed in the presidential gardens. Somehow, I doubt they have hosepipe bans either.)

London has won the Olympic bid. Celebrations all round. And, hopefully, a vastly improved Underground system.

I went to pick a friend up from Leeds General Infirmary: she had been admitted for some routine observations. For a couple of days I gave lifts to her children, to and from hospital. During this time, out of the blue, I felt very unwell myself — with flu-like symptoms, aching, hollow legs and strange stomach cramps. When I entered the hospital today, I felt a real resistance to going inside. Everything in my body told me not to do it. When I mentioned this to Clare, as we were leaving, she said, "Your symptoms are what I get when I have eaten something I'm allergic to. After all you've been through, perhaps you're allergic to looking after people now."

7 July There has been tumultuous rain, and several really cold days, followed by sudden, intense heat. Thanks, Mr Bush.

Something has happened in London. The news reports are garbled to begin with, and then slowly the facts emerge. Suicide bombings — on the Underground, and in a bus at Tavistock Square. Unimaginable horror. I do the usual thing, and start ringing all my London friends, to see if they are all right. I am ringing from Leeds to London. As the day turns to evening, more information comes. The bombers are from Leeds. One of them was a teaching assistant at a school my friend works in. The clear trace of the bombers seems to send a stark message from the North of England — Leeds and Bradford — to the soft, white South. But this is not the city I recognize, not the Muslim community I walk among, whose hospitality nourishes me, and whose children make me smile (and gently drive me up the wall). The mood becomes tense in the whole neighbourhood over the days to come: what on earth will happen here now?

London feels a million miles away to me now, even though I lived there in my formative years — arriving, fresh from university, at twenty-one, and leaving just a few months before I was forty. For several years after our move north, I felt very split: there was a London-me and a Leeds-me. Every holiday we would head south, to our past, and then career back north into a barely formed present. When I was in Leeds, I found it impossible to recall how it was — who I was — in London, and vice versa. The "then" and "now" seemed like two different countries. (Indeed, when Molly was small, she believed that we had moved abroad.) But slowly, integration happened.

The whole process was curiously like a bereavement. Even though the choice to move was positive and life-enhancing, the physical dislocation took a long time to absorb and assimilate. These days, when something happens in London — particularly something danger- ous, like the bombings — I feel an immediate alarm, as if someone I love has been singled out, struck down.

180

But I am not a Londoner now: that city sleeps quietly inside me. I have given my heart to Leeds.

11 July Monday morning. The first time in a week — and what a week — that I have been up to the allotment. It's 8a.m. and already hot, but blissfully still and quiet. I can't help thinking that Bob Geldof would like Mondays rather better if he spent them here. July equals abundance; profligacy, even. The red *Crocosmia* by the arch are in full cry now, scarlet flowers growing from tall curving stems like the plumage of some exotic bird.

Closer up, near the shed, the planting around my little pond is looking full and vibrant. This is a difficult area to cultivate, as the soil at the top end of my plot is very dry and impacted. But just two summers after planting, the loosestrife (yellow), verbena (purple), plume poppy and alliums (dusky plum and pink) are bonny and well established.

Occasionally I see a lazy frog basking on one of the stepping stones in the pond, put there to give them a leg up out of the water. Most of the time, however, they prefer to lurk in the manure heap under the tarpaulin, where it's smelly, damp and dark: waiting to leap out when I take the cover off, and scare the living daylights out of me. It isn't the creatures — I love frogs — it's the sudden JUMP out of nowhere that unnerves me. Alas, no basking frog today.

The grass, as usual, is too high, but the flowers and vegetables are holding their own in the growing stakes. I make an exception: the pea patch has been a great disappointment. Despite all my efforts with pea sticks and companion planting, the crop has been desultory. There are just a few dried-up pods now, hanging from droopy stems and tendrils. My father was right about peas being too much fuss for too little product. How galling. I cleared the whole patch in a fit of pique.

More success elsewhere. The giant yellow and medium-size red sunflowers are sporting fat, promising flower heads. They will look wonderful, come August. I harvested broad beans (just a handful of pods, but precious none the less), more gooseberries, blackcurrants, and some fabulous, juicy red onions.

12 July Once again, I went up to the allotment early, for an hour. It was cooler today, but calm and soothing. Molly, along with the whole of her school, has to run the Roundhay Marathon today. Tall and slender, with a healthy contempt for all sport (except swimming), she is dreading it. I sympathize. I remember the misery of aching joints, a stitch in the side, the gasping for air, which accompanied all my long-distance efforts at school. I thought they had abandoned corporate torment like this — vetoed, surely, under the Geneva Convention? — but no, the English school system still loves to tease.

My tasks this morning were more manageable than Molly's. I cleared the broad bean patch, leaving the roots where they were to "fix" nitrogen into the soil. A good thing, apparently. (Don't do this with any brassica roots, however, for fear of clubroot disease. Which is a bad thing.) Then I hoed the onion patch, where I have high hopes for the white onion. The leeks I planted in May are beginning to swell nicely, their girths thickening with appreciation in the sunlight. They won't be ready for ages — needing a long growing season in which to fatten quietly. Like onions, leeks offer little in the way of decoration on a plot — no frothy foliage like carrots, or showy leaves and flowers like the squashes — but they are hard workers, hiding their treasure at their roots, deep in the soil, where it counts.

In the middle of summer, when growth is so profuse, it is easy to overlook the subtle changes going on in the middle of all that crazy green. But I looked carefully today, and saw plenty. There are priapic heads forming on the red-hot pokers — ready to glow like fire in August — and tassels on the sweetcorn, like the batons of drum majorettes. Behind them the row of Jerusalem artichokes, which produce very humble little tubers in autumn, has grown into a (frankly disproportionate) six-foot screen of foliage. Easy to overlook, underneath, are small canary yellow flowers, just beginning, on the courgettes. The poppies at the base of Tim's tree, which I thought I had lost in the mess following the leaky water pipes of June, are throwing up tiny new leaves. They were the real triumph today.

I had some strawberries to pick from between the wild grasses. They shone bright pillar-box red, and were quite delicious. Darker red, almost to purple, were the raspberries I took home (with her permission) from Sumi's neighbouring plot. She grows the summer-fruiting varieties, which drip perilously off tall canes.

My "Autumn Bliss" wait until September, and grow on a smaller, less spectacular, shrubby stock. Some of the garlic in the herb patch (planted to sweeten the lavender) was ready to pick. I roasted two fat "elephant" bulbs that evening, and they were very good.

13 July I had lunch with Sumi at our favourite restaurant, Quantro, in Roundhay. It is a rare treat to eat out, and it was hot enough to sit outside — an extra bonus. We talked about the bombings of 7 July. There have been sporadic gatherings on the streets in Harehills, and isolated incidents of trouble, with police arrests. It's worrying. The waiter overhears us talk. "It'll get worse," he mutters gloomily. "This is just the beginning."

16 July I teach regular Saturday workshops now, while Molly meets up with friends or relaxes at home. At rising thirteen, she seems genuinely to enjoy her own company, which will stand her in good stead for the future. Solitude: a great gift, if you can settle down and enjoy it.

After teaching I drove down to see Grant — my Alexander teacher, and now a good friend. He and his partner Lucy live on a narrowboat moored in Kirkstall, on the other side of town, amidst an urban sprawl of leisure complexes, industrial sites and an electricity substation. The approach is inauspicious, but when the gates of the boatyard clang shut behind you it is quiet and green. There are a fair number of boats moored there — like a small floating village, colourful and serene. The canal itself has an intensity of stillness peculiar to man-made waterways, helped by the mass of natural planting which spills over the towpath and muffles the sounds of the city. I am so full of (hot) air, I need firm ground under my feet: otherwise, this floaty, slightly other-worldly *Wind in the Willows* existence would suit me just fine. No garden? There are plenty — on boat decks, roofs, and under the trees, along the path where the boats are moored. They've got it all.

17 July I have written something for the *Guardian* about the allotment, and they are sending a photographer on Tuesday. This is Sunday, and I am panicking. Suddenly my little piece of paradise looks a bit shabby: I fear it will be judged and found wanting. But I am just wearing the wrong eyes.

Still, it galvanized me into action today, strimming the grass, watering and rewatering the parched earth, cutting back some of the wilder excesses on my perennials, and planting a few pretty extras (pink *Cosmos*) here and there. It feels like having someone to stay: that's about the only time I clean the house properly, and assess it with a critical eye. All the domestic idiosyncrasies we take for granted (the bathroom door that doesn't lock properly; the joke handle which comes off in your hand every time you pull it) seem like glaring faults when the visitor is due.

The front garden is a complete jungle in July. You have to push your way through the branches and foliage

185

to get into the centre of the little lawn. I quite like this — it feels like a mini-expedition — but perhaps it has got a little out of hand. The arch is thick with honeysuckle and red jasmine, their stems knitting and twining together with passionate intent. I got the secateurs out and cut them apart. Killjoy.

There are two empty beds on my plot now, since harvesting the onions, peas and beans. This immediately induces guilt. If I were organized and clever, I would have things waiting in the wings, straining in their trainer pots, ready for successional planting. Magazines and gardening programmes urge us to make the best possible use of our space — and my plot is reasonably small, with only half of it cultivated. But actually I enjoy blank, brown places just as much as bustle. Everything rises to excess in summer. A part of me longs for it all to slow down. So the presence of a fallow patch somewhere, left just to rest, is perhaps no bad thing.

19 July The *Guardian* photographer, Kal Lathigra, a young Indian guy, came and shot his rolls of film in both my gardens. He liked what he saw — his keen eye alighting on the most inauspicious corners, and finding something quirky and photogenic. (I worried, as usual, over nothing.) He was just back from a long trip to some Native American reservations, where he worked alongside two tribes, photographing and documenting their culture. He felt passionate about their struggle to survive, and wanted to return. He was also about to do a project on women in India. From the great plains of Native America to Oakwood Lane Allotments, Leeds, and on to the Indian subcontinent; all in a day's work. He told me he was the cook in his house, so I sent him back to London with a bag of onions and stinky fresh garlic, newly dug, to spice up his dishes.

My dad is feeling some local effects from his radiotherapy: burnt and tender skin where the powerful rays have penetrated. I send him a little pot of rose, lavender and chamomile cream, which I bought from a herbalist at the Otley Show. Also some Honeysuckle Bach Flower Remedy for helping with sadness and nostalgia. Just little packages of love, really.

22 July Andrew Motion, biographer and poet laureate, has written an intimate memoir of his mother, who lay immobilized for many years after an accident. In an article about his work, he quotes William Wordsworth's description of memory as "spots of time". These are significant moments from the past, which become illuminated in our minds when everything else fades to shades of grey.

This day, in 1989, is a particularly bright spot for me. My relationship with Tim — after a shy, brief courtship — began here in earnest. On this Saturday, 22 July, there was a concert at Kenwood House, on Hampstead Heath. Four of us packed a picnic (plenty of wine) and took a taxi from Primrose Hill. The evening was warm, the sun still clear and high. We camped on a hill, beyond the enclosure where the paying posh sat, and listened to the strains of the orchestra drifting across the lake. I wanted a closer look, so Tim and I wandered to the gates. He gave me a piggyback so I could see more clearly, but only for a few minutes, as his shoulder was hurting.

Hours went by. The sun went down. The orchestra went home, but we did not. We picked up our picnic and wandered across the Heath, heading south. After dark, the Heath is a bacchanalian paradise, *A Midsummer Night's Dream* come to life. People flitted here and there — some dressed, some not — and we just wandered along in the middle of it, drunk and happy.

When we came to the mixed Bathing Pond, Jean-Pierre (Tim's flatmate) decided he would take a dip, fully clothed. At two in the morning. With severe rheumatoid arthritis, he knew that any fall could be serious. Wading out of the pool and up the hill, he tripped and broke his arm. By three o'clock in the morning, we were in the Royal Free Hospital, Accident & Emergency wing ... still happy and drunk. (Jean-Pierre carried on drinking, claiming it was an effective and necessary anaesthetic.)

Eventually, Tim and I left Jean-Pierre with his patient girlfriend, and wandered down Haverstock Hill to the flat. I rarely remember my dreams — they are mostly just flotsam and jetsam, surfacing from an untidy psyche — but some stay with me, powerful and symbolic. That night, at dawn, I dreamed of wild geese, flushed with the red of the rising sun, flying in an arc overhead; and a curving rainbow, which started at the house where I was born and ended here, where I was now, in the flat of the man I would later marry. Spots of time — and light. Home at last.

23 July There have been too many funerals in the past year or so: Tim, my mother, my aunt, my father-in-law. The only time the full tribe of my extended family seems to meet is to mourn. My niece Ruth thought this should change. So she persuaded her mum and dad — my elder brother Martin — to host an annual summer party. The first one was today. People from the furthest reaches of the clan — people I had never met before — came to his Berkshire house and great big garden. There were barbecues, hammocks, silly games, music, and juggling with fire . . . It was a lovely event. But I wandered around the edges of it somehow: there seemed to be a gap, an absence right at the centre. I realized the source of this absence as the one person who would have enjoyed such a celebration most. Kathleen. My noisy, laughing mother.

Tim, unlike my mother, was not a party animal. He could usually be found, at an event like this, in a quiet corner with a drink, or, more likely, in the kitchen being helpful. His absence is harder to register than that of my mother, but is still palpable. One of those people who provided a kind of gravitas to any occasion — a still point in a madly turning world — he is a missing ingredient today, making the dish that little less flavoursome. Molly, like her dad, disappears in a crowd. Today, she hides in a tent in the garden for most of the proceedings. Her cousin Mary, equally unimpressed by the razzle-dazzle, keeps her company. Would Molly appear more often if Tim were here, sitting somewhere in an easy chair? This is a question which has no answer.

The last week of July has seen the rain start to fall. We are away, in Berkshire and Somerset. I hope it's raining in the North — not from chagrin, but with a thought for my parched vegetables. Every year this happens: the allotment reaches a fever pitch of production just as the school holidays begin. Invariably we are away for at least two weeks. Who will water if drought sets in? Who will pick the ripening fruit and stop it going to the birds, or to the bad? Once again, the garden seems lost and out of my grasp. Just letting it go, and finding it again later, is a difficult matter of trust.

25 July In 1994, five years almost to the day after the midsummer night's dream of Hampstead Heath, a darker journey began. The left shoulder, which caused Tim sudden pain when he hoisted me up at Kenwood to watch the orchestra, revealed, under X-ray, a major tumour, pushing down from shoulder to left lung, and spreading across his chest and deep into his back. The cancer site was so extensive that only surgery could excise it, and even then the tumour could only be "de-bulked" and not fully removed. A holding operation. Tim's surgeon was frighteningly robust in his assessment.

"The operation is not without risks," he told Tim bluntly. "You could bleed in any one of a thousand places. It's my job to see that you don't." This was Friday. "I want you in on Sunday. I operate Monday."

I remember looking at the consultant's hands — big, fleshy, confident and clean — spread out on the desk in front of him. "I trust those hands," I thought. I had no choice.

On Monday morning, I planted sunflowers in a pot. At the other end of the city, Tim went in for a five-hour operation, came through the other end, and was moved to intensive care. In the evening, I left our hot little flat to travel by tube to the Royal Brompton Hospital to visit him. Friends were looking after Molly. They gave me gin and tonic for courage. It tasted like weedkiller. People wanted to come with me, but I chose to go alone. Sometimes, it's better that way.

The intensive care unit was like a small subterranean cave, dark and hushed, with the occasional bleep of a monitor and the soft pad, pad of the nurses' shoes. The nurse in charge of Tim was kind and friendly. Did I need a chair — some visitors can feel a little faint? I shook my head.

I knew Tim immediately by his feet — they were so big, and he was so tall, that they overshot any bed — but by little else. He was a shaven mass of masks, wires and tubes, softened only by a single cotton sheet. He had been cut from sternum to diaphragm, and from front to back on his left side. The wounds were considerable, but dressed beautifully — not a spot of blood in sight. The surgeon had come true.

Tim was conscious, and when he realized I was there, he started speaking, in an urgent morphine-soaked whisper. At first I could make out none of his words, but soon recognized them as a list of

191

commands. He itched dreadfully, he was thirsty, he was boiling, he was sore. I did what I could, which was little, almost nothing, and moved to the bottom of the bed. Suddenly I needed air. I felt myself falling. The nurse, with admirable speed and precision, placed a chair beneath me and broke my fall. Soon after, I left.

The corridors upstairs — after the twilight zone of intensive care where all is poised between illness and recovery, between life and death itself — felt light, clean and normal. This was a new part of the hospital, and was decorated with taste and care. As I went into the entrance hall, I noticed a rill of water passing over stones through a long, shallow trough: leading the eye, and the imagination, out to a central courtyard, where there was a deeper pool, planted in green, and surrounded by benches, secluded and serene.

Over the coming days and weeks, this graceful place, like a little Arabian oasis, became the whole family's focus for recovery. Tim moved from intensive care to the high dependency unit, and then on to a ward. Soon he could walk — pushing his tubes and trolleys with him — and would sit with me by the pool, whilst Molly (just a toddler) played with the stones and the shallow water, delighted at the plops! and splashes! that she made. When I recall those arduous days, of July heatwave and hospital crisis, this garden shines at my mind's surface — like the gentle standing water in the green pool itself — and somehow turbulence turns to calm. Gardens do make a difference. They heal.

★ ★ ★

31 July We drive back to Leeds after our week away. I hardly dare look at the garden: it's scruffy, but OK. With only two days until another trip, I leave the allotment to fend for itself. Out of sight, out of mind, maybe.

The dire predictions of riots or unrest following the London bombings have come to nothing. We are all rubbing along nicely, as usual — chatting about the weather, trudging off to work, trudging back, mowing the lawn, and yelling at the kids, and each other. It's hot. It's July. Life goes on. I feel proud of that, and hopeful.

Jobs for July

- If you have strawberry plants, they will start to make runners soon — long stems with a flurry of leaves and tiny roots at the end. These can be potted up, and the stems snipped off, making lots more plants for next year. (Plant the runners in autumn.) If you don't have strawberry plants, buy some. Yum yum.
- Red, yellow, orange — hot colours have a place and a time. July is the time; any container, or sunny spot in the garden, is the place. Marigold, montbretia, and good old nasturtium — "Empress of India", a brilliant jewel red.
- Harvest whatever you have — including flowers for vases. Bring the outside in. Fill the house with colour.
- Eat outside, if you have a garden, or even a step. Meals always taste better in the open air.

- You can grow tomatoes easily in big pots or growbags (better to buy the starter plants in late spring/early summer). Feed them regularly with tomato food, and water them copiously. They love to drink, and they love the sun. Same here.
- Clear any vegetable beds of early summer crops. Put something else in, or be daring and leave them BARE and well dug. The earth will smell rich and fruity.

August

In the park the dreamy bees
are droning in the flowers among the trees
And the sun burns in the sky . . .

Ian Campbell, "The Sun is Burning"

August is when I lose my mind: it is the month which most entirely belongs to the body. No matter what work needs doing, whatever daily drivel needs sorting out — the bills and paperwork and unanswered telephone calls of domesticity — August is for scattered senses, for disappearing into dream, for sunbathing and forgetting. I never know where anyone is in August. Friends who are normally bound and gagged by the predictability of the office, who can be tracked within a five-mile radius for eleven months of the year — or found, unfailingly, on the allotment, come Sunday morning — suddenly send postcards from different counties, countries, even different continents. Everyone and everything becomes unreliable. There is a wonderful contagious madness in the air. It is essential to give in.

1 August In our little household, there is chaos, as the three of us are about to go our separate ways for a week: the dog to my cousin's house; Molly to her friend in London; and I am going to Ireland. The logistics of this — three separate itineraries, laundry and packing (Muffin's bedding is the worst, hairy, smelly and difficult to dry) — all in the mounting heat of high summer, with body and brain in meltdown, are a nightmare. I cannot imagine having a big family to organize; even our little nucleus is maddeningly complicated. No wonder my mother shouted all through our childhood. Raising the voice is a tremendous coping mechanism.

There is as always a last-minute drama. One of the car tyres has a rip in it — not what you want when belting up and down the motorway. A friend comes to the rescue, and takes me to the tyre man in Harehills. This guy has a corner house, back to back, in a little side street off Harehills Road, tucked between the Asian groceries and Yorkshire Fried Chicken (YFC), and filled, from door to window, floor to ceiling, with reconditioned tyres. He found and refitted the tyre I needed, at the roadside, in ten minutes. He was cheerful, efficient and cheap.

"Just don't look at the calendars on the wall inside," advised my friend. Pneumatic in an entirely different way.

2 August No summer is really complete for me without Ireland. One of my dearest friends, Liz, lives in Ballinavary, near Enniscorthy in County Wexford, and I have been visiting her smallholding there since 1997. I first met Liz twenty-five years ago in Brixton, immediately fell for her sly wit and compassionate intelligence, shared a flat with her for seven years, and missed her badly when she moved back to her native Dublin and, later on, to Wexford. She is the person who perhaps knows me best, and accepts me most: we are always present in each other's minds.

During the years of Tim's illness, we had several holidays in Ballinavary. It was one of the few places where Tim felt totally at ease, and accepted, with all his physical difficulties, whether blown-up and bloated on steroids in 1997, or bald and gaunt on morphine in 2002. Out in the bonny Ballinavary garden, shaded by umbrellas from the August heat, he would sit with his gin and tonic (retreating to the kitchen only when the late summer thunderstorms broke), and visibly relax.

Sitting in this garden now, in 2005, I see the influence it has had on my own growing plans. The half-acre plot, complete with long, productive polytunnel (full of tomatoes, courgettes, melons, squashes), outside vegetable patch (with cabbages, potatoes, peas and beans) and hen run (full of plump, clucking birds, spoiled rotten on wild strawberries, juicy lettuces and choice grain), shines with the polish of a decade's continual labour.

But it is the flower garden and patio, gracing the outside of the old stone cottage, that I notice most. Here is a billowing butterfly bush, a vibrant *Crocosmia*, a palm-leaved *Fatsia japonica*, just as I have at home. In pots and hanging baskets bright nasturtiums trail and tangle. And on the wide kitchen ledge two pots of basil (far more successful than mine) are fattening aromatically in the August sun.

I had no idea the subliminal influence had been so strong. When we first visited Ballinavary, in 1997, I had gardened for less than a year. My borders boasted nothing except some little lavender bushes and a fallow apple tree. Over the next eight years I filled the borders tenaciously, subconsciously planting in parallel: me in West Yorkshire, mimicking Liz and Fi in Wexford. Forget RHS Wisley and the stately homes of England. Learn how to garden (the way you learn to grow up, have relationships, to parent, to grow old) from your friends. They will share seeds and cuttings and expertise for free. In this way we make a collective garden, to walk in and remember — a shared and generous space across time and place, as well as an intimate, solitary retreat.

Ireland has a wildness that draws me, especially the southwest coastal fingers of Cork. But it has a softness too: the cornfields and rolling pastures of the east coast, and Wexford in particular, bring a nourishing taste to my mouth. Liz and Fi are prodigious with their hospitality. Their food and drink is lipsmackingly good. This suited Tim, who was epicurean in his taste; despite long periods of nausea and sickness, as the cancer took hold, his delight in a groaning table lasted nearly till the end.

There were four kitchen gardens — apart from our own — where he loved to sit on long hot summer evenings, places where women friends would spoil him with attention and an ever-full plate and glass: Sumi's beautiful high billowing borders in Leeds; Frances' elegant terrace, with herb pots and rising meadows behind, in Ampleforth, North Yorkshire; Beverley's tall London kitchen, leading through stained-glass doorways on to a pretty sloping lawn and summerhouse in Muswell Hill; and Liz's Irish smallholding, set in the middle of wide fields and rounded corn bales, lilting and discreet.

Tim was used to being with women. He had two older sisters — who made him, at five, dress up as "Lady" and scream for help as the robbers (played by them) came to abduct him — and he flourished in female company. Deep voiced, tall and imposing, with a love of football and cricket, and a hatred of small talk, he remained a stubborn archetypal male in many ways. But the presence of women made him happier than that of men, I think. And Ireland, like Yorkshire, had a special place in his heart.

On this visit, the first since Tim's death, Liz, Fi and I scattered a few of his remaining ashes under a big bush near to where he had always sat, drink in hand. We did this with little fuss or ceremony, as he would have wished. The moment, and the sadness, shortly passed. But as soon as we had finished, Pickles — Liz and Fi's little rescue dog — pointedly rose from the other end of the garden, where she had been snoozing, and went straight to the bush where the ashes were strewn, lay beneath it, and refused to move till nightfall. After I had left to come home, Pickles visited the same spot every day for a week, lying beneath it, guarding.

6 August Back to Leeds to collect my own dog. The drive from Leeds-Bradford Airport takes me through countryside which is remarkably similar to the fields and hedgerows of Wexford. Maybe their green is a little more intense, but the Yorkshire landscape is full and beautiful too. Early August has a voluptuous feel — before the plants and trees begin to gasp with the effort of all that productivity. There is a sensual charge in the air, a pulse in the hot ground.

7 *August* Another day, another city. London always feels too warm to me, even in the winter. Come the summer, and the heat rises in a welter of fumes and bad temper. Muswell Hill is always gridlocked with traffic (this was the first place where I encountered the joys of triple parking) but it does have plenty of trees to absorb the noise and pollution, and they lend grace to the city streets. The house where Molly is staying has a garden, front and back, is close to parks and the ancient Highgate Woods — a different world entirely from the south London estates we once lived in.

8 *August* Back in Leeds, and the weather is changing. There is an uncharacteristic coolness suddenly. As soon as the temperature dips, my brain switches back on — and that is not what August is for.

9 *August* I grit my teeth and visit the allotment. Like an orphaned child, with uncombed hair and an empty belly, I expect my plot to offer a mute rebuke at my return. Sure enough, it is overgrown and neglected after my summer absence. But it is also productive, seeming to have done it all on its own. My runner beans and

courgettes, in their pale and darker shades of green, are plumping up nicely. The French bean, which I planted far too late in the season, is forming a few reluctant pods. But the star of the show, in the vegetable stakes, is the pointy-headed "Hispi" summer cabbage. In fuzzy stripes of crisp cream and yellow-green, the leaves are full of bite and juiciness, and taste delicious when I braise them in butter for our tea. Cabbage is normally a chore to eat. This was a positive delight.

There are hollyhocks in full bloom — white and blush pink, clashing nicely with the fire-red *Crocosmia* alongside. I don't give a damn about refinement up here: anything that produces a flower or a vegetable — even a few interesting leaves — is OK by me.

Edwin, my allotment neighbour, likes to feed the magpies — not that they need any encouragement. I notice two there today. In June I saw sorrowful singletons everywhere. If the old rhyme is right, and two is for joy, then things are definitely looking up. Confused as I am, still, and struggling towards cohesion of mind and body, I *do* feel more optimistic. The inevitable turn of the wheel towards the top. It cannot be stopped.

It rained hard in the night. There is no sweeter sound for the gardener in August: a good soaking for the ground, without the bother of hosepipes or watering cans, and without any interruption to a day's gardening. I just lay in bed, listened, and relaxed. The smell outside next morning was enchanting: fresh water on hot earth; like a desert oasis.

One of the most beautiful professional gardens I have visited — often going in August, when staying with my mother, who also loved it — belongs to Beth Chatto, and can be found in Colchester, Essex, near to my parents' home. Chatto has a reputation as a fiercely dedicated gardener, and pictures I have seen of her, gazing like a hawk over the top of her half-moon glasses, are enough to inspire awe, if not instant retreat. She looks as if she does not suffer fools gladly. Certainly, her own achievements have been formidable. She has worked since the 1960s on a large and difficult site, part of it dry and parched, the lower part water-logged, and has transformed it into a series of gardens, each with its own enchantment. A dry gravel garden, where the car park entrance used to be, leads down to a curving, sensual waterside walk, and then into softly shaded woodland.

It is the gravel garden which shows her forward thinking — she was working with plants that can survive drought, such as verbascums, sedums, lavender and yuccas, long before climate change became such an urgent public issue. Over the past decade, this sculptural, desert-style scree has acquired a spare elegance: her experiment has become both a showpiece and a lesson in ecology. Away from this, deeper into the gardens, by the water, a more traditional mood of shade and privacy comes, under the shelter of swamp cypress, and the boggy *Gunnera* and spiked *Phormium*. Then finally, the wood takes over.

The mood of the garden changes with the planting; everything is managed in harmony with the natural conditions, rather than the gardener imposing her will on her surroundings. This is what gives the garden such great power: its personality is unified, deep and complex, singing its own clear song. My mother was discriminating in her tastes, and she loved this garden above all others (except her own). I think she and Beth Chatto would have got on well.

One of the chief delights of high summer, for me, is to get away from my own garden for a while (even if I carry my guilt for neglecting it along with me) and to walk into someone else's. The National Gardens Scheme, which started in 1927, in aid of charities that now include Macmillan Cancer Care, Help the Hospices and Caring for Carers, all dear to my heart, offers the perfect excuse to be nosy in a good cause. Under this scheme hundreds of people every year open their private gardens for a day to the paying public (a princely £3 per head).

Some gardeners now offer their own version of the idea. One August, two summers ago, I visited a tiny plot only two streets away from me, where the gardener, a delightful, friendly woman who suffered badly from Crohn's disease, had opened her garden to raise money for research into the condition. She told me that gardening offered one of the few escapes from the constant debility she suffered.

There was nothing particularly exotic in her little garden, but there was skill and love and brightness in everything — from the fish pond by the back door, with its soothing flow of water, to the colourful tapestry of flowers in the border, calling forth the whole spectrum of summer, with its reds, yellows, pinks, blues and purples. There was a little table on a neighbour's lawn selling her propagated plants — I added a few grasses to my collection — and a steady stream of family, friends and well-wishers wandered around in the hot sun, just enjoying the day and the diversion. I had walked past this small house countless times without ever realizing what treasure lay concealed behind its gate. The garden and the gardener together bring illumination. I came away with a special regard for the flowers I saw, having heard the story of the woman who grew them.

Sometimes, not just individuals but whole villages open their gardens for a day. These occasions are not to be missed. Thorner, a small, well-heeled community north of Leeds, tucked away off the main road to Wetherby, has done this for several years, and it is a revelation. One hot summer's day in 2002, I went for the whole afternoon with some friends. It was almost comically blissful, wandering along the quaint main street with a swelling festive crowd, and diving off here and there into gorgeous cottage gardens, licking lollies and ice creams among the delphiniums and hollyhocks, the rambling roses and old established apple trees.

Some of the grounds were small, and some enormous. They were all lovely — except, maybe, for one, which I think had joined in for the hell of it, and had nothing to show except a little bit of turf and a couple of pot plants! Generally the standard of gardening was high, with plenty of time, effort — and hard cash — poured in.

At the far end of the village was a stream and a ford. The children with us had a paddle and chucked a few stones about. Set back beyond this ford, up an overgrown winding track, was one of the last gardens on show — slap-bang in the middle of the farmer's fields. Sitting outside in this garden — and there were artfully placed seats at every vantage point, of which I made full use — was like drowning in a billowing sea of flowers and summer corn.

The whole experience was of being transported back in time to a graceful Edwardian idyll, one I am sure never existed then, let alone now, but a mirage I am happy to have participated in, just for a few dreamy hours. (My more pragmatic husband and daughter missed out on the whole thing. They stayed at home and watched the football.)

Such different tastes we had, Tim and I. He loved watching sport — I loathe it. He stayed up late (insomniac by nature, even before the onset of illness), whilst I go to bed early. He mooched indoors, ironing, cooking, snoozing: I dive outside at any opportunity. Increasingly, Molly took her cue from him, the two of them quietly at home, together. In later years, natural inclination was reinforced by the vicissitudes of illness, pain and physical incapacity.

I cannot decide whether I feel sad that they would not come to events such as Thorner, or am liberated, a little, by time on my own, enjoying undiluted my particular passions. It is probably a mixture of the two:

regret diffused by resignation. Strong-minded individualists and stubborn to boot — all three members of this little family have always done their own thing. So my summer garden delights were solitary then, and remain so today.

13 August It must be time for the allotment summer barbecue because it has rained all day, non-stop. We have friends to stay, both with high-powered city jobs — one a barrister, the other a university lecturer. When I mooted the idea of going to the barbecue last night, they were quietly appalled — a sentiment my daughter shared. However, a reprieve for them seems possible. As the day goes on, the rain keeps bouncing down. I ring organizers Moira and Don at 5p.m. It has just stopped raining. The event is at 5.30p.m. Will it be cancelled?

"Oh no, we're going ahead," comes the cheerful response. This is Yorkshire, after all; we should be used to bad weather by now. As it turns out, the evening is hilarious and enjoyable — a mix of fiercely competitive volley ball and croquet games, shed painting (murals, not creosote), and vast quantities of food and drink. Edwin turned up swinging a pole of gleaming, freshly-caught trout, their eyes round and glassy with astonishment at being landed.

"I don't eat them," he says, aghast at the thought. "I just like fishing." He doesn't eat the vegetables he grows either, just tends them for fun and then gives them all away.

My visitors end up chatting to everyone happily, and visit my plot to make the requisite appreciative murmurs. They're good at humouring me.

I just wish it would stop raining. It is meant to be August, after all.

17 August Late summer, abundant in so many ways, has one special arrival: blackberries. How I love these dark and ruby fruits, bursting out from every bramble — such lowly, invasive, unprepossessing stock. The hedges which skirt the top and bottom of our allotments are full of blackberries now, ripe for the picking. But we'll have to be quick or other gardeners will get in first. I am not the only one with a taste for blackberry and apple pie — and fresh fruit for free, with none of the hassle of planting it! Tesco's have started selling blackberries in tiny punnets for big prices. I wonder how much they paid to the growers?

Today I send Molly and her friend Emily off with plastic containers to fill — DVDs and popcorn from Blockbusters being their reward for a good harvest. Meanwhile I get busy hoeing and picking on my plot. Despite my disaster with the rotting potatoes, I did manage to find a few in the ground — enough to feed three for tea — and I picked runner beans, French beans, and more delicious "Hispi's".

August is rampant with growth. Despite the cooler than usual temperatures, there has been a dazzling array of colour all through the month. I have a picture of my allotment, taken in August 2003 when I had just signed the lease. Molly sits on the step of the shed and looks down, eyes shaded, towards the camera. There is nothing before her except rough brown grass and a covering of mouldy carpets. It is a derelict scene. Today I sit in the same position as Molly, and feast replaces famine.

The purple *Verbena bonariensis* has been flowering all summer, and they are still at it. Further down, the medium-sized sunflowers, "Fiorenza", sown at home in spring, are in full shout, their intense, rusty red faces floating in the mid-distance, just high enough to shine over the crops, but not so huge as to overwhelm. They are a particular triumph this year — exquisite in detail, petals fading out to pale yellow from their fiery centres, and vivid in both tone and depth. At ground level, the nasturtiums, which have bloomed prodigiously throughout July and early August, are now almost over, but there will be plenty of seed to collect for next year; and the pink and blue geraniums just do and do and do.

Add to this the tripods of beans, and rows of cauliflower, cabbage and broccoli; the jungle of Jerusalem artichoke and the soaring thistle heads of the cardoon — and I feel rich with the swell of it. (Of course, the old grass is still there, digging its coarsened heels in, and threatening to take over the minute I turn my back — but I am watching, strimmer in hand.)

The year 2003 was a time of dying for Tim, for our family. It was a dry, arid summer that year, and the plot, when we visited it for the first time in late August, felt that way too. (This was one of the last few times that Tim could walk anywhere unaided: by September he was confined to a wheelchair — and bed.) Yet, despite the debilitating heat and the almighty effort he had to make, on these initial visits to Oakwood Lane there was a feeling of welcome in the air. If it had been a person, this place would have had a twinkle in its eye for us — something plentiful to whisper in our ears. At the time, this hopefulness was an intuition, born out of need. Now, I know it to be fact, and I see the promise spread before me, beautifully fulfilled.

The year that Tim first became ill, in 1994, and was suffering the many after-effects both of chemotherapy in spring and major surgery in July, we were sent on a recuperative holiday, paid for by Tim's parents, in the late summer. We went to the South Coast. Our friend Mike had particularly recommended a house to rent in a strange little place called Pett Level, between Rye and Hastings, in East Sussex. He drove us there himself (we had no car at the time) in one of his wonderful dilapidated old vehicles.

There was almost nothing in Pett Level, as we approached, except a single row of houses, built on stilts to rise above the sea defences. Little to look at from the front, but once inside our building — what a difference. The rooms were huge and open plan, with massive French windows opening on to a balcony, which in turn looked out on to a strip of shingle beach, a flat, moody sea, and big, big skies. Being a city-born girl, and living in a tiny, upstairs flat, Molly, at just under two, was astonished at the proximity of the great outdoors. "In — Out*side*!" she would shriek in delight, as she hopped between living room and balcony through the ever-open French windows. As the sun set each evening, the sky, framed in these windows, filled with deep pinks and reds. After dark, the stars arrived. In the morning, there was a confusion of clouds, clearing to all perceivable shades of lovely blue. It was like living in the sky itself. The immediacy of such a vast space — sea and sky, uninhibited by buildings or city lights — was soothing for Tim, still so wounded from his operation, and for me, overwrought and panicked at the events we had recently endured. Molly, in her unfettered child's way, just accepted it as a gift she was due as of right.

Across the road from the house was a strip of wild land, grass and hedgerow. It was blackberry season, and this was Molly's first introduction to pick-your-own fruit. She could hardly believe her luck, staining herself black and red, chewing hard, with a little frown of pleasure. To this day, she retains her love of currants and berry fruits, like a foraging woodland creature — sophisticated and urban now, on the brink of her teenage years (and needing bribes to pick the blackberries), but scratch the surface . . .

Looking back through the tunnel of years, I gain more and more respect for the resilience Tim showed after he became ill. On this little holiday in Sussex, he was still very fragile — had been warned not to lift anything or exert himself in any way so soon after major surgery. But he could not be stopped. One day, paddling at the water's edge with Molly, a freak wave came and threatened to engulf her. Without a second's hesitation he swept her up, despite my shouts of alarm lest he rupture the deep wounds still healing in his chest. With his daughter, there was no question: her safety came before his own always. Less dramatically, he managed to walk, to dig a few sandcastles, to participate in the seaside holiday, physically impaired though he was. He could still flinch at a touch too close to the chest — there was a force field around him, a hyper-sensitivity, a jumpiness. But that never communicated itself to Molly. She was his lifeline, and the irritability he showed to me, the tiredness and volatile tension — which I inevitably reflected back to him — disappeared when they sat in the sunshine and played.

I can look at one plant for an hour. This brings me great peace. I stand motionless and stare . . . Dungeness is at its best in the golden light of summer . . . Twilight here is like no other. You feel as you stand here, that tired time is having a snooze. (Derek Jarman)

In August 1994, before arriving at Pett Level, we visited Jarman's cottage and garden in Dungeness, Kent, and then returned several years in a row. Artist, writer, film-maker, agent provocateur of the avant-garde London art scene, Jarman was an inspiration to me, both as a writer and a gardener. He documented the long story of his illness (he died of AIDs in February 1994) in words, pictures and celluloid. Most of all, the essence of the man emerges from his garden, which he started to create as his illness began, and which sustained him, even as his vision dimmed (a cruel privation for a visual artist), and as his world diminished.

I believe that you can make a garden anywhere. Derek did, too. He chose a fisherman's cottage in the shadow of a nuclear power station, by the salt-bitter shingle of the water's edge, in which to plant his unlikely, apocalyptic vision.

I have pictures of our August visit. Tim, myself, two friends, Molly — all a little distant from each other — are sitting or standing, and silently looking, much as Derek Jarman frequently describes himself doing in his garden. What we see is shingle. Curving silvery beds of lavender and santolina. Tall fennel and poppy heads; sharp *Yucca* and curly sea kale. Comfrey, corn-flowers, and pinks. Pieces of rusty metal, standing sharp and proud amidst the flowers. Pebbles in intricate circular patterns. Driftwood. Stones pierced with holes, worn through by generations of tides, hanging from spikes or leaning wearily against wood. The black pitch of the little cottage, sitting in the middle of it all, is lit by two big yellow window frames, like bright suns in darkness. The feeling is palpable, even through the lens of the camera and the distance of memory: reverence is here, and also an alchemy, a furious witches' brew. This is like no garden I will ever make, but its stark, singular aspect remains a primary inspiration.

20 August We have to go to London to look after my brother's house in Chingford. I feel tense about travelling on the tube so soon after the July bombings — even though this is cowardly and defeatist — so we

212

drive everywhere, and take little local buses. Buses are never a problem, but driving through London from Chingford to Catford on a visit to our friends Richard and Neil, under the erratic navigational instructions of my twelve year old, becomes a waking nightmare. At one point, after the third time of driving through the same junction (the wrong way), I stop the car briefly to look at my map. The second I do so, someone leaps out of a house on to the kerbside, and shrieks, "You can't park there! This is residential only!"

"I'm not parking, I'm just lost, and I'm looking at my bloody map!" I shriek back. Molly shrinks in her seat. Not road rage this, so much as house-and-parking-space rage. That's a new one. Do people now stay at home all day, peering out of their window at the small, car-shaped spot they have carefully carved out for Their Use Only, guarding against hapless interlopers like me? The stress of it all . . . I vow never to drive in London again. I don't have the stamina.

23 August We are still in London, and I am taking the chance to revisit some old haunts. For many years, while I lived in Brixton and Stockwell, with little or no access to a garden of any kind, Brockwell Park — which stands, sloping and elegant, on the borders of Brixton, Tulse Hill and Herne Hill — became an essential green playground for me. It is a beautiful space, designed by landscape gardener John Sexby in the 1900s, and open to the public since 1892. From the entrance by the old Lido (now revamped and fully functioning, although permanently freezing, even in a heatwave), the grassy slopes rise up to Brockwell Hall (which has become a café at the top of the hill, giving panoramic views of south London), before sweeping down again on the other side to a walled garden, paddling pool and pond — well populated by visiting birds. Brockwell Park has a grandeur which sits in defiant opposition to the rough and ready streets which surround it. It is well used and much loved by the local population, just as Roundhay Park is in Leeds. Parks play such a vital role in a city: lending their generous green lungs for health, and serving as a shared and surrogate garden; one you might not be able to dig or plant, but which you can certainly inhabit and enjoy — the primary function of any garden.

Brockwell Park is potent with past associations for me, and today I bring some of them into the present by strolling through the space with my T'ai Chi teacher, who has taught his classes here for twenty years — both outside and in the Lido building. Al fresco T'ai Chi always takes place by the pond, on a patch of unspoiled green near some trees. Andreas is hardy. I have trained with him in January, dewdrops hanging from our noses, as well as in August, when the heat — as it is today — makes the sweat pour out, and the flesh melt on the bones. No one ever hassles Andreas when he performs his T'ai Chi in Brockwell: the peace and concentration he brings to this public space seem inviolable, part of the landscape somehow, like the trees. Once again today, in a ritual we have performed over twenty years, we rehearse our slow motion T'ai Chi sequence, and afterwards walk and reminisce.

In the walled garden, there is a bench dedicated to two dead friends, John and Stewart, and we sit on it for a while. The walled garden is beautifully tended, with beds cut into geometric shapes and filled with opulent summer planting, in English Cottage style — pathways leading all around the edges of the space, and then diving off in diagonals and curves towards the little circular pond in the centre, where our memory bench is placed. The park is often noisy in high summer, but somehow the noise fades away when you enter the walled garden. It is an artful place, and perfect for reflection.

On our way out we pass the children's pool once more, and I have a flashback to when Molly was a toddler, sitting in the pool one day, in the middle of a heaving mass of small children, all screaming, splashing and running around her. Everything was in motion. But not Molly. She just sat and passed little trickles of water from one fist to the other, wordless and content.

There is a tree planted, in 1994, also in memory of my friend John, right at the top of Brockwell Park hill: a flowering cherry. It is still quite small, but healthy. I saluted it today as we walked past. When the tree first went in, I hooked an earring over one of the branches — some tasteless purple paste thing, which John would have loved — and when we went back the following year, the earring's hook had worked its way into the flesh of the tree, which seemed strangely symbolic. The friendship John and I had was not always easy — "thorn in the flesh" describes it well. He had a fierce temper and found me tentative. I was an introvert and found him demanding. We were opposites: fire and water. But then, straightforward friendships are not necessarily the best.

30 August Today Molly and I travelled from London to Essex — and stepped straight into my parent's back garden, in the sunshine, with some relief at being out of the city. This garden has remained relatively unchanged in the forty years I have known it. The planting has become more established, and the vegetable patch somewhat diminished, but still its long, familiar rectangle welcomes me back like an old friend. Although the garden is at its most colourful in spring, I connect it more with summer.

Throughout the years of my growing up I played in it; in my twenties I retreated to it during sporadic visits home; by my thirties, it was a playground for my own child; and in my forties I have returned to it as often as I can, this time for consolation when times have been tough — both for Tim and for my parents, as they have grown old. But I don't really associate the garden with Tim. He rarely sat in it, and in the summers, when he was well enough, and working, I would come here alone or with Molly. (When he became frail and ill, he used to stay with his parents or sisters, while I went to Essex.) No, this garden is more about the family I came from than the family I made myself.

The lawn is where I threw the ball for our dog, when I was eight, on long, light evenings. The patio still has the low breeze-block wall — embarrassing this — that I sat astride for hours, when I was ten, pretending it was a horse (the holes in the bricks were stirrups). When I heard I had passed my A levels, and would be going to university, I lay on a sun lounger under the tamarisk tree, down on the left beyond the wall, feeling a huge wave of relief and anticipation. During convalescence, after minor surgery at twenty-eight, my friend John drove me to this garden to recuperate. And when my daughter was little, we would come to the garden every August, park ourselves under the huge weeping willow, and play with a plastic tea set, and a bowl of water to splash in.

The willow is gone now, chopped down because it grew too huge, but the pretty tamarisk remains, and as I look out of the back window today, at dusk, I see two reclining chairs that have been left, empty, beneath it: where my father and I were sunbathing earlier in the afternoon. The sky is turning pink and orange as the sun begins to set.

A hot air balloon suddenly appears and drifts past in stately fashion. How odd. My mother always wanted a ride in one of these when she was alive. It is a little late now for one to be turning up. But it looks a picture, and seems to be carrying a belated message to me from Kathleen: whether it's "hello" or "goodbye", I don't know, but either way the greeting gives me pleasure. The balloon is low enough for me to see a flash of red as the fire is stoked, making it fly a little higher. So like my mother, this — to take another risk, to burn a little brighter, with fire in her very nature, and red her signature colour.

★   ★   ★

31 August I got married on this day, in 1991. I should be sad when this particular anniversary comes around, but I am not. Some days burn bright in my memory, sustaining rather than pulling me down, whatever has happened since then. (Another of these sustaining anniversaries, bizarrely, is Tim's funeral: such was the outpouring of affection for the man, the sense of celebration. I drew great strength from people as they spoke at the service, and at the gathering afterwards. The occasion felt complete, and I was at peace.)

As for the wedding, it was a gas. The day, 31 August 1991, was boiling hot. The civil ceremony was in west London, at Ealing Town Hall — the borough where Tim lived, until he moved in with me — and we set off late from Stockwell, on the south side of town, and got stuck in traffic. Since I had already been at the champagne, I didn't care too much, although running through the town hall car park in wedding gear, and then belting up several flights of stairs to a room where a rather stern registrar and all our friends and family were twiddling their thumbs, and getting restive, *was* a little nerve-racking. Anyway, we rattled through the vows efficiently. At the end of the ceremony, John, my witness, made a great play of kissing the bridegroom, then his mongrel dog ran amok on the town hall steps, as people took photographs, and Tim's mother shooed him away, thinking he was a stray.

The reception was held at Tim's workplace — a studio theatre at the Central School of Speech and Drama, which meant another cross-city dash, from west to north this time, in the Saturday crush and ever-rising

218

temperatures. Not very clever organization. Anyway, everyone made it, and the party began. This, for me, was the point of the day. Official vows don't mean much to me, but personal declarations do. So we had our own readings (shamelessly sentimental), music and dancing from my brother's ceilidh band (chaotic), and more drinking. John got so drunk, he was completely incapacitated. Several of the guests followed suit.

At around midnight, a whole crowd of people walked with us from Swiss Cottage down to Soho, where our wedding gift from friends was a night at Hazlitt's exclusive little literary hotel in Frith Street. Tim and I arrived on foot at about two in the morning, together with an entourage of eight — and, of course, the jolly black and tan mongrel. Hotel staff did not turn a hair. The dog sat behind reception with a laid-back, smiling clerk, and the rest of us piled on to the big four-poster bed, and carried on drinking. Chef Anthony Bourdain says of Hazlitt's: "It's like staying at a potty English uncle's, when he's not at home." And that suited us fine.

As the years go by, the memory of this day becomes less detailed in my mind — but more vivid. I am gradually starting to replace the many horrible images of illness, the attrition of Tim's long decline, with more nourishing pictures from the past. Such is the work of grieving and loss — it takes time and application, but is a necessary process of reclamation. This rewind to the beginning is just as true a story as the fact of Tim's death. And as the days pass, into weeks, and months, and then into years, the pain in my heart becomes a smaller part of a much bigger picture: I start to believe that love really *is* stronger than death. Yes, it is. And that although those we have loved *do* leave us, sometimes brutally, in sudden death, or, as with Tim, in a slow fading out, they will come back again, if we let them, and settle down, invisibly, beside us.

Jobs for August

- Runner beans and French beans will crop all through August, and if you pick them, they will make more.
- Sweet peas will also produce more and more flowers, but only if you keep cutting them. They need loads of water. (Mine often end up looking scrappy, because I am away too much to keep them tended.)
- Keep on strimming. Grass just keeps growing.
- Visit at least one garden through the National Gardens Scheme. The Yellow Book, with details, can be found in every library. There are little local brochures to pick up too. They're not only a great day out, but often a cheap source of plants and cuttings — from little stalls in the gardens (next to the tea and biscuits).
- Blackberrying is a must. The fruits start to turn from red to beautiful black this month. Pick, pick, pick.

September

There is a whole world in a single leaf.

Andy Goldsworthy, "Hand to Earth"

3 September A few days' flurry of winds have blown August clean away. The warm, limpid evening spent, less than a week ago, watching a hot air balloon drifting over my parents' garden, is already a memory from a different season. The switch has been clicked, from summer to autumn. Change is coming.

Melancholy by nature, I normally find this transition rather sad. Something about the sweetness in the air, an atmosphere ripened by long summer days to a fullness that can only preface a fall (the heavy red of the apple before it drops to earth), pulls me close to myself, intimate and rueful. But this year, though that melancholy moment is present, it is fleeting.

Maybe I have had too much real sorrow to indulge so readily in the inevitable autumn gloom. (I don't get so down in the winter these days, either — which could just be the dull pragmatism of age.) Actually, these early September winds have blown energy into my bones. There is work to do, and plenty of it.

Today, my aims at the allotment are threefold: picking, pruning, and the pond. All summer I have watched my little pond be steadily sucked dry by an adamant and invasive bulrush. I toyed with the idea of splitting it, but it looked as sturdy as my nemesis, the bamboo, and warning twinges in my back persuaded me otherwise. Then I thought I would ask someone to help me move it, but allotment people are always busy with their own lifting, splitting and digging. (It's when the work gets heavy that I wish I gardened in a team of two rather than grumpy and alone.) Today, I took matters into my own hands and heaved the whole thing out myself, thumping it down with triumphal grunts on the tarpaulin near the shed, for future dumping and disposal. Victory.

This dinosaur out of the way, all that remained of my wildlife water feature was a scrappy black hole: pond liner (mercifully intact), and a few old stones to weigh it down. Undaunted by the destruction I had inflicted, I filled the hole with rainwater, and thought about some marginal plants which might go in, to fit the outsized shoes of the tough old bulrush. Bog iris and marsh marigold will do the job nicely. (By the time I left the allotment, a couple of hours later, there were already insects inspecting the new water: a pond rejuvenates itself astonishingly quickly, with the smallest intervention from the gardener.)

I picked some French beans and some tiny squashes. The latter looked pretty enough, but would not be fit for cooking: I did not spoil them sufficiently, with the rich compost or prodigious watering they require, and now I am paying the price, with minimal returns. Vegetables are so damn choosy.

Sandra — queen of cuttings, and owner of a beautiful, festive plot down by the main gates (far from the scrubby outreaches of the uplands, where I garden) — offered me some fat beef tomatoes from her polytunnel. Delicious for a fry-up. Sandra has given me countless plants over the past two years, nurtured from cuttings and seeds: tall foxgloves and verbascums for punctuation; miniature borage and blotchy-leafed *Pulmonaria*, for tricky shaded corners. She seems to grow plants from the ends of her fingers, and as fast as they come, she gives them away, with a canny Glaswegian quip and a twinkling smile. How do people get to be so kind — and so *capable*?

While September demands that plenty be done — harvesting, clearing and cutting back — it also asks for attention of a different kind. September days sometimes breathe in and wait, creating a lull quite different to the exquisite quiet of May. Late spring is all about burgeoning: September prepares to let everything go. But not quite yet. On some days, it just stands still.

Today, when I had finished with my pond and done all the pruning, I sat on the shed step and stared. The wind of recent days had dropped now to nothing. My eye, in the calm, was drawn to the buddleia, still full of purple flowers drooping, in their lazy way, over dark green stems and leaves. I do not find this plant particularly beautiful — it becomes scruffy too quickly, even for me, as the flowers go over — but it is functional and willing, growing tall and full with little fuss, and (chief reason to grow it in any garden) is deeply attractive to butterflies. After some minutes of gazing intently, I saw it: a single butterfly whose mauve spots perfectly matched the shade of the particular flower on which it was feeding, in a cunning blend of disguise and deep natural attunement.

Sometimes, when Tim sat in the garden at home, quiet and fragile in the autumn of his life, he became, like this butterfly, almost invisible: a wistful figure in one way, and in another, a perfect fit with the world he was about to leave. It is his quietness — the silence I so often fought, angrily, to break, in an attempt to draw him closer — that I miss most.

5 September First day back at school for Molly. Now I know autumn is really here. It is also my first day of teaching regular T'ai Chi classes. The anxiety this provokes exasperates me — I am running around in a frenzy, producing posters and flyers, and planning each session with laborious intensity. Have I learned nothing over the past ten years? That too much worry is a waste of time, and only corrodes? It is as if a habit of anxiety (which cancer seems to encourage, both in the sufferers and those around them) has become so entrenched in my carer's make-up that I cannot shake it off. It floats around, and attaches to the nearest activity, in this case my teaching, and won't let go. As soon as each class begins, however, the fear recedes and I move into smooth, familiar territory. Anticipation is the terror: reality can be grasped and grappled with. It was fear of

Tim dying which ate me up. The fact of his death simply had to be accepted.

6 September I have an appointment with my acupuncturist. As he takes my pulses (subtle, energetic ones, along the "meridians of chi", quite different to western medicine's measuring of blood as it pumps through the veins), he registers my anxiety, and interprets it as a deficiency in the kidneys and the spleen. Then he plugs me in: needles in the balls of the feet to draw on the "bubbling well" of kidney energy, and several more in the lower leg — plus one in the centre of the crown of the head for uplift. The sensation is amazing. My feet feel as if they have been planted, like eager saplings, directly into warm spring earth. My head feels open and light. There is an immediate, pervasive sense of well-being. Acupuncture is an esoteric art, particularly strange for sceptical westerners, but if you are not afraid of needles, it can be enormously beneficial as a means of fine-tuning the body and the mind.

Mike Freeman, the practitioner I see, knows the world I inhabit only too well. He treated Tim and me for five years, and was there all through the final stages of Tim's cancer. It was Mike who talked to Tim about dying, who sat with him in the autumn of 2003 in our front room, refusing to fuss his body with any more needles, but just acknowledging the reality of Tim's exhaustion — allowing him the luxury of letting go long before anyone else was ready or willing to do so. And it was Mike who supported me in the physical and emotional catastrophe of grief from which I am still emerging. He knows, perhaps better than anyone, exactly what cancer costs (he worked in oncology for many years before setting up practice in acupuncture), and how long the journey is: for the sufferer, the slow, tortured unravelling of illness into death; and, for the survivor, the painful re-emergence, from a dark cave of bereavement, into the bright, bewildering world of the living. I treasure him for that.

10 September The first of my immediate friends to become fifty — Catherine — throws a noisy party. That's it now: we are the Saga Set. How would Tim have been at fifty? Cranky and stubborn (and inwardly convinced he was still a glamorous twenty-nine). Just like the rest of us, then. A major difficulty of his illness was his premature ageing: by his mid-forties he looked a decade older. At forty-seven, the year he died, he was coughing compulsively, wretchedly, as if he had smoked like a chimney all his life, and was forever complaining that nothing tasted nice any more (no wonder, with all that morphine clogging up his insides). His manners, always meticulous, began to lapse a little. The bright eyes, ever set to shine at a guest in years gone by, became veiled and suspicious. His greatest love, his honesty, was reserved for his only child. He demanded much of me — as I would, were I in his shoes — and we became functional, pared down to basics, surviving, all energy blown, in a waiting game with death.

But still, ravaged as he was, his mind seemed to quicken and race in the last year of his life. He read voraciously, watched films and listened to music in a tidal stream. He tuned in to his own brain and memory, even as he tuned the outside world out. I sometimes wonder if his mind travelled on, after death, untrammelled by the body which let him down so badly. Where does consciousness go — the spark which ignited him into life in the first place? All the great religions would have a theory for me, but I remain mystified. On the morning he died, Sister Brigid Murphy, spiritual mentor at St Gemma's Hospice, came to meet me. These were her first words, spoken confidently, and with a humorous smile:

"Well, he knows it all now."

I hope so.

12 September The rain has been coming down in torrents. This, together with the winds at the start of the month, has fast-forwarded autumn. The leaves, still green for the most part, have begun to crinkle and fall. The rain is so bad, I don't go to the allotment; there are things to do at home. I pick the last of my pot-grown tomatoes and put them in a bag in a bottom drawer to ripen. I walk around the garden, slowly, in between the showers. This does not take long, the space is so tiny, but so familiar, so loved. We might move house at the end of the year, so it's time to put the little garden to bed. Tidy up, cut back, let it go.

Now that the gaudy summer flowers have died away, the basic bone structure of the garden re-emerges: the shapes of bushes, the architecture of branches, and, especially, the lovely simplicity of leaves. Artist Andy

Goldsworthy first alerted me to the particular beauty of the leaf. He works with found objects in nature, to make exquisite, ephemeral sculptures, sometimes with sticks and stones, and sometimes simply with leaves. He pins them with blackthorn, places them in delicate spirals and curves, against earth or on water, to illuminate their rich, sappy greens or autumnal reds and oranges, their latticework of veins, and supple arteries.

The leaf is too often handmaiden to a flower. In my garden, I grow shrubs and trees where the leaves themselves are the crowning glory. Purple curving *Cotinus*; frilly, fringed sumach; shiny, palm-leaved *Fatsia*; shimmering bamboo, and spiky cordyline. The character of each is quite different. They add a quiet depth and tone to the garden. Shouting, thankfully, is not in their repertoire. The brassy pelargoniums have had their day — let leafy subtlety prevail.

13 September I have a nasty tooth infection, and am sick and groggy on antibiotics. Poison is leaking from the rim of a back tooth into my gum, and it's knocking me out. I am wary of ascribing metaphor or symbol to physical ailments. Is there really a "cancer personality", more repressed and secretive than the rest of us? Clearly this is nonsense. But my teeth do seem to flare up, like a danger signal, at times of heightened stress and worry.

After I had my wisdom teeth out, when I was twenty, my teeth caused no problems at all for another twenty years. They aren't particularly straight or pretty, but they always functioned well enough, until I was forty. We had just moved to Leeds then, in August 1996; we had found somewhere to live, and Tim had secured a brand new job in arts administration. In October, he went for routine scans in London. He had been in remission for two years. A letter came swiftly after his check-up. Significant regrowth had occurred in all of the tumour sites. He would need extensive radiotherapy as soon as possible.

At exactly the same time, I started having horrible toothache: an abscess had formed under a molar in my bottom jaw, and I needed root canal work, whacking great painkillers and several courses of antibiotics to sort it out. Ever since then, I have been prone to infection in my mouth at difficult times. It seems that all the corrosive thoughts that I can't quite put into words — lucky for those around me, perhaps, but not so great for my insides — convert themselves into poison. "Toxic grief", one homeopath called it. I have even been treated, homeopathically, with a remedy based on volcanic lava which resulted in a rash of boils and abscesses — leaving the skin under my arms seething like something out of Hieronymus Bosch.

Grief does not always wait to be expressed until after a death. I was grieving, to some degree, for the whole ten years of Tim's illness: regretting the life that might have been, missing the man who disappeared from view the moment he received his diagnosis, to be replaced by someone much more wary, careworn, withdrawn.

I tried to use the allotment as tooth therapy today, but every gust of wind burrowed into my jaw like an animal with sharpened claws, so I gave up and went home.

14 September I have just had a phone call from school, to say that Molly fainted in assembly. She was standing at the back, then suddenly turned a whiter shade of pale and keeled right over, bashing her head on the corner of a table on the way down, giving her friends and teachers a rare old fright. It is the day before her father's birthday. Something odd happens to her with every such anniversary. Just when I think it's getting a little better — that we might slip past these significant dates in the calendar, and carry on regardless — WHAM! A fall, a faint, a sickness . . . One way or another, we are called to attention.

15 September So, Tim's birthday. He would have been forty-eight. I have a favourite photo of him at forty-two, sitting on our couch beside his mother, father and Molly, gleefully blowing out candles on a Silly Sheep birthday cake. It was taken in 1999, just after a summer holiday in Wales, so sheep were very much the theme of the season.

Despite his terminal diagnosis in December of the previous year, 1999 was a good year for Tim. He was still working — albeit from home, to conserve his fluctuating energy — and he was well enough for us to go away twice: once to Wales and, in October, to Crete (financed by my generous brother Nigel).

On this photograph he looks the picture of health: strong, with plenty of meat on his bones and a

230

luxuriant head of hair, parted in the middle, with a dandyish quiff at the front, and tumbling down under his ears like a true bohemian. He even has a goatee beard, a complete departure from the Mr Cleanshaven I had always known.

Tim was proud of his hair and fussed over it constantly. (In the Chinese astrological calendar, he was a Rooster, and in the early days of our relationship, he did indeed have a mass of thick ginger-blond hair, styled with stiff gels to tame its waywardness. When he was offended, his fringe would quiver like the comb of an indignant cockerel.) As the cancer took hold, this hair became a barometer of his illness, and changed, in length and texture, waxing and waning like the moon, before the final wintry baldness of his last years.

In 1989, when we first met, he had a full head of hair, cleanly cut and carefully styled, with a side parting, from which a few artful strands broke loose to brush his forehead. Five years later, after his diagnosis and a rigorous regime of chemotherapy, his hair started coming out in clumps: so he shaved it right back to a Number One cut. The nurses reassured him that it would grow back, but that it might look rather different on the first regrowth. It certainly did. As surgery followed chemotherapy, and he was recuperating from both, he began to sprout tight little curls all over his head, completely at odds with the thick straight hair of before. He was quite delighted at this Adonis look, but it did not last. The curls gradually disappeared, leaving him with his normal barnet. By 1999, when the birthday photo was taken, it was the longest he had ever grown it in his life. But, by December, on the eve of the new millennium, it all fell out, for ever, leaving him completely bald.

We assumed this baldness was a delayed physiological reaction to all the medication he had received, but were assured otherwise by his consultant. It was a simple case of alopecia — possibly brought on by the stress of his illness, but not by the illness itself. (His father had lost most of his hair in his twenties, with shock at the death of his mother.)

Molly never seemed to bother about the changes in Tim's appearance — she just accepted him as he was; but I mourned the loss of his hair deeply: to me, it was the ultimate symbol of his youthful good looks, vanity and hope, now gone for ever.

We still buy a cake on his birthday — Tim had a sweet tooth, and loved chocolate cake in particular — and raise a glass in celebration. Happy Birthday, dear boy.

16 September Molly's best friend at school, Ellen, and her parents, Lynne and Paul, live fairly close to us, in Roundhay. Over the years, since meeting at the nursery class door, we have shared many meals, child care and celebrations, as well as a significant amount of illness and death in both households. Lynne's father has recently moved into a nursing home, and she wants to rent his house out to me. The new place is only a few streets down from where we live now, and the house is a similar size. The difference lies outside: there is a lovely large garden, front and back — a bigger canvas for me to throw my paint at! The restlessness I felt in the summer is now a reality. We will definitely be on our way at the end of the year.

Today I went round to visit the new house. Inside will be completely redecorated, so lots to do. But my eagerness, as ever, is for the garden. It is large and overgrown, with established shrubs and trees at the far end — holly, viburnum, flowering currant, *Kerria japonica* — and a thick planting of bulbs, in generous borders, hidden temporarily under a mass of sprawling growth. It was Lynne's mother, Iris, who was the gardener, and she died a few years ago. Since then, the garden has been left, perforce, to its own devices. My task here would be quite different from that at our present house, where the front garden was empty on arrival, save for grass and a small fallow apple tree. This new garden has plenty going on already, and will need cutting back, taming and tidying — then a year or so of watching to see what will emerge. Like an archaeologist, I am ready to dig for treasure.

17 September This autumn, as part of my push for more work, I have started to teach early morning T'ai Chi on Saturdays, as well as during the week. It's always a trial, getting up and over to the other side of town on time; otherwise, this is a perfect way to start the weekend. The stillness of these mornings; the soft September light, which filters by stealth through the high chapel windows; the quiet contemplation of a new day beginning — exactly the time when this "slow dance" of old China was traditionally performed, its opening movements dedicated to the Rising Sun.

As with any meditative practice, T'ai Chi always brings me closer to myself — and the serenity I feel this morning, with the ebb and flow of synchronized movement between all the different bodies in the room, offers great satisfaction. People — doctors, alternative health practitioners, friends, family — always urged me to use my movement skills on Tim, to keep him mobile, to help him relax. I tried, but it never worked. For a while, I attempted to teach Molly some yoga too, and got nowhere. Both husband and daughter steadfastly refused all my offers of help. It takes distance, I think, to create a teaching or therapeutic environment. Put another way: at home, I lack all worldly status. Wife and mother and "What's for tea?" takes over.

The weather was fine all day, so I gave my garden an autumnal haircut. Nothing unusual in that, but I was aware, as I worked, of a new finality. Someone else would be doing this next year. There are some gentle yellows and oranges appearing on some of the leaves, although the more vivid colour changes will come in October; and the apple trees and buddleia are shedding gently on to the grass. I scoop up a few crinkled leaves into a scrawny heap, with the twiggy offcuts of my pruning. I am beginning to detach; I can sense it happening. I have a strong survival mechanism and it is kicking in, even with regard to my little outdoor domain. This has been a lovely garden, but already it feels as if it is no longer mine.

234

My neighbours are unhappy to see us go. Molly, too, is stricken that we are leaving. This is the house she grew up in, the place she most associates with her father. But as the weeks start to go by, and the moving date (30 December) inches closer, I grow more and more steely. We have to go now: it is nearly two years since Tim died. Staying here any longer is almost like waiting for him to come back. We must make a new life without him, trusting that he is a strong enough presence inside us for that to be possible. And he is.

18 September Sunday morning strimming. Probably my least favourite job in gardening, and the most essential. Everyone is up at the allotment, looking for some peace and quiet and a healthy hour or two outdoors. Here I come, with my plastic goggles and this big beast on my back, petrol engine chugging, rearing — at the touch of the red button — into a siren screech which shatters the sweet idyll into smithereens. Has to be done. Every Sunday someone powers up some bit of nature-destroying kit, in the name of tidiness and human productivity. I always curse them. Today, I am cursing myself.

Edwin gives me a load of maincrop potatoes from his plot. "I don't know if they'll be any good," he says in his self-deprecating way. The fact is, Edwin seems to grow things by remote control. He sits, with his can and his cigarette, and watches, as potatoes, broad beans, peas — all the crops which have failed me this year — start appearing before his very eyes, and grow and grow. I begin to think that he is practising some kind of white witchcraft under that midnight moon he loves so much. Anyway, his potatoes (like the beans and peas before them) taste fine.

I started work on tidying up Tim's corner. His sumach tree is tiny, but healthy. There are good green leaves on the poppies. I cut back some grass and nettles, and will put some kind of plastic covering down, as a base for wood chippings and small stones. In 2002 — one of Tim's miraculous years, in which he recovered from the deathly weight loss and sickness which nearly killed him the year before, to become quite sturdy and rosy — he decided we should take a break together. Once again, our combined family had been generous with a gift of money (by this time, he had stopped work altogether, and we were skint), and I wanted to show him the Beara peninsula in south-west Cork. A quintessential North Yorks Moors man, he took immediately to the bleak, granite landscape of the peninsula — the high cliff tops, and perilous swooping falls, over a wild, unforgiving sea — and, in several photos I have of Ballydonegan Bay, close to the house in which we stayed, he stands like a mountain himself, a powerful part of the landscape. At one end of this bay, on the strand where we walked every day, there was a cluster of sharp, slated rocks; beneath them, some pebbles and stones. One day he scooped one up — it was large and heavy, pale grey, with a circle of white inscribed around its knobbled top. "For you," he said. It came back in the car boot, all the way to Yorkshire. Soon I shall take it and place it under the sumach tree,

236

by the poppies, on a bed of white pebbles. For him, now.

Why do daddy-long-legs suddenly appear in September? They are bouncing around our house at the moment, in their scuttling way, freaking Molly out as they hurtle towards her bedroom light, singeing themselves to death. Apparently they are more properly called crane flies, which I never knew until I looked it up today. They spend most of their life underground as larvae, and then emerge as adults: lifespan three whole days, spent tottering around on six spindly legs. Hardly seems worth the effort.

21 September I am starting a new class in Harrogate, and take some flyers over to the venue for a bit of pre-publicity. Harrogate — the town of the "ladies who lunch" — always feels a little chillier than Leeds, although it's only twenty miles to the north. The road to Harrogate is delightful, passing the extensive grounds of Harewood House, down the steep and swirling Pool Bank (eyes left for the herds of Harewood deer), and then bowling along, through Pannal and Collingham, fields to either side, leading to bijou villages with tiny churches and fabulously overpriced houses.

Perhaps the best thing about Harrogate is the Royal Horticultural Society garden at Harlow Carr. Given a boost over recent years by the arrival of curator Matthew Wilson, who has brought his own particular energy to the place — with subtropical borders, swathes of meadow flowers, a kitchen potager and high, swishy grasses — Harlow Carr has a spacious sloping terrain, with wide pathways leading down to woods and water. The relative steepness of the incline is fine for walkers, but tricky for those in a wheelchair — as Tim and I discovered, when we paid a visit with my parents in the autumn of 2003.

This was shortly before Tim was admitted to the hospice, and already his legs were failing. We decided to take a trip out, since our world was becoming dangerously small, and borrowed a wheelchair from the garden staff when we arrived. I have enough trouble managing supermarket trolleys, let alone a chair on a slope, with a six foot five passenger sitting in it. Our progress was slow to the point of farcical, with frequent veerings off into the flowers — coming dangerously close, many times, to upending chair and human contents into the showcase borders. It was tiring and exasperating, both for me and for Tim, and was an object lesson in how difficult ordinary life is when you are confined to a wheelchair. I remember how vulnerable the trip made Tim feel and how hard it was for me to be sympathetic under the effort and strain. I wish it could have been otherwise — one of his last days out blessed with more gentleness and humour. The flowers were lovely, but we were viewing them as if from Mars.

My friend Nick moved to Kendal, in Cumbria, today. He was very kind to me and to Tim, in the months leading up to Tim's death and in its immediate aftermath. I sent a friend to him for lessons — he teaches the Alexander Technique — and she had a shock when she first saw him: tall, with a fine head of thick blond hair and a wry smile.

"He looks just like Tim!" she said.

I had not noticed that at all — not consciously, anyway. Since Tim died Nick has met a new partner — soon to be his wife, and to have his son. He hiked with her through India, and walked through the mangrove swamps of Northern Australia. All that adventure and action. Things happening that Tim will never know about.

It is hard to accept the onward swing of events, when my life still feels mired in the past, in the constant visiting and revisiting of memories and emotions about the one who is lost: the hidden and constant work of grief. This is not work which can be chosen, or put away by conscious decision — anyone who grieves will tell you that. Often, this work cannot even be described — it is just a murky feeling, a weight at the back of the brain. Sometimes individual scenes — of Tim's illness usually, and his last days in particular — are replayed in my mind at odd times of day or night, with a piercing and unwelcome clarity. It is like a haunting, and always comes with regret: at words unsaid, at actions clumsy or undone . . . at the way things might have been. But these visits in the mind come more rarely now, the replay is less raw. Slowly the silt is settling: clear water coming to the surface, into which I can look, from time to time, and see Tim's face — a peaceful face; smiling.

★   ★   ★

22 September Still the garden takes me forward. I turn my thoughts to next year. What shall I grow in 2006? The new garden remains an unknown quantity. The allotment, meanwhile, must be rotated: so, broad beans where the onions were, French bean and sweetcorn in the potato patch, and runner beans where the courgettes grew. I drive myself crazy with these charts — I shall revise it all in January, when I am stuck inside and bored, and then abandon the whole thing when I come to do the planting. But it doesn't matter; the function of the doodling is one of connection. The September harvest and tidy-up means that the garden is soon to disappear beneath its own tired surface. Although it's partly a relief to let it go, I must, at the same time, project myself towards another beginning. This is not just about the garden, of course. It is a means of staving off depression, as the nights get darker and cooler. It is the storing up of hope.

September cobwebs are shining in this week's morning mists and dew, strung from the front hedge at crazy angles and stretching, gossamer fine, across the corner of the kitchen window. What beautiful woven artworks they are. We have our usual autumnal invasion of huge spiders, seeking rescue in the bath. I don't like to hurt them, although I am not keen on touching them either (their terrified scamper is unnerving), so I spend many bleary minutes each morning fussing about with cups and tissues, trying to evict them out of the bathroom window, and then putting the plug in the bath to stop them climbing back up through the water pipe. Molly

240

has the usual youngster's fear of spiders, and these September visitors are immense. I learned recently that spiders have no sight and no hearing: their world is predicated on a supremely delicate awareness of touch, filtered through the hairs on their long, incey legs. I vow to be more careful with my catching cup in future.

25 September I cleared out my allotment shed this morning. This is a job which rarely gets done — there is too much hard graft outside — but when I do get round to it, it is always immensely satisfying. The detritus of a whole season was in here — seed packets, plant pots, compost bags, crusty old gardening gloves, and bottles of drinking water from the summer, now turning mouldy green. Chuck, chuck, chuck. Out it all went. This was a miniature rehearsal for moving house. Then I sat on a folding chair and stared out of the window at the tall, decaying, thistle-headed cardoon, and brown faded teasels, feeling as if I had the keys to a glorious, shabby kingdom.

I love those September mornings — and we have had a few recently — which start with moody mists, and then gradually clear to a luminous sheen, blue skies vaulting overhead: the sun, in a subterfuge, telling us it is still really summer. But September can be very grey, too. Auntie Ella died in September last year, and her funeral, in Ashton-under-Lyne, took place under leaden skies. This seemed unfair for a person so sunny. The clouds were disrespectful.

27 September Molly and I went swimming after school, but it's not much of a pleasure these days. Now that Molly is nearly thirteen, the water has lost its appeal. She spent most of the time sitting at the poolside while I swam, which was not the idea at all. How things have changed.

We used to go swimming regularly as a family. When small, Molly's greatest passion was the Disney film *The Little Mermaid*. It became the inspiration for many make-believe water games.

"You be King Triton!" she would shriek at Tim, who willingly obliged — roaring and splashing through the water in a very unregal fashion, delighting his small daughter. I usually had a bit-part — Ursula the wicked sea monster, or something equally unflattering — and never quite filled my roles with the requisite enthusiasm. Tim had far more patience for these meanderings than I did, and, at home, was more than willing to dress up in ridiculous hats, and be surrounded by beanie toys and Barbie dolls, enacting complicated, interminable dramas with solemn-faced conviction.

For a while, after his surgery, Tim became self-conscious about undressing to swim, afraid to expose the livid scars which ran from collarbone to diaphragm, and around the left side of his chest from front to back. But in time he overcame this and got back into the water. Nobody ever seemed to stare or make comments — except an elderly German man, once, on a beach in Crete. This was in 1999, five years

242

after Tim's operation, with his scars paler now but still distinct.

"You have been in the wars," he remarked, as Tim sat on the beach, watching Molly cavort about in the water. The man's tone was respectful, not intrusive, and Tim — unusually for him — found himself telling some of his story to the stranger.

"You have been very brave," the man commented laconically. Then he pointed to Molly, the only person swimming on a cool, windy day, with the waves whipping up around her.

"And she has courage too." Then he walked off at a brisk, determined pace, not looking back. Tim was disconcerted, yet bolstered by this man's words, his penetrating attention. Tim never once believed in the astonishing strength he showed throughout the ordeals of his cancer. But the few pointed words of this stranger went deep, and neither of us ever forgot them.

I woke up at one in the morning and could not get back to sleep. This is becoming a regular occurrence — on the dot of one, like an internal alarm clock. It is the time of night which governs the liver channel, according to Chinese medicine. And liver disruption means ANGER. The recent flare-up of my tooth may be a flash of fury too. How dare all these things happen? So much illness, so much death.

It is hard to admit to these darker, more destructive emotions — sorrow is socially sanctioned, frustration and bitterness less so — and it's harder still to find a

243

channel for them. You can't shout at a dead person (and expect a reply). But pouring all this out, in confessional style, which seems a contemporary obsession borrowed from our transatlantic cousins, does not sit easily with me. Small outbursts of anger, short and sharp, are all I can manage, usually with some absurdly trivial domestic upset as a trigger. I just have to get used to this internal turbulence: make more space for it. And keep on digging.

28 September Last Christmas Molly bought me a voucher for a day at a health club in Harrogate. I used it today — with more swimming, and a lot of loafing in a robe on the poolside recliner. Water is very good for frazzled nerves. So is loafing.

The Cox's apples on my little tree in the front garden look shiny red, fading into a green gloss round the stalk. The tree is laden with fruit, and the neighbour's children are desperate to eat them. But it is a poisoned chalice, I fear. I took a bite out of one today and it is eye-wateringly sour — a bellyache in a mouthful. So any eager scrumpers will have to be kept at bay. If the winds stay mild, and the apples hang on to the tree, they may ripen more by October.

I love apple trees. Once, years ago, Tim, with his lip curled in a sneer, read out a Mystic Meg horoscope for my sign: "Libra — happiness is a garden with three apple trees." I became obsessed with this little morsel of pastoral advice. When we moved to Leeds, there was one apple tree *in situ*, grown from seed by the owners,

244

but it never produced a single blossom or fruit. I bought another for the opposite corner — and since the variety was grafted on to a different rootstock by the nursery, I counted this as two trees in one, thus making my mythical three. It's certainly true that this little garden has brought me deep contentment. And there is no more cheerful sight than a tree full of bright bonny apples.

29 September Another visit to the new house. No apple trees here — although the next door neighbour has a huge one — but the ornamental trees are beautiful. I am itching to get my hands on my loppers and secateurs, to sculpt my way into the space.

Up to the allotment for an hour. My sprouts are producing tight little buds in neat upright columns: but they are very, very small. Still, they might furnish a few chicken dinners as the autumn proceeds. There is a plague of unsightly whitefly on them: they rise up in a sickly grey haze whenever I shake or water the plants. So are the sprouts still edible? I won't use any sprays.

"Yes," says Maria, on the plot above me (whose sprouts are already the size of Fabergé eggs). "Just knock 'em off before you cook 'em." I like this low-intervention gardening, and give the thick stalks a kick for good measure to dislodge a few more of the pests — and vent my spleen — before I leave.

I cooked a cheese and onion pie today — good, solid autumnal fare. My grandmother used to make this dish, and it could not be simpler. Line an oiled dish

245

with pastry — half fat to flour, lard and butter mixed, and a minimal amount of water to make it stick (plus very cold hands to mix it with). Gently simmer some sliced onions, with black pepper and mixed herbs, till tender, drain, and season some more. Mix the onion with grated cheese — a good strong Cheddar — and fill the pie lining. Cover with more pastry. Glaze with milk. Cook in a medium oven till the pastry is golden. Easy. There are, of course, many more complicated versions of this dish. But the original works fine for me. It helps if you are good at pastry. I am not bad (I worked with a pastry chef in a local kitchen when I was eighteen, and learned a few tips) and Grandma was supreme.

It is time to start the slow process of sorting out the house ready for our move, and I begin work in the front bedroom: tackling a large, ugly filing cabinet, relic of the days when this room doubled as a study for Tim, and full of redundant, ancient papers.

I can feel myself deliberately censoring any response, as I wade through files for Tim's work, salary and (short-lived) pension; the MA he started and could never complete; the endless forms for Income Support and Housing Benefit; the hospital appointments and medical information; the abundance of helpful brochures on cancer support, bereavement and humanist funerals. Tim was methodical. This is like an A-Z of his adult life. But it is functional — not the real man at all. I keep back personal letters and cards — start to read a few, feel a little queasy and upset, and then stop myself (this is not the time). Some of the bureaucracy gets refiled, but most of it is bundled up in piles for recycling.

From time to time, I peer out of the window at the front garden below — the leaves are starting to drop at regular intervals now. I need a bin liner up here for all these old papers, and a bin liner down there, for the dying leaves of a finished season.

Jobs for September

- Bring in any tender plants before the first frosts threaten. Pelargoniums over-winter well on a cool window sill. Cut them down to size, and they should come back next year.
- Make an autumn pie! Cheese and onion is easy and tastes good (see page 245).
- Look at the structure of the garden. Now the flowers have settled down, it's a good time to invest in some shrubs or small trees, to give it shape and definition.
- Tidy up sheds and greenhouses.
- This is the month for harvesting. Autumn-fruiting raspberries may be producing; apples are ripening; late planted potatoes, squashes and the last of the beans are ready for picking.
- Sweep up leaves as they start to fall. If you put them in bin liners and stack them somewhere out of sight, you can make your own leaf mould for next year.
- Digging begins now, as the vegetable borders empty of their treasure and the flower borders die back.

Turning the earth exposes it to the invigorating frosts that can strike any time now, on clear nights, and kill off any lingering earth-borne pests and diseases.

October

A springful of larks in a rolling
Cloud and the roadside bushes brimming with
      whistling
Blackbirds and the sun of October
      Summery
On the hill's shoulder . . .

Dylan Thomas, "Poem in October"

2 October I was born in October, and so was Molly. Perhaps this is why it is my favourite month. Fruitfulness, birth and beginnings are my seasonal associations, even as nature starts its slow retreat. The very look and sound of the word, OCTOBER, has a richness to it. It is a beautiful month, vibrant in colour, and precious for what that colour represents: a final, glorious flush, before the world turns grey and old. There is a festive air in October, even the gaudy leaves pronounce it. Time to celebrate the harvest, and to party.

This morning there was a party of the working kind up at the allotment. New plots were being prepared and neglected ones resurrected. There is a growing waiting list of prospective tenants — since I signed up in 2003, allotments have become distinctly cutting edge — and room must be found for them. Sadly I have had to relinquish the bottom half of my plot, which has sat and sulked for the past year under mouldy carpets — wild grass even seeding over the top of the coverings in the relentless march of nature. My part in the chain gang of workers is to help dig this over, roughly, in readiness for a new tenant.

I do not feel too defeated by this. Originally I only took on a half-plot, then got greedy and gobbled the lot. But the greed has given me indigestion: I cannot manage this big space single-handed. Twice I have tried to dragoon friends in as co-tenants, but each of them has fallen by the wayside. The allotment demands commitment and a certain consistency. The average size of a full plot is "ten rods", or one sixteenth of an acre, of tough, grass- and weed-infested land. It does not sound much, but it is. Most people are just too pushed for time. It will be a relief to see this lower piece of ground properly worked: it has oppressed me to see the grass growing ever higher, sticking out its ticklish tongue and mocking.

The people who have turned out to help are doughty and determined regulars. They do not mess about. It is a somewhat scary experience, watching Peter, one of the committee members, wield a pickaxe and attacking the intransigent ground with grim determination; and his son is equally zealous, slicing through the hedging and undergrowth with his machete. By the time the group have finished, at noon, my half-plot has been dug, and two other plots have been cut back for eager newcomers. The far hedge has had a severe haircut, and brambles and bushes beyond the path are now strimmed into submission. Gardening in gangs is formidably productive.

With a little time left for individual activities, I went up to Tim's corner, near my shed, and covered the ground with a blue tarpaulin. Next move, as planned, a bark mulch and decorative Cotswold stones for cover. Another small step towards repair — of neglected land, and injured memories.

There are few months in the year that I do not associate with Tim receiving treatment or suffering some new twist in his illness. October is one of them. Spring and summer were often dangerous times for him: diagnosis in April; surgery in July. Winter, too, was hard. He became terminal in December; had extensive radiotherapy in January, chemotherapy in February. But early autumn was often treatment-free. We were, all three of us, allowed our birthdays in relative peace.

5 October The process of throwing things away continues, ready for the house move. I took bin liners of stuff to the local tip, and boxes of books to the hospice shop. I am not sure how saleable some of these were: *Learn Hungarian*, and several Hungarian poetry books in the original; plus plenty of Soviet and Russian history and politics; and some strange Eastern European novels.

I went through an extended Slavonic phase, which started when I was eleven, and saw David Lean's film of *Doctor Zhivago* (even though it was filmed in

Spain), and ended in 1976, after studying subsidiary Russian at university, and spending a strange, hypnotic summer as a student in Leningrad (now St Petersburg). Fixed in aspic as it was, under the antiquarian Brezhnev regime, the city and its people were — under the surface — still irrepressibly wild and beautiful.

Old, irrelevant, or just plain obscure as these volumes may be, I can hardly ever bring myself to throw a book away. It is a wrench. The elderly ladies at Oakwood Charity Shop look a little nonplussed, but feign delight none the less.

I notice, as I get older — and with the house move a definite spur — that I have a yearning to start discarding things. I crave clarity. Offsetting the complications of mind and memory with material simplicity has great appeal. Molly, at nearly thirteen, is at the opposite end of this life process. She busily accumulates as much stuff as possible: clothes, books, make-up and trashy magazines — layer upon layer forming her own landfill site in miniature, contained, just, within the confines of her bedroom. Harmonious in many other respects, over this we clash mightily.

I took the dog for a walk in the woods, to get away from my bin liners for a while. This time of year can be a trial for Muffin: one dive into a bush (in search of that ever-elusive squirrel) and her hairy spaniel ears and tail are riddled with burrs — tiny spiky seed pods and bony, sharp-spined plant stems, which have to be painstakingly brushed or pulled out between finger and thumb on our return home. Although she does an admirable job, redistributing the wild seeds of the wood throughout the estate, both dog and I could do without this tedious daily chore. Today, I notice the mid-afternoon light slanting through the trees, just as it did in spring. But now, in autumn, the light is not so soft, or hazy, or promising. It has a metallic edge — just as the clouds do, sharply delineated against a dark, steel-blue sky. There is a cold clarity in the air. I like it — it has determination and vigour.

Among the treasures which drip from local trees in October are two in particular: shiny conkers and sweet chestnuts. Each has a specific memory for me. The conker — that fat, glossy seed in its green spiky case, fruit of the horse chestnut — reminds me of Molly as a child. Her primary school was built on a beautiful avenue of cherry and chestnut trees. In spring the pink and white flowers appeared, and every autumn it was conker time. Walking to school with her friend Ellen, the competition was always fierce: who would collect the most? Every available pocket and bag was pressed into service. The stash was always immense. Once gathered, some were strung for playground conkering, but most were placed in a bowl in Molly's room, their shiny red-brown coating slowly fading, as the season turned, to a dull, woody blur.

There is the occasional horse chestnut in our wood, but the sweet chestnut holds greater sway. Muffin and I step over several empty cases on our way out today. Some greedy squirrel, or hungry human, has taken all the nuts already. Sweet chestnuts take me back to my own childhood and one of the few seasonal rituals my family observed. Before puberty interfered with the very notion of family walks, I would go with my parents and two brothers to a little village — Stisted, in Essex — every October, to collect chestnuts for roasting on our open fire. I remember the dilemma — gloves for protection from the sharp, slender spines of the casings, or bare fingers, to prise out the nuts with greater skill and accuracy? I think I usually went for the gloves option.

In my mind, these walks are always cool and misty, and atmospheric: any damp discomfort offset by the lure of the roasted chestnuts once back home — their mouth-watering smell in the embers of the grate, and sweet nutty taste on the tongue, a sign of the season closing in towards Christmas. I have let this ritual slip in my own small family: it's not the same with central heating — there's no open fire to roast them on.

6 October Paul, one of the people who took on a strip of land at the bottom of my plot, came up with me today to dig up his cabbages and broccoli, ready for the next tenants. We transferred them into a corner of my brassica patch. These winter cabbages will keep going through the cold weather — and the purple sprouting broccoli, which has a long growing season, should produce tender, multi-stemmed florets (delicious lightly steamed) next spring. Paul was sad to let his cabbages go, but I promised to take good care of them.

8 October Molly and I had a long drive down to Berkshire today, to spend my birthday (which I share with my father) at brother Martin's house. Of the three children in the family, Martin, the eldest, has been the most steadfastly rustic, leaving his civil service job early in his career to train as a master thatcher, and choosing a house in a tiny village in rural Berkshire in which to settle with his wife Mig and their offspring. (He, too, has Barney as a nickname. I stole it from him when I was eighteen, and went careering off to university with a new identity. I'll give it back one day, but not yet. Barneys have more fun than Elizabeths, I have found.)

The house is set in land given over to agriculture and forestry. To the side is a little orchard, and the back garden rolls, grassily, down to a hedge. Beyond that — fields and trees as far as you can see. Although their neighbours grow flowers, and have a neat and flourishing vegetable patch out the back, Martin and Mig are not big gardeners themselves. Their land is given over mostly to grass and trees. It blends beautifully with the surrounding countryside; is welcoming, relaxed and comfortable. In the summer, there is a hammock slung between two trees. The space is big, for tents to be pitched: when summer parties occur, the garden resembles a mini-Glastonbury. It is a dreamy sort of place: its climate soft and soporific, very different to the sharper, colder air of Yorkshire.

9 October Today my father is eighty-two, and I am forty-nine. It is the first time for years that we have been together on our birthday, and it feels particularly important to do so this year: both of us having lost our spouses so recently. It seems right to acknowledge our own survival, and to celebrate something for a change.

Tim was big on birthdays. He always made elaborate birthday dinners, and bought expensive, beautifully wrapped gifts (I held the purse strings — he regularly cut them loose). His whole family seem to share this skill for buying tasteful presents, in marked contrast to mine, who tend to resort to a crumpled banknote inside a card, or just the card, with the notorious procrastination scribbled at the bottom: "Present to follow." It does — maybe six months later. Food and drink, however, is something the Bardsleys rate as highly as did Tim, and we feasted well today. Brother Martin keeps a Hogarthian table: the huge wooden table in their dining room groans under locally made sausages, bacon, eggs, mushrooms, black pudding, for breakfast, and hunks of roast lamb for lunch. Vegetarians need not apply — although there are brave exceptions in the household, and they seem to survive.

In the afternoon, just as we were leaving for the long drive home, Martin beckoned me to his workshed — the outside den where in his spare time he beavers away, turning wood into lovely objects such as bowls, signs, walking sticks. Earlier in the year, feeling fretful at my lack of progress in creating a suitable memorial for Tim, either at home or on the allotment, I had asked Martin if he would consider making some kind of wooden seat in his honour. Time passed, and I put it to the back of my mind, half-assuming that the request had been forgotten, half-forgetting, indeed, myself.

256

"Close your eyes," he said, as he led me through the door. Some rustling and shuffling ensued. "Now open them!" came the command. When I did, I was dumbfounded. There in front of me was a majestic bench, four square, blunt and sturdy, its curved side arms still bearing the bark of the ash tree it had been sculpted from. He had designed it himself, for flat-pack assembly, so that he could put it on his pick-up and drive it up to Leeds, to be placed wherever Molly and I might choose.

Ash is particularly loved by wood turners and wheelwrights, for its pliable nature, coupled with a tremendous ability to withstand shock. (The description seems apt, for Tim, and for his bench.) Martin has worked his wood with precision. The grain runs deep through its pale flesh — dark lovely streaks through the white planks, deftly constructed into a strong, upright bench. All the time that I had been dithering, wondering how to symbolize Tim's life, how to make his presence felt, my brother had been quietly labouring, making something tangible and powerful — almost a monument, and certainly a work of art — which captures Tim's spirit (a tall, silent tree of a man) more nearly than anything I could have hoped for. It is far too desirable an object for the allotment (which gets thieved on a regular basis), but will be a perfect addition to our new garden.

11 October One of the women who comes to my T'ai Chi class is trained in Thai yoga massage. Having only the faintest notion of what this might be, I book myself

257

in for a birthday treat. Feet are important to me, as one of the tools of my trade, so I asked Tanja to concentrate on them. She proceeded to pummel and knead, and push and squeeze each foot, with a vigour and determination that left me gasping for air. Forty-five minutes later I emerged from her little room, feeling as if I had done three rounds with Mike Tyson and had come out the victor. The soles of my feet buzzed and hummed. I had wings on the back of each heel, and practically flew to the car. It took me days to settle down: I skipped everywhere.

Feet are my thing. Hands epitomized Tim — together with his deep, resonant voice. Hands say much about a character. Tim's were large and capable, his fingers long, tapering elegantly from square palms, nails neatly clipped and always meticulously clean. As a gardener, I struggle to keep the soil at bay — a thin line of it is often left jammed into the space where the nail turns pink, as it fits to the finger. It won't be budged, no matter how hard I work with scrubbing brush and soap — but Tim's nails glowed. He had warm hands, too, comforting to hold, like bear's paws. It was sad when those hands turned cool and dry, the nails flaking from the chemical stress of drugs and disease. Like his voice — which moved from the baritone of his chest, to a whisper in the throat — his hands diminished: a mirror to the life force receding inside him. But those hands stayed clean, right to the end.

★ ★ ★

258

12 October Molly is thirteen today. A teenager. Uh-oh. Tall and willowy, with a great sense of style and grooming, she could pass for sixteen at least. In letters he wrote to her in 2001, when Molly was nine and he was already anticipating his own death, Tim said that his great ambition was to see her become eleven. He succeeded — she was eleven the year he died. I wonder what he would make of her now, as we head off to a local restaurant to celebrate, Molly in perfect outfit and make-up? He would be proud certainly, and uneasy maybe, at the sudden growing up of his girl. I don't doubt that he would have been over-protective: they would have clashed over that.

She was born a week early, at ten in the morning, in St Thomas's Hospital, Lambeth, 1992 — in a delivery room that overlooked the Thames, just down from the Houses of Parliament. Although we left London when she was three, Molly still feels a great love for the city. Perhaps being born there has bound her to it in a way I don't feel (even though I lived there for nearly twenty years). After a textbook beginning, in the manner of the Natural Childbirth Trust, her birth went on to be difficult and long. I was exhausted. So was Tim. We had been up for two solid nights. At one point, just before some last-minute dramas — a late epidural and ventouse delivery in the second stage — Tim rested his head on the bed and fell asleep. This did not go down well with me. But after that he was an exemplary "new dad", cooking, changing nappies, and cuddling his baby daughter with quiet joy. Tim had an affinity with babies. They liked his stillness, and settled easily against his big frame, nestled in the crook of his arm. Whenever he was holding Molly — and photographs testify to this — he melted away. She made him utterly content.

13 October The sumach tree in my front garden is glowing in its seasonal coat of orange, yellow and vermilion. In a couple of weeks this tree will be nothing but bare sticks. But today it is breathtaking, like an exotic bird in full plumage. Round the corner of the house, lacing its graceful way up the stone cladding towards the roof, the Boston ivy has turned a deep, enchanting red. I try to drink it all in with my eyes and imprint it on my memory, before winter — and our move away — obliterates these rich autumnal traces.

For many years, I wore nothing but the colours green and blue. Tim too was always drawn to cool blues, steely greys, and the palest of greens: both in his clothes and in furnishings. There was something austere in the way he presented himself to the world — the great, largely untapped warmth at his core was something only small babies and animals could reliably unwrap.

But the older I become, the more I am pulled to the earthier, more autumnal end of the colour spectrum: scarves and socks in reds, deep russet browns, flashes of yellow and orange. The ancient grey and white striped curtains which first adorned Tim's flat in London, and have followed us from flat to flat, and from London to Leeds, are going, in the new house, to be replaced by ones in brilliant orange, like the fire of the setting sun.

As a joke, for Christmas 2003, which Tim spent between hospice and visits home, I bought him a jester's top hat, in squares of jet black and crimson red. (Silly hats are something of a festive tradition in our house.) He was delighted with it, and wore it all through Christmas Eve and Christmas Day. "That bloody hat!" the hospice doctor said, as he administered more doses of painkiller, his patient refusing to take it off as he was examined. He wore it in bed, he wore it in his wheelchair. He wore it out on family visits, and he wore it in. It was this hat which graced his coffin, four weeks later, and which still sits on top of the dresser in the back room. Vivid, defiant red. The colour of life.

15 October Molly had a big party in a local hall to celebrate her birthday. I drafted in her aunts and grandmother, from Tim's family, for moral support. We stayed in the kitchen, well out of the way, making endless mounds of sandwiches, and pouring giant pink smarties into bowls. Before long, the guests arrived. The girls looked knowing and sophisticated in their glamorous outfits; the boys seemed awkward and young. They spent their time swarming from one corner of the room to another — alighting on food one minute, then rushing over to dance, or compete in a noisy floor game, the next. When one girl went to the loo, five more joined her. Clandestine groups clumped in the corridors, and outside. I don't recognize this species: the territory is a wild one. When Molly was four — her first birthday in Leeds — she had a tea party in the back room: seven girls, in pointy party hats, munching happily on tea cakes and penguin bars. I knew where I was with the world then.

16 October It rained in the night, and everything has been revitalized on the allotment, which is now enjoying a mid-autumn flush of colour and growth. The pond is full and fat, pondweed gathering in speckles of green, filling the empty spaces left after the clear-out of bulrush and stagnant water in late summer. In the bed devoted to grasses, the mini pampas is boasting soft fluffy plumes of white, and the giant oat, *Stipa gigantea*, sends up tall curving stalks from its grassy base, flower tassels fluttering from their tips in the breeze, like a fanfare of wild, tiny flags. At the other side of the plot, the cardoon — its huge thistle heads desiccated now, on fat, hollow stems — is already sprouting vibrant new growth from the ground: sharp jagged leaves, green on top, silver-grey underneath. Next to it, the sunflower heads droop: the birds are enjoying their honeycombs of seed.

I plant garlic in the fruit patch, to encourage juicier fruits on my raspberry canes. "Autumn Bliss" has not been as prolific as I would have liked, but today there is at least one long branch dripping with dark red jewels, as I dig at its feet with my trowel. Every so often, I rip off my gloves and stuff a few fruits in my mouth. It's me or the birds. Behind my back, where the beans and potatoes were planted, one or two rogue nasturtiums, orange and red, are still managing to bloom. I am struck by the ragged loveliness of these late harvest treasures. How different my plot looks now to the scene

262

in January, when I first started digging. It would not win a medal at Chelsea, that's for sure, but I have created a garden here. Its life has been established: even in my absence the cycle will turn.

17 October This afternoon I gave a talk and demonstration on T'ai Chi at the Robert Ogden Macmillan Centre, based at St James's Hospital, Leeds, which offers complementary care and support to people with cancer and their families. In 1999, after Tim had been given his terminal diagnosis, his care was transferred from Cookridge, the centre for radiotherapy, to St James's, which offered a drug-based approach and had a special palliative care unit. From 1999 to 2003, Jimmy's became a familiar hospital to us, and the whole family used the Macmillan Centre for information and support.

Tim had one particularly kind and friendly oncologist, who agreed to meet Molly and explain some of the facts about Tim's degenerative condition. He went with her to the Macmillan Centre library. Carefully he tried to steer her towards the fact that Tim's illness was incurable: she, at nine, was already absolutely clear about what she would and would not discuss. The death of her father was definitely not on the agenda. In desperation — and probably relief — the doctor turned on the computer, and they ended up playing on-line games, Pokemon and Solitaire, instead.

Today the boot is on the other foot. I am the one supplying information, and offering techniques which may be helpful: breathing, movement and basic meditation. One of the people taking part was Tim's Macmillan nurse who looked after him while he was in the hospice. Things turn full circle eventually, and it felt good to be the teacher, for once, rather than the needy supplicant of so many years.

18 October An overnight stay in London. Molly is sleeping over with friends in Leeds. My friend Melissa has bought tickets for a play at the Royal Court. This theatre was like a second home to me when I was a theatre journalist in the 1980s. I interviewed a string of playwrights, actors and directors, who came from the stables of this small, defiant art house, which sits, brooding like a predatory beast, sharp teeth, sharp claws, on the edge of Sloane Square, only too willing to bite the hands of the well-heeled punters who feed it. Alan Rickman, an actor I first interviewed in the bar of the Royal Court in 1984, has directed this particular production of *My Name is Rachel Corrie*, the powerful story of a young American peace activist bulldozed and killed outright by an Israeli tank in Gaza.

Although the material is no less controversial than in my day, the theatre itself has had a makeover since then, the whole of the basement now given over to a swanky bar. I arrive, hot and dusty, from a long journey south and a frantic rush-hour dash across London by tube. I am not used to this any more. When I go down to the bar, artfully lit and packed with people, I am temporarily flustered and disorientated. The urban chic of London is unnerving; I feel as if have dirt on my shoes. I live in a big city still, but feel like a country girl. I do not polish up as well as I used to.

20 October Molly has quarrelled with her Guide leader about some petty point of protocol. I cannot see her sticking it much longer. She managed Brownies, and has had a couple of attempts at Guides. But, like me, she is hardly pack material. We are two awkward cuckoos in the nest.

22 October It is half-term. For once we are not dashing up or down the A1, visiting family (mine in Essex, Tim's in Newcastle). Except for two days away at the end of the week, we are staying at home.

It was 22 October 2003 when Tim was finally admitted to St Gemma's Hospice, where he stayed till his death the following January. His care had gradually been transferred there from St James's over the previous year. We had visits from Macmillan nurses, and frequent hospice appointments with a wonderfully witty and skilful consultant — palliative care his speciality — and Tim remained an outpatient for some time. But I felt increasingly besieged by the physical and emotional demands of his condition — and his health deteriorated so badly during 2003 that, for me, it was a relief when he was finally admitted on to the wards.

Throughout the years of his illness Tim and I were often left to fend for ourselves at home, having always given the impression that we could manage. Our middle-class manners let us down in that respect. If we had screamed and shouted, care services may have intervened more, and sooner. But we did not. In the end, sleep deprivation and acute anxiety over all the unmanageable symptoms — Tim's weight loss, his persistent retching cough, the frequent, appalling bouts of pain — took their toll. When the determinedly cheerful Macmillan nurse came to visit, on this particular October day, I wept. I had walked to the end of my path, and so had Tim. Beds were at a premium in the hospice, which is a small, immaculate, highly specialized and cost-intensive unit. But Tim was given a place.

Molly, understandably, did not share my carer's relief at a burden being lifted. She was quiet and sad. Although she came to love the hospice — which was more like a hotel than a hospital — she missed her father deeply. From October to January 2004, we visited nearly every day. I watched the autumnal colour of the hospice garden change to the dull grey of winter: what happened outside the window was going on inside, too. Tim was helped, with infinite kindness, slowly to let go.

25 October It was very windy and rainy today — the spectre of November moving in, to blow us all sideways. The leaves are beginning to drop. In the wood, the paths are stuck with the first of the sheddings from oak, beech and chestnut. The first casualties of the season — sunflowers and Jerusalem artichoke, on my allotment — have keeled over in the wind. It's startling, this sudden switch from colourful abundance to bare branches. I chopped down, and tidied, and cleared the different beds: throwing everything on to my bottomless compost heap which, despite endless applications of helpful urine, is steadfastly refusing to transform itself into the "black gold" upon which champion vegetables thrive. Two years after starting this heap, it is still a pile of dead sticks and recalcitrant foliage. I persevere.

To combat the general mood of change and decay, I left some dried stalks and old flower heads in the ground — verbena, fennel and globe artichoke — as mementoes and silhouettes of summer. I still managed to find something growing — two new courgettes — as I uprooted the mother plant. Next year this will be the bean patch. I turned the soil over, and took the courgettes home.

27 October Thursday is always my singing day. Just like adolescents, adults can behave in an unseemly fashion when gathered in a pack. My singing group are lively and giggly, and often very naughty. Since most of us are over forty, this is ridiculous behaviour. Brian, our teacher, is frequently exasperated. We seem to get nowhere — failing to master a harmony, talking and yawning when we should be concentrating — and then, suddenly, it all comes together. We open our mouths, Brian close to despair as he directs us, and a beautiful noise fills the room. "Famba Naye", a Zimbabwean call and response of peace and welcome, is my particular favourite. Tim could not sing a note, but encouraged me to do so. Molly won't sing — and cringes at my efforts. No matter. This singing group unlocked my heart when it was deeply mired in sadness, four years ago, and it continues to do so now. If gardening were a song, it would be rich in tone, the melody soaring free. If singing were a garden, it would start with soft shady colours and fragrance; then swell into bright open spaces of delight.

28 October We end our half-term holiday with a trip to Mike and Nina's boat moored at St Ives, on the River Ouse. They are great water people, and have chosen a beautiful spot for boating: the flat, wide fens of Cambridgeshire; banks full of graceful willows, bending their arms over and brushing their fingertips in the water, as big, big skies roll overhead. The river offers up treasures as we sail: an otter bobs its head up in the distance, before diving down to catch a few fish; and a lone bird visitor, all the way from the Mediterranean, a purple gallinule, stalks in the shallows on its spindly, incongruous legs.

The clocks go back this weekend. I hate it — the arbitrary messing about with time and light, which invariably leaves everyone feeling dazed and disconnected. The light is snapping off before five now. October is being frogmarched into November; winter is rearing its dark head. But I am not ready. I am never ready.

31 October Back to Leeds, and the season is even further on up here, as usual. Wind. Rain. Cold. My glowing sumach has shed its leaves, and the Boston ivy is nearly bare. The wood is on fire with orange and reddish-browns, but most of the leaves are underfoot now; the branches have dropped their load.

I dash to the supermarket to buy sweets for the inevitable gangs of ghoulish Hallowe'eners. The varied celebrations people make through autumn and winter — Hallowe'en, Bonfire Night, Diwali, Eid, the Winter Solstice, Christmas — are welcome lights in the darkness. Without the sun to do it for us, we have to make our own bright rituals: bulwark against the gathering storms, the long nights.

Jobs for October

- Bulbs. Plant plenty. Daffodils should go in by the end of the month, if possible. Some of the tinier narcissus are particularly appealing and withstand the spring storms rather better than their blowsier relatives. White daffodils are my favourite — so discreet, and charming.
- Collect conkers. Just because they are there. Also, apparently the horse chestnut trees are dying off in this country, having reached their allotted lifespan. So we need to plant more. See if you can sprout one for the future.
- Roast sweet chestnuts — on an open fire, if you can find one.
- Plant garlic, for a bumper harvest next summer. It will easily survive the frosts.

- Prune off old branches and the dead heads of old flowers.
- Dig up anything you don't like — and live with an empty space for the winter, until you can think of something nicer to replace it with.

November

My very heart faints and my whole soul grieves
At the moist rich smell of the rotting leaves,
 And the breath
 Of the fading edges of box beneath,
And the year's last rose.

Alfred, Lord Tennyson, "Song"

1 November The texture of November is immediately different. I feel it. I see it. The wind is sharper and more determined: it rips the remaining leaves off the trees with a savage bite. And, in the woods, the leaf matting underfoot is less vibrant — oranges paling to yellow, then dying into browns and blacks. The rain, too, is colder. It sticks the leaves together, clogging to shoes, slimy, loathsome. Pathways are unclear — everywhere littered, as the month progresses, with the discarded coats of trees. The root of the word "bereft" means "to be shorn" or "torn open". The November landscape feels bereft to me.

Annie paid us a visit this afternoon. This is the social worker who befriended Molly for three years, from 2001 to 2004, during the last, difficult period of Tim's illness. She worked for the Castle Project, a unit which came under the auspices of the redoubtable children's charity Barnardo's, and focused its attention on children in families where a parent was seriously or terminally ill: dealing head-on with issues of death and dying, and steering children through perhaps the most complex and daunting process they might ever face. Annie was a remarkable presence in all our lives — sunny, kind and thoughtful — and has become a dear friend. She is now pregnant with her first child and has left Barnardo's. In the face of financial pressure — and despite a deep, continuing need (people *will* keep dying) — the Castle Project has been closed. I honestly do not know how we would have coped without it. Tim, who came to love Annie, and who benefited from her gentle insights as much as did Molly, would be horrified to hear of the Project's closure. He would, on the other hand, be delighted at the news of another baby arriving. Just in time, as the November light begins to die: the spark is reignited.

3 November I went up to the allotment to do some digging and weeding, just avoiding the rain either side of my visit. The ground was wonderfully soft — plenty of rain lately, and not too many night frosts — so the weeds yielded easily, except for docks and dandelions, which have such deep, stubborn taproots and always put up a fight. I concentrated on the little herb patch, cutting back the mint, which is starting to die off above ground, and tidying up the lavender, snipping at its old, dead flower heads but saving this year's growth beneath. Next door, on the brassica patch, the whitefly were still swarming around my little sprouts. The way they stick to the plant is disgusting, but I refuse to spray — even the parasites must have their day. Behind them, by the shed, Tim's valiant little sumach still boasted some colour, the leaves hanging on by a slender desiccated thread.

After this, there was just enough time to race home and change before teaching a class in town, at a leisure centre built into the bowels of the vast government edifice of the Departments of Health and Social Security. I am not quite sure how I fit in here, the slow deliberation of my style contrasting almost comically with the shrieks and yells from the squash court next door, and the intense aerobics of the gym at the end of the corridor. Still, I seem to have a little following — of stressed-out employees, and older people who use the centre to stay mobile and fit.

I have a horror of gyms: all those machines, redolent of the torture chamber rather than healthy living. The body itself is the only equipment I use. Tim had a brief attempt at joining a gym, in the autumn of 1993. He was fed up with feeling tired all the time, and used to go after work and tread a few mills. This only made him feel worse. Six months later, he discovered a tumour the size of an enormous fist obscuring much of his left lung. No wonder the guy was tired. It was a wonder he could stand up at all.

5 November Bonfire Night. Not a popular event with our dog, who is terrified of the sudden bomb blasts, which these days pass for fireworks, and which start going off in our neighbourhood around late September

273

— culminating in the day itself, when the air is thick with screeches and bangs, and the reek of gunpowder, from early evening to the small hours of the next morning. It's madness. Molly is not that keen on fireworks either — so we refuse invitations to the allotment barbecue, and eschew the ritual walk to Soldiers Fields, to watch the massive public bonfire and display in Roundhay Park, staying at home instead, peering occasionally out of the window as cascades of colour shoot through misty skies. Muffin is a gibbering wreck by the end of the night, and sleeps upstairs at the foot of my bed for creature comfort.

6 November More digging, more weeding. Even on my patch — far away from the main gates and the scene of last night's bonfire — I find shreds of rockets and Roman candles, and loathsome bangers, thrown over the fence by the local kids. Goodness knows what my little frogs made of the racket. Can they hear? Even the vibrations in the pond water must have been seismic.

I laid some thick black plastic between the rows of sprouts and calabrese, pinning it down with metal hoops before the winter gales let rip. I want to cover as many of my paths as possible, in an attempt to keep down some of the ever-invasive grass. I like some green underfoot, but it will keep trying to take over. I do not want to reduce everything to dirt, however, and am happy to keep some turf around the arch, pond, and near the shed. This is a second garden to me, not just a vegetable patch.

One of my longest-flowering plants, the tall, proud, purple verbena, has finally gone over. I cut it down to the ground: there is already new growth, abundant at its base. Beautiful *and* tough. What a winning combination. One solitary nasturtium — brilliant orange — remains. Jaunty little thing. I have collected the fat, wrinkled seeds from its dead companions to plant again next year.

November is a messy month. The leaf fall clogs path and pond. I skimmed the water's surface with a rake, hoiking out thick layers of weed and dead foliage, but taking care to leave some protection for any slumbering pond life — and to decapitate as few frogs as possible. The light is dying quickly now. Even by two o'clock the afternoon starts to dim. I feel less and less incentive for being outside. There is plenty to do, but decreasing willpower and energy with which to do it.

8 November I love my dog, but I do not love her toilet habits. As she has got older, she has started to leave small puddles of wee where she has been lying asleep. This began happening when Tim was still alive. Tired of running around with a bowl of scalding water and lavender oil, to clear it up, I decided to have her checked out, and persuaded Tim to come along. At the time, Muffin had a rather severe woman vet, in her fifties, face permanently pinched like a squeezed lemon, manner not designed to put a nervous dog (or owner) at ease. So we went as rarely as possible, and always hoped someone else would be on duty. On this particular day, we were out of luck. Muffin trembled and shook as she was gruffly examined, and we explained the problem.

"How old is she?" barked the vet. Muffin was seven. "Oh well. It's hormonal. Very common problem. Middle-aged bitch."

At this, Tim turned his penetrating gaze on the speaker, with an infinitesimal raise of the eyebrow, the ghost of a smile on his lips — all irony lost on his victim, but not on me. As ever, he said nothing. It was all in the body language. We came away with anti-wee drops for Muffin — effective so far — and a decision to change surgeries, which we have done. Kindness matters.

It was highly unusual for Tim to have come with me that day. He generally left medical care of both dog and daughter entirely to me: I think he found it hard to bear their suffering. When Muffin seriously ripped her paw, as a young dog, he *did* help; but the sight of Muffin's panicked face, as she was put in a small cage before her operation, haunted him terribly. I was the one who turned practical, pushed the cage door shut and pulled Tim away, making the exit short, if not sweet.

When Molly was four, and still at nursery, she fractured her arm badly at the elbow. She was ashen with shock, and in a lot of pain. Tim was at work. I phoned him from Accident & Emergency to let him know, and he chose not to come home early, leaving me in charge. This was 1997, not long after he had undergone a bout of radiotherapy. Work needed him, after a month's absence, and — I am sure — he was protecting himself, consciously or not, from more distress. So it was me who sat with her for hours at the hospital, and spent sleepless nights nursing her, as she cried and moaned. (We read story after story in the dark hours together — the magic of books being the only thing which took her mind, albeit briefly, off the hurt she suffered.) I don't blame Tim for this — he had to work, to keep going, to conserve his energy, psychic and physical. But it did feel lonely. Another way the cancer prised us apart.

10 November Ricky the computer man came to sort out our sick machine. Ricky is a useful man to know — cheerful and competent. He mends cars as well as computers. He met Tim many times, and never knew he had cancer; just took him — baldness and all — at comfortable face value. There was a big gap in his visits during Tim's final months, computers being fairly low on our agenda at the time, so he was shocked when he heard of his death.

"Tim never looked ill to me," he said, which I found comforting somehow. It was a tribute to the astonishing capacity Tim had for keeping going, for making things as normal as possible, all the way through.

During the years when Tim had stopped work completely, from 2000 to 2004, and we were thrown on to the hardest times, some unexpected, no-nonsense angels came into our lives. These were not family (who always supported us), nor friends, but helpers on many levels. Ricky was one. He built us a computer. Surinder Singh was another. He taught me to drive.

Surinder was a philosopher Sikh, as well as an expert driving instructor, and the lessons he gave me — at a time of extreme pressure — were ones in life as well as road management. I learned to drive late, at forty-four, chiefly because the disability living allowance, which Tim received, offered the special component of a Motability hire car. Having a car would make our lives so much easier. Tim's mum and dad paid for lessons. It took quite a few, but I got there in the end.

To begin with, I did not mention Tim's cancer to Surinder. I always faced this dilemma with new people — what to tell, and when? The story was so huge, the appropriate level of disclosure always a puzzle. But once I knew him better, and there was a level of trust, I did confide in him. He realized immediately how important it was for me to pass this test. Taxis, buses and trains were hard work for Tim: the dog an extra complication.

Apart from expert tuition in the car, Surinder also offered his own unique perspective on life. My driving lessons became animated discussions on the very nature of mortality. He had a laid-back fatalism which I found strengthening and funny, and we had some fascinating chats. I passed the test. We got the car. And I learned a lot more than how to drive. I still see Surinder, driving around with a hapless new pupil, the initials "SS" emblazoned, with complete lack of irony, on the roof of his long-suffering car.

Once more I find myself sorting through papers and clothes — the detritus of daily life — in the front

278

bedroom. The best view of the garden is from up here, and I notice that it, like my house, is layered with old stuff: leaves, dead flower heads, weeds left too long under hedges and in borders. It needs a good clear-out, but the house must take priority. We move in a few weeks, and I am far from ready.

November, I have come to realize, is the least rewarding month outside. At least December has a clean, gaunt quality, with none of the left-over sprawl I see below me now. I remember the first visit my American friend Laurie paid to Leeds — it happened to be November, a year after we had moved up north. I had long enthused in letters about my new garden, and what joy it had brought. When she arrived, to see for herself, the front was a total mess, much as it is today. It was cold and wet, the lawn was churned up with mud, and there were leaves everywhere. I had not been in the garden for days. There was the reek of neglect in every corner. "*That's* your garden?" she exclaimed, her disbelief barely concealed. Gardens — like pets and children and spouses — can let you down sometimes.

11 November Like Tim, I am vain about my hair. For years, I spent nothing on it — but still wanted it to look fabulous. It fluctuated in length, from skinhead/punk, to shoulder-length curls. Now that I grow older and greyer, and the condition of my hair deteriorates accordingly, I have started going to a posh salon — the Cutting Room, in Chapel Allerton (self-styled Islington of Leeds) — and spending a small fortune, trying to keep it in trim.

Hairdressing is the new rock and roll, it seems, and this particular salon is dauntingly chic — a huge flat-screen television on one wall, replaying lavish London award ceremonies, where the salon's cutters and colourists are frequent winners; tasteful, expensive, slightly avant-garde flower arrangements on the waiting-room coffee table; a bar for drinks (complimentary); and an army of perfectly coiffured young things, flitting about, washing, cutting, drying, primping, gossiping. My own hairdresser, Jamie, is young, cynical and smart. The conversation is always hilarious.

"So what have you been up to?" He asks the obligatory hairdresser's question.

"Oh. You know — digging and stuff . . ." I always reply. He humours me on the gardening thing, but compared to him — demon cutter/late night barfly/boy about town/urban cowboy — I know I come from a different planet.

12 November I went to the new garden to clear a space for Tim's bench, underneath a window in the side of the garage. There are big old plants here, sprawling and overgrown. *Kerria japonica*, with yellow pom-pom flowers in spring; a flowering currant, *Ribes sanguineum*, with pink racemes, blue-black berries, and a pungent fragrance; *Viburnum davidii*, more a tree than a bush, and boasting white scented flowers from summer through to late autumn. In between these monster beauties, Tim's bench will fit snug, and a little bit secret. Just as he would like.

★   ★   ★

280

13 November Sunday: allotment day. Bright sunshine and the usual bustle of weekend gardeners hard at work. I cleared the fruit patch, always weedy and overgrown, and pruned the currant bushes and raspberries, for neatness' sake. As I worked on the ground at the base of the plants, and dug the neighbouring beds to "air" the soil, a satisfying bareness emerged. I love the look of this fallow earth. It is full of potential. And restfulness.

14 November My diary is starting to fill with panicky notes about moving: complicated timetables for shifting bits of furniture; lists of people (poor suckers) who might help; and further, longer lists of measurements, fixtures and fittings, and urgent Things to Do. I am not good at all this, and miss a significant adult other to share the load. Tim had a particular gift for calm, last-minute organizing, which would come in useful right now. I can manage the motor of everyday life, and can fit in a lot more now that my energy is improving. But a big thing like moving house daunts me.

I went for an Alexander lesson. This technique works on the brain quite as much as the body — tidying and ordering my insides, much as I am trying to order my house. My teacher has worked with me for five years: he has seen me in the worst of shapes, reassembling me, when necessary, from many tiny fragments back into a coherent whole, with skill and humour. Curious little comments, like "Head forward and up", "Knees spiral out and away" and "Think into your right hip", feel quite commonplace to me now. My daughter, who is already very tall, is complaining, at thirteen, of backache. She sits, slumped, in the wrong-sized furniture all day. They should have Alexander lessons at school instead of long-distance running. It would save the National Health Service a fortune.

15 November The days are exquisitely sunny; the nights, treacherous with frost. I see my garden mostly through windows, as more and more boxes of belongings are filled and stacked in corners. Just when I found the ground under my feet, I am being unearthed — again.

16 November Today was the anniversary of the death of Tim's father, Leslie. He died in 2004, the same year as his son. (The first twelve months after a loss so huge are always critical. Some doctors in hospices talk of a "broken heart syndrome".) He found the long years of Tim's cancer very hard, always looking for good news about it, which we always tried to find for him. He and Tim were very different — Tim quiet and withdrawn, Leslie chatty and extrovert. He loved a party: and put his family above all else. I think he would have been happiest, were we all to have lived under the same roof, as a huge extended family, himself as pater-familias.

Although father and son sang such different tunes, Tim did come to resemble his dad, in aspect and demeanour, as the cancer accelerated his ageing. It is the same for me. I look in the mirror some mornings, and there is my mother, Kathleen, staring back at me. This is an unnerving process — but is also a clever trick of nature, ensuring that our parents never really leave us.

Some people move in a single day — hire huge pantechnicons and a team of removal men, and shift the lot in one fell swoop. My budget being what it is, I have to do things in stages, and grab beleaguered friends and family, whenever they are available. The process is much longer, more drawn out, like pulling teeth. The house we are going to is already empty, and being redecorated, so there is room for some large pieces — a dresser, some book-cases — to be installed tomorrow, when my brother arrives with his trusty pick-up truck. The clock is ticking. It is time to move forward.

Suddenly my life is in a new phase. My insides are turned into tight little knots of tension and foreboding. I have been stuck in a womb-like state of grief and bereavement for the past two years. Now it feels as if I am being forced to come out and face up to the world, and it is distinctly unnerving. I am pale and thin and losing weight. Get a grip, girl. At least you have a house to move to.

17 November To the tip, with lots of filled bin liners. This place — just down the road from St James's Hospital, in Harehills — is becoming a second home. Goodness knows what treasures get hurled into those huge yellow skips and crushed to pulp by the comical spiked cylinders, attached to noisy diggers and operated by bored machinists who spend their days in nonchalant destruction.

Even the small tip by the storehouse at the allotments, supposedly just for "pernicious weeds" and unwanted, non-compostable vegetation, yields frequent surprises. Don, the secretary, keeps a tight ship, and regularly scrutinizes the scrap for anything untoward. The most valuable piece he has found was an old bronze draw hoe, dating back to the 1600s — probably used in some big old kitchen garden, and dumped by a long-gone plot holder who had been billeted to various country estates during war service, and must have picked up the hoe on his travels. It is now held, for exhibition purposes, at the magnificent Hall and Duck Trust, a museum for vintage lawnmowers and garden implements, whose avowed aim is to "save and preserve artefacts of turf care".

A less arcane addition to the tip was a dirty blonde mop head — or was it a wig? — flopped, one morning, on the top of a pile of weeds. The mop moved when picked up, and turned out to be Rosie, a blind Schnauzer who lived locally and had lost her bearings, ending up after three days of wandering, filthy and cold, by the allotment sheds. She was traced back to her owners eventually — who seemed less than thrilled to see the scruffy mutt returned home.

19 November A bitterly cold morning. A crisp rime of frost underfoot. A metal blue sky. And some very reluctant helpers, being amassed to move a few large objects to the new house, on the back of my brother's truck. First and foremost, there is the shed. It is small enough to be tipped on to the truck without being dismantled. When we have finished heaving, there it sits, up high, at a perilous angle, secured by guy ropes, like a rustic Leaning Tower of Pisa.

The truck makes slow progress along the treacherous black-iced roads of the estate, its ludicrous cargo perched neatly, swaying slightly, but arriving safely at its new destination. This little shed means a lot to me — not for its contents, which are few, but for its context. It was a trademark feature of my first little garden. Bringing it to the new place is a way of filtering the old and comfortable into the new and unknown. Shed as transitional object. It is also a statement of intent. I will make a garden here as lovely (to me) as the first one. My shed will be like an eye, a window on new green territory.

We are only a few streets away from the old house, but the perspective is quite different. On the hill where we were, the skyline at night was the city illuminated: tall office blocks, cranes and glittering lights — the Parkinson Building of Leeds University most distinctive of all, its pale learned tower rising above a typically grand stone edifice. (Even municipal buildings in Yorkshire seem to have the magnificence of old mills hammered into their fabric.)

Here, at my new address, standing in front of my shed as it faces the long lawn, I can see no city at all — just the trees of our beloved wood no further than a stone's throw away. Muffin will be thrilled. She can almost take herself for a walk from here. And although

285

we are still in the middle of an urban estate, it feels as if we have moved to the country.

Brother Martin has one more important job to do. Tucked away beneath the shed, on his truck, is Tim's flat-pack bench, waiting for assembly. Within a couple of hours it is up, solid and secure, flagstones beneath it, trees and bushes to either side, with a discreet view over the hedge tops to the wood that Tim loved as much as does his dog. The trees visible from here shade the furthest corner — where the bluebells will be most prolific, when next spring comes around.

20 November Every year Molly makes a pilgrimage to York with her aunt Philippa, in search of Christmas presents and treats. Today is the day. Quaint and pretty though York is, I am happy to stay away. Crowds of shoppers worshipping the great god Commerce only make me cross — so I try to do my Christmas buying closer to home, and at odd times, when no one else is around. I am an antisocial shopper. Besides, I have a garden to attend to — a garden on the move.

I take advantage of Martin's truck to transport some of the large earthenware pots from my ugly old concrete drive — which is already looking abandoned, without the little shed perched in the middle of it — round to their new home. Not every pot will leave: on the back terrace, three honeysuckles will continue to wind up the trellis, a potted conifer will stay in the corner, and two brutish cordylines will also remain. Coming along, for old times sake, are the red camellia, a fat-leaved bamboo grown from an offshoot from a

286

friend's garden, the lace-capped hydrangea (which desperately needs repotting) and assorted herbs for the back door — sage, rosemary, mint and bay.

People often dig up half their gardens when they move house. To me, this seems rude — and wrong. A garden is specific to a time and a place. To move it, in substance, is like taking the living room with you. Where will the new inhabitants sit? What will they see — how will they know what to alter and remould (or neglect)? It is important, on a psychological level, to leave something behind. The pretty apple tree that the neighbours' children coveted; the rosemary bushes in remembrance; Mum's smoke bush; John's sumach; the little weeping pear tree that Tim and I bought together — and the bamboo in the opposite corner, planted to shield him from the gaze of the neighbourhood, while he sat and read the last few chapters of his life. None of these pieces will carry any such associations for the tenants who will come after us. And that is exactly as it should be. I will take a few softwood cuttings and leave it at that.

22 November There has been a deep, persistent pain in my left arm, from shoulder through to thumb, for several weeks. Always a reluctant visitor to doctors' surgeries, I make the effort today. My GP — no stranger to health scares herself, and a stalwart, no-nonsense ally to Tim and myself through years of attrition — tells me I have a blocked medial nerve. Given the amount of box-shifting currently in progress, the news of any kind of physical blockage or stress is hardly surprising. There is nothing she can give me for it. No surprise there, either. Ever since she read my *Guardian* article about the garden, she has urged me to keep working outside. Today, when I mentioned I was about to move house, she said, in consternation, "You *will* keep the allotment, won't you?" I will.

23 *November* The weather is tempestuous, highly strung. Out in front, all the plum leaves from the smoke bush have been scattered to the winds; leaving strong, naked branches pointing purple to the sky. At the back, in the corner, where cordyline and conifer are jammed in together to camouflage next door's conservatory, the usual thing has happened. At the slightest gust of wind, the twelve-foot tall conifer, vertiginous and unstable, topples towards the house, the pot wedging itself against the old stone Buddha, huge branches and lacy greenery brushing, too familiar, against the wall and wide back window. No matter the direction of the wind, or angle of the fall, the two-foot smiling Buddha beneath always emerges unscathed. The worst damage he has sustained, in nine years of battering by trees and windy weather, has been the occasional smattering of bird poop on his head from a passing magpie. The statue smiles, implacable, throughout: infinitely reassuring, and slightly superior.

24 *November* I am running around with a tape measure, sizing up windows and curtains, and getting in a dreadful muddle. Where *was* my head, at school, during Needlework and Home Economics? Dreaming,

288

dreaming, dreaming. Desperate for light relief, I soon abandon the house, and attend to the garden.

I take some cuttings from the smoke bush, dip the ends in hormone rooting powder, and tuck them into the outer edges of a little pot filled to the brim with J. Arthur Bower's John Innes No. 1. Then I sow some broad beans in toilet-roll tubes, for a good long root run. These will start on my cool kitchen window ledge, and be planted over winter at the allotment. If they fail, which they might, I can sow some more in January. There is always another chance.

There are still some dried flower heads on my rose bushes, and even some tiny buds which put in a late, unsuccessful push for growth, only to be nipped by the first frosts. Roses are remarkable plants. They flower prodigiously, if treated nicely. I have never been much of a fan until recently, with too many memories of childhood gardens where roses were often placed in formal arrangements — sterile rows of stiff bushes and harshly clipped trees, their thorns too off-putting to a little girl, the blooms too poor a reward for such severity. But I am coming round, slowly.

I started a few roses off in pots when I moved up to Leeds. Bad idea. They like space, depth, richness of soil, and were very unhappy to be so contained. Then I moved one or two into the garden, and had a little more success. The white rose, "Iceberg", with its awful name but exquisite scent, has done particularly well. And to my delight, the new garden I have inherited has several large established roses: a pink rambler in the front, which currently sports fat red hips; and two beauties in the back — a yellow "Easy Going" floribunda, and a dark red hybrid tea, called, alluringly, "Deep Secret". When I went to the garden recently, I knelt down and studied all the labels at the roses' base. On the evidence of this, and judging by the healthy branch and stem growth already in action, next summer should be a joy.

25 November The singing group — always keen on a party — have organized a weekend away in the Dales. Molly is staying with her aunt in Newcastle, so we have an early drive up the A1, and then I shall dive off across country to Kettlewell, North Yorkshire. Anthony Gormley's sculpture, the *Angel of the North*, looks stark and splendid as we thunder along towards the River Tyne — its vast rusty wings outstretched in permanent welcome. If I had to choose one piece of art (appropriately scaled down) to transport to my allotment, this would be it. Stark, impersonal, imposing: the Angel brings a prickle to the back of my eye, each time — on countless drives past — it swoops into view.

Later I head south-west, through the rain-washed, shining scenery of the North Yorkshire Dales, and down the cunning, windy back roads to Kettlewell, Burnsall and Appletreewick. We are staying in a converted barn near Burnsall: singing, walking, eating and drinking. It is the Yorkshire way. Set back from the road on a steep incline, wild pasture on one side and a clear rushing beck on the other, the barn is a perfect blend of comfort (light, warm, airy) and savagery. Step outdoors

290

and the wind and wet instantly whip your cheeks to a stinging scarlet. Although the Brontë Parsonage in Haworth is some miles south of here, the territory is similar. It is easy to see how, to a fervent imagination, a *Wuthering Heights* could be born among the snaking stone walls, ridges, steep valleys, sharp rocks and sweeping high terrain — beautiful and pitiless — of the Yorkshire countryside.

27 November Molly arrives home a little after me, along with a high metal bed-cum-sofa, in complicated pieces, which she has inherited from her cousin. Each piece has been carefully numbered and lettered for easy (!) assembly in her new room. The taking apart and putting back together of things: this is the territory we live in now, and I feel permanently disorientated.

28 November The puddles on the floor are back. Muffin's medicine is not working. Back I go to the vet, who suggests a hormone tablet, Incurin, which sounds a little too much like "incurable" for my liking. Muffin is small and androgynous — a boy-girl look I have always, since the days of Ziggy Stardust, found particularly alluring. But the vet sounds a warning: "She may change shape on this stuff — could end up looking a bit like Mae West." This is not what I want to hear. But the piddling has to stop.

29 November Annie's baby is born. Edie-Mae. Tim will be beaming, wherever he is, and holding out comfortable arms to claim his cuddle.

In the evening I go to Molly's Parents' Evening. Roundhay School is a huge comprehensive. The main hall is brightly lit, teeming with eager parents and row upon row of teachers. The desire to bolt is immediate. I was a studious girl, at school and university, but still felt immense relief when I left institutional education for good, kicking over the traces for life as a freelance thereafter. Late to parenthood, there was one thing I had failed to foresee, worse than teething, sleepless nights and tantrums: when you have a child, there is a need to educate them, and you have to *do it all again*. Back through the school doors, from nursery to sixth form. The teachers, this time round, are roughly half my age. But they still say the same things, bless them.

30 November I pick up "new address" labels from the local stationers and walk through the woods on the way home. All camouflage is gone now — I can see through the bare branches to the main road below. The wood feels exposed, less mysterious, in its denuded winter state. There is a dank smell rising from the leaves as they lie rotting under my feet. This was the time when Tim, during his illness, would begin his long hibernation, and I feel a strong downward pull myself, an urge to curl up and rest. The mornings are dark now, walking to school. The sun does not bother getting up until eight, and the night begins at four, light suddenly switching itself off with no gradual slide to sunset. But just as the sun withdraws its favours, and with Bonfire Night over (thank goodness), the festive lights have arrived in town. I used to curse the early onset of Christmas: now I feel glad of the twinkle.

Everywhere I go I look for illumination. When I walk the dog down the street for her evening run, I find myself staring in through undrawn curtains at people's lamps and fires. When I visit friends, I linger near the kitchen, greedy for comforting smells and nourishment. Like a moth, I am pulled towards heat and light; like a scolded child, I seek consolation.

Jobs for November

- If it's not too cold and wet, you might want to plant some bare root roses for next year. (You can do this right through to March, if you don't have time now.) This is the best way to buy roses, although they will look like a bunch of mouldy brown sticks, not bothering to advertise their wares. Dig deep, add loads of fertilizer or muck, and they will astound you, come summer.
- Broad beans can be sown now, or in January.
- Tulip bulbs can go in now. They flower later than daffodils, and do not mind the cold.
- Before the great rains rot everything, have a last look round for seeds fallen from old flower stock — poppy heads and nasturtiums — and store them for next year in airtight containers.
- Empty flower and vegetable beds could benefit from a layer of manure. The worms will take it down, and break it up nicely, before next spring.

December

That same loneliness that closes us
Opens us again.

Anne Michaels, "Land in Sight"

1 December All too soon the season is turning. Autumn bows out to winter, and the darkness has come. When I go out walking, I see shapes loom in the half-light: houses in shadow, trees in mist, the world squeezed between late, reluctant sunrise and early, eager night. Any moments of light are squandered today in the interminable details of our move. I prepare myself for a visit to the council's Housing Office.

Those fortunate enough never to have claimed state benefits will have no idea of the hoops which must be jumped through — the fat, long forms to fill out, the provision of documents (original only), the full accounting, the disclosure of bank statements and savings, and the accompanying anxiety of interview — before help is provided. Every six months the procedure is repeated, in painstaking detail, with home visits from council officers and reviews of every personal particular. Any change in circumstance — such as our imminent move — kick-starts the whole procedure again. So off I go to Leeds City Council's Housing Office, in the centre of town, armed with a big file of personal details. The office is new, clean and efficient, its staff invariably polite — which helps enormously. But even though my entitlement is clear, I still feel I am coming cap in hand. Fortunately, because I am working part time now, help with housing and council tax is the only thing I need to claim, in diminishing amounts — and not for much longer either, thank goodness.

These days I am at least spared any contact with Income Support — the bowels of the means-tested benefit system — whose offices I had to visit when Tim was very sick, and which was an experience grim beyond belief. The building was shabby and neglected, the staff barricaded behind thick glass and locked doors. Claimants brawled in the corridors, there was spit running down the walls, total desperation and fury in the faces of the people waiting, and blank apathy in their children, who were strapped into their buggies for hours on end, looking as trapped as we all, staff *and* supplicants, felt inside. Pure chance and bad luck led me to these places, and I have become immune to the indignities involved. At least I kept my home together, when I feared, many times, that I might not. Cancer is so greedy, it feeds on all you have, and challenges your resources, every single one, without compunction or reserve. Fight it, all the way.

Thank heavens for the trusty dogwood. This is an unassuming shrub in the summer, with pleasant enough leaves and an open, upright habit. It does not grow too unwieldy, and makes no particular demands of care. But come winter, when the leaf fall and November sprawl is finally over, the dogwood steps centre stage, its denuded branches glowing with a rich deep-red lustre. (There is a yellow-green variety too, but it does not have the same sheen.) It is always worth planting two or three of these little beauties together, as I have in the corner of my front garden, where they shine like beacons as I walk through my long green gates, tight and weary, from my bureaucratic exertions.

2 December I drive out to Harrogate in sparkling sunshine — but am not fooled by the glitter outside the window, because it is freezing. I still teach a class in Harrogate, but my numbers are dwindling, so I have decided to stop at the end of the month. It always feels like a defeat, finishing a class early, and there is inevitably one person who has benefited, and will struggle to replace the experience. But I must keep to my resolve: it is a weakness of mine, to carry on with something long after it has stopped working, out of a misplaced sense of duty.

In 1997, I taught a Performance Skills workshop on a Monday morning at Harrogate College, to a group of teenagers who loathed and resisted the physical demands I made of them (even taking their shoes off was an affront to their adolescent sensibilities). I could barely keep them in the room, let alone teach them aspects of *Macbeth*, a brilliant play for testing physical and emotional extremes, but one which demands focus,

296

dedication and clarity. The project was doomed from the start, but I still stayed to the end of my year's contract, and it nearly killed me. It was a sad swansong for my drama teaching — and a million miles away from the wild enthusiasm of those drama students and actors I worked with in London and Hungary not so long before. But something came out of it. Above all else, I realized, many of those Harrogate kids — messed up and highly chaotic — needed movement as therapy rather than theatre. Thereafter, movement for health became my sole professional concern.

Responsibility for someone else's health — this time a promise made in my private life — kept me with Tim, through years when I was tested more severely than my imagination could ever have foreseen. I stuck it out, at some personal cost. And this cost, the invisible price of caring, should never be underestimated. I personally know women whose partners died of cancer, and who suffered severe physical and emotional breakdowns as a result of the burdens they shouldered. But there was no running for the exit. Tim depended on me utterly; Molly still does. I stepped up. It is love's work.

The journey to Harrogate today is as scenic as ever, a panorama of fields rising and falling gently to either side of the fast (sometimes bad-tempered) road, low-lying mists soon clearing to a bright vault of sky. Space everywhere. For a child brought up in the small, contained countryside of Essex — pretty villages, small fields, discreet woodland and messy London over-spill — the grand open landscape of Yorkshire still amazes.

✳ ✳ ✳

I must remember to buy birdseed. I do feed the birds in winter, although somewhat haphazardly, which is not ideal — and indeed feeding them at all (encouraging a false dependency) has become controversial. Still, it is rewarding. And I seem to have the same old gang returning happily to the garden. The blackbird is my particular delight, and he does not need my bag of food at all, as he bounces along the ground with that powerful yellow drill of a beak, hauling up insects and worms at every opportunity. Higher up, in the branches and bushes, I have lots of quarrelsome sparrows and acrobatic blue tits, who love to hang from the fat balls in the apple tree, turning themselves upside down and inside out to find the juiciest lardy morsels. Two robins come regularly, cheeky in their scarlet singlets, and very territorial. Lurking on the chimney pot across the road are a mischief of magpies, who gatecrash the garden regularly and, like boorish old drunks lumbering through the undergrowth, wreck everything in sight. The smaller birds are crafty, though. They pick their times, arriving early and flitting away quickly before the bully birds start their raids. Birdsong, which goes on all summer long in our tree-filled neighbourhood, is rare at this time of year, and all the more thrilling when it comes. If I hear a songburst, it is usually early in the morning, in woodland: a solitary note of defiance, like a blazing torch in the darkness.

3 December I pay a quick visit to St Gemma's Hospice Christmas Market, which has its usual crush of festive

298

stalls in the conference centre, and a row of Christmas trees lined up outside. There are too many people to browse properly, so I beat a retreat to the tea stall, and take a breather. I never was any good at pushing my way through crowds, although with my height and long, gangly arms, I have the equipment — just not the willpower.

When Tim was an in-patient here, we came to this market together. One of our daily treats was the little restaurant reserved for staff and patients. If he felt well enough, the three of us would have an evening meal here. On the day of the market, he tottered down to see a few stalls, then quickly withdrew from the crowds to the tea room, just as I am doing today. I remember his consultant coming up to say hello, accompanied by his tiny daughter, who had blonde plaits and a sweet, shy smile. When she was introduced to Tim, she gazed wordlessly up at his tall, painfully thin figure, and he gazed down at her, pale-faced and equally tongue-tied. I wonder what on earth they made of each other, creatures from two such different worlds?

St Gemma's garden is lovely in the summer — and I know it in all seasons — but winter is the time that I connect with it most. The December days of St Gemma's in 2003 — short, dark and bleak — were spent mostly in Tim's hospice room. This was a serene space, luxurious, comfortable and quiet. Its small balcony, on the first floor, was like an eye on the whole garden. I am not a very good hospital visitor — it feels a bit like being in church to me, with hidden rules that

299

I don't understand — and I become monosyllabic and lethargic almost as soon as I arrive. Molly always managed it better — she would climb into bed next to her dad and watch television with him, or play on the electrically powered armchair — whilst I looked out of the window, at the cut-back borders, the neat rectangle of the shallow water feature below, the big, brooding trees — and longed for it to be spring. But the desire I felt for new life, for the flower bursts and fresh breezes of March, was shadowed, my hands tied — metaphorically, tightly — behind my back. I longed to be free, the way spring always sets me free. The price of that wish was a knowledge increasingly certain and stark: Tim would not survive the winter, as I expected to do, to see another season ripen and unfurl.

4 December I am changing the venue where I teach, to the local Quaker meeting house. It is, in true Quaker style, simple and unadorned — different entirely to the grandiose chapel I have used all year. I like it. The meeting room looks out on to a little garden. The space is clear, the atmosphere calm and unpretentious. The warden gives me a key. On my way out, I notice a poster on the wall. It is a circle of stones: symbol of the stillness you will find at a Quaker meeting. Pale, on a simple white background, these stones resonate for me. Outside, a bird swoops on to a bush, lingers, then soars away. I can watch it flying, through big, plain picture windows. It is possible to cope with anything in life, if we remember to come back, always, to quietness and

contemplation: waiting for the meaning to clarify itself. I look forward to teaching here.

5 December I taught at the new venue in the afternoon. Before that, I had a half-hearted look at the garden, but my desire to work out here is near to zero. This is not just because I am moving house: I never want to garden in December. Those stalwarts who do something outside on every day of the year, come what may, will be horrified, and I am rather shocked at myself. It is not as if there is a shortage of jobs — cutting back, clearing and digging — particularly in the new garden, which is shaggy and overgrown. But the will is not there. And as the years pass, I realize that this is not entirely a dereliction of duty. It is not only humans who are exhausted at the end of the year. The earth is, too. Nature's production line has stopped; it needs a rest. Why not leave it alone?

Of course, there are the wonderful exceptions to the rule. In among the brittle sticks — the trees, like old men, holding their arms up tight, for fear of falling — are red berries on the cotoneaster, orange hips on rambling roses, and white flowers on the plucky viburnum. The Christmas rose (*Helleborus niger*) which I have never grown, but which my Auntie Ella used to show me proudly in her winter garden, its subtle white bloom blushed with pink like a shy, old-fashioned bride, chooses December and January — the fallow time of year — in which to blossom. But despite these occasional jewels, the trees, the bushes, the ground underneath, are all in a doze. My green-handled, mud-encrusted spade (one of the last gifts Tim bought me, and much treasured for that) leans against the back wall of the house, temporarily redundant. It will not be used for a while.

6 December Housing Office — tick. Library books — tick. New ink for the computer printer — tick. My diary is full of jobs, crossed off in thick biro every time one is finished (like a child's school exercise book) to promote some sense of achievement amidst a steadily growing urgency, as life at this house (nine years of it) speeds to a close. The more jobs are added to the list, the more complicated the marking system becomes: asterisks and underlining, brackets and arrows abound — the contents of my brain spilled, like garbage, on to the crowded page. The mists which gather, as the day progresses, only oppress my mind further. I feel like a walking litter bin — the sort you see just after Christmas, lid hinges groaning with the effort of containing all those black bags of useless refuse.

8 December This is a job I have written in my diary and scrubbed out several times already. I am not keen. It's a trip to Ikea for flat-pack furniture. Colourful, cheerful, low-budget heaven, but the store itself is hell to negotiate. I can remember visits to Ikea, in London and Leeds, at pivotal times in my adulthood — it has become almost a rite of passage: when I married Tim (living-room furniture); when I was heavily pregnant with Molly (nursery stuff); when we redecorated the back room and bathroom (mirrors and prints); and now — furniture for a house, and an era, that Tim will never know. The store itself is not difficult to find, and not far away, just off the M62, but because of the way the roads fit together, I invariably miss the turning, and end up going down the M1 towards London, or along the M62 to Manchester, either road a one-way ticket for miles. Today it was the M1. I toyed with the idea of going to the Yorkshire Sculpture Park in Wakefield instead, to gaze at the gargantuan Henry Moore and Barbara Hepworth collections, but bowed to domestic duty, and came back — eventually — with a fold-up desk and a stack of incomprehensible shelves.

10 December My last Saturday class opens a small window of calm on to a busy day. December mornings like this — the sun rising just as I leave for the drive across town — are mysterious and lovely: the day veiled from itself, everything held in careful abeyance; energy conserved in soft grey skies; skeletal trees outlined along Meanwood Ridge in fuzzy black charcoal — and then, a beautiful flush of pink coming through the clouds, as the dawn quietly spreads.

After teaching, the annual tree hunt commences. If Molly had her way, we would buy our Christmas tree at the beginning of December, but I managed to beat her off until now. We always have a real tree. It is one way to bring the lost outside world into the house itself, and I love the incongruous magic of having a great tree in the front room, dominating the small space with its thick prickle of branches. Like Birnham Wood to Dunsinane.

The size of the tree is always in dispute, Molly wanting the largest one available, regardless of proportions — tree to car, tree to house, tree to narrow front door — and me negotiating her down, until we reach a compromise and struggle home with the booty, netted up like a huge green fish, its endless sharp fins pointing savagely through the holes. I no longer buy the rooted specimens — having reluctantly surrendered to the reality of trees bred for Christmas, and then recycled — and have long since stopped trying to plant hapless little firs that don't fit in their surroundings, and are not suited to the shock of coming outside after two or three weeks of being in a warm house. There is a guilt factor in buying trees made purely for human pleasure, but I love them none the less. This year we bought a Nordman Fir — a handsome creature with a particular deep green gloss and wide needles, bred specifically not to shed. Sadly, one thing remembered from childhood (when the tree had to be big and real too) is missing: the gorgeous aroma of pine. These non-drop varieties, unlike the smaller, traditional Norway Spruce, have no scent at all.

It is, as usual, an almighty struggle to get the tree into the house at all, let alone assembled and displayed to our satisfaction. Both Molly and I have a keen eye for symmetry — nature, alas, is more lopsided. So there is plenty of snipping and pruning before the tree is finally ready for dressing. Some hours later, we are finished. Our Nordman Fir shimmers with silver, and a draping of tiny white lights. Perched on one branch is the battered little pink and white house which my mother kept from her own childhood Christmases. Hung up, high and golden, are two specially inscribed baubles — to "Dad" and "Tim" — which we made for the first Christmas without him. When the house lamps are off and the tree is lit, it lends a silent, graceful presence to the room. A simple comfort: light in darkness. To me, this tree — symbolizing life, hope and continuity — is the true spirit of the season.

11 December I manage a rare Sunday visit to the allotment, which looks pretty sorry for itself: cold, waterlogged and messy. The fruit patch has converted itself into a shallow pond, as it always does in winter, bare raspberry canes sticking up valiantly above the waterline. The pond itself is full, and thick with weed — plenty of hiding space for slumbering frogs. The ground squelches underfoot as I lumber around ineffectually, too frozen to do much except pull a few dead sticks from the perennial sweet pea at the base of my arch. I find myself looking down all the time: as if the sky, thick, grey, oppressive, is pushing on the back of my neck. I cannot believe anything will grow again on this sorry little mud patch. But it does — it always does.

12 December I drove down to Tesco's for boxes to pack up my books. I have given away stacks of them, and still they multiply. How does this happen? I have a library mutant within itself. Then I went to the post office for a form to redirect my mail, and drove the car over for its service. (Three more things to tick off in my diary —

I'm using a black felt tip now, it looks more satisfyingly final.)

The garage which services my car is out on the busy ring road, and I drive past the hospice to get there. How familiar this road is — the broad majesty of Princes Avenue, leading past the open spaces of Soldiers Fields, to Canal Gardens on the left and Roundhay Park on the right; then on into Street Lane, to Moortown Corner. On the left, at this busy junction, is St Gemma's. Today I speed on past. Two years ago, in December, I would take the left turning practically every day, then swing into the hospice car park, and pause to peer at the gardens through a round ornamental window, before walking upstairs to the brightly lit ward. A short journey. A graceful place to visit at the end of it. And such a desolate feeling inside.

Sometimes, when the frost has come and the air is bitter — the ground crisp underfoot, blood pounding in fingers and toes — it feels as if the weather is biting right into me. I like those days, they clear the brain. But December is often damp and foggy. My breath hangs in wreaths around my face when I walk out with the dog into the grey morning. Everything droops in a strange malaise. No wonder we whip ourselves into a frenzy at Christmas with shopping and parties and feasting. Something very dark stalks us in December, and I can feel its presence creeping down my spine, in the woods and in my garden. Nature sleeping, dying even, offers a cold embrace.

15 December Carpets are being laid at the new house. An electrician is doing a total rewire at the same time. This is an unhappy combination. I show my face around the door, encounter utter chaos and considerable bad temper, and beat a hasty retreat. When I go back home I notice some sturdy tips of daffodils (startlingly early) just beginning to push through the earth's surface. In the middle of nothing, it all starts again.

I take a trip to do some Christmas shopping. This is not an easy undertaking in December, since the city is always busy. Leeds is a consumer's paradise, with all the major stores (from Primark to Harvey Nichols) concentrated around one compact, pedestrian-only centre. The regeneration of the city from black-stoned survivor of the Industrial Revolution to a smart and elegant ambassador for the North of England has been successful and complete. It was already well under way when we moved up here in 1996. Now, new shops, offices and smart apartment blocks appear on every square inch of inner-city space. The outskirts may tell a different story, but the centre shines with opulence and excess.

I usually stick to the same well-trodden path, wandering up and down Briggate, a wide pedestrian precinct with avenues of shops off to either side. Today, as I pass a large jeweller's on the left, it sparks a particular memory of Tim's last Christmas in 2003. Although he was already very weak, and had to use a wheelchair for any outing, he wanted to do his own Christmas shopping — a task he had always enjoyed, just as much as I dreaded it. His sister Philippa took him into the city once or twice — not an easy job, with such a big man, plus wheelchair, in her small car — and then he came in with Molly and me.

At the end of October 2003, when he was finally admitted to the hospice, he gave Molly his watch: a highly symbolic act, since this was a watch she and I had bought for him, ten years before, just after the shock of his diagnosis, and his major operation. By passing this watch to Molly, it was as if Tim were giving her a piece of her history — and a piece of himself. "Look after it for me," he said, and to this day, she will not remove it from her wrist, although it now runs seven hours late. But Tim always liked to know what time it was, so in December, on one of our Christmas shopping jaunts, we stopped at the jeweller's, to buy him an inexpensive replacement. As usual, progress was slow with the wheelchair, and people's attitudes varied, from kind to downright rude. I remember the slight disdain (real or imagined?) of the young shop assistant as he came round the front of the desk to show Tim various watches, and remember also the stubborn determination on Tim's face as he refused to be rushed and, with much deliberation, chose exactly the item he wanted. Molly has that selfsame strong streak: it is her father's legacy to her.

16 December School finished today, and so did my teaching. Now nothing stands between us and moving house — an unnerving thought, since this process is far more than a physical uprooting, it is a psychological breaking of bonds. And freedom is scary. On a practical level, it is the worst possible time to be moving: the end of the year is so draining. I can feel a dull ache, right down to my bones, and it is nothing but simple, deep-rooted tiredness. I have no choice but to press on. It will be worth it.

Moira, the allotment bee-keeper, has kindly donated a little green sofa for the new front room, so in the evening I helped move it into place. Molly and Muffin stayed at home. The dog is resigned, by now, to this abandonment, climbing into her basket with a sigh as I rush out of the front door without her, yet again. Molly curls up in a big chair and watches unsuitable nonsense on the television. Both of them, in my opinion, have the better part of the deal.

17 December Yesterday the sofa was delivered in a single, wobbly wave of torchlight (the electrician is late with his rewiring, and the new house has no electricity). Today is an even trickier proposition. My friend James is coming, late after work, to erect Molly's big metal bed. There is no light and no heat, and it is freezing. Temporary solutions are found, to save us from frostbite, and the bed construction proceeds, but it is hard and heavy work. Just as the final pieces are slotted into place, James realizes that a vital set of screws is missing, chucked out by mistake amidst the rush to redecorate. The bed is up, but not safe. Another job, for another day. I go back home to the welcome fug of proper heat and a glow of light from lamps and tree. It seems almost wilful to give this up: the safe, cosy inertia of an established house, for the cold, blank canvas which awaits us.

18 December Another sofa is delivered to the new house — in daylight this time — by a group of homeless people who run a shop selling second-hand furniture. They are cheerful, quick and efficient. Their sofa is cream, and very pretty. While I am here I have a look in the back garden and am delighted to find bright red berries on one of the holly trees. I must have inherited both male and female plants for the pollination to succeed like this — and the berries are juicy and shining, the holly a free and welcome resource for our Christmas garlands, if the birds do not get there first.

I like Christmas wreaths: arrangements in a circle, of bright colour against deep green, are always appealing. One year I took the advice of *Gardeners' World* magazine too seriously, and made a funky arrangement of red and orange chilli peppers, strung on a circular necklace of branches against trails of ivy. It looked fabulous and festive — but the whole thing withered within a week. These days I stick to holly and moss.

Although I have little time, energy or patience to spare, I promised I would go to the allotment today, with trowel and gloves, and help plant a hedge of hawthorn. This is an attempted long-term solution to the permanent problem of break-ins to the site (people push down the perimeter fence on a regular basis — usually just to spoil and wreck, since there is little of value to steal amidst the cabbages and couch grass). The hawthorn — a tough, heavy wood with white blossom and red haws, which can live for 250 years and grows to ten metres — will certainly look prettier than barbed wire. Since I turn up later than anticipated, the long row of bare root plants is already in place when I arrive. Shame. Just time to share a thermos of tea with the ever-resourceful Sandra on her tidy, well-managed plot.

19 December Molly and I went to see *Alice in Wonderland* at the West Yorkshire Playhouse. The Christmas show is always an event, with rows of little girls and boys in brand-new party outfits, ready to enliven proceedings by shouting out at inappropriate moments and generally unnerving the poor actors. Molly enjoys the theatre but does not seem mesmerized by it, as I was when a child. She is used to the sophistication of films like *Harry Potter* and *Lord of the Rings*; real people standing on a real stage must be an anti-climax by comparison. When I was in my twenties, and working as a drama critic in London, I took Vicky, the little girl who lived in a house I shared in Brixton, to see *Peter Pan* at the National Theatre. It was a spectacular and magical show, with the mercurial Mark Rylance as Peter. At the end, Vicky walked to the front of the stalls, as close to the stage as she could physically get, and stood rooted to the spot, staring at the now empty space in front of her. I went and stood beside her. I knew where she was, in her head. Far away. We were the last two to leave the auditorium. Molly does this sometimes when we go to the cinema: only when the last credits have rolled, will she get up and leave. So long as the magic grabs her somewhere, the seed is sown.

* * *

20 December My friend Lucy gives up her free time to do a big lumbering job: moving my boxes of books and unpacking them all at the other end. When we have finished and our new front room is full of book-lined shelves, I feel content. Now this is a house I can live in.

21 December Winter Solstice — the shortest day of the year. It is cold and dark. A few people gather at our old house, and we have our last celebration here. Molly has stuck cloves in oranges, and I burn cinnamon and citrus oils, so a mixture of warm aromas — lemon peel shot through with pungent spices — penetrates the air. Candles. Warm mince pies. Mulled wine. Nothing original here, all very low key. Just comfort and tradition.

22 December The trees in Canal Gardens on Princes Avenue are always laced with simple lights throughout December. Since Molly was little, and Tim was with us, we have gone to see them, taking a short walk in the dark, steam on the breath, feet stamping with the cold. These days we go with friends from down the road. It is strange how quickly things become a ritual at this time of year — points of reference as time gallops by, small sources of solace and delight. The lights in the gardens are not as carefully strung as they used to be — these days they just line the branches nearest the road, where once they danced through the whole of the small gardens. But the entrance to Tropical World, Leeds' collection of exotic creatures and fish, at the top of the gardens, is still well lit, the atmosphere festive and full of anticipation.

In the pub across the road, the Roundhay Fox at the edge of the park, fires are lit in a cunning approximation to Christmases past. The glow of yellow and orange is especially alluring — they are both deeply grounding colours. That is why the Asian grocer's on Roundhay Road, which sells satsumas by the box complete with stalks and glossy green leaves, always merits a pre-Christmas visit. And that is why the baking of a seasonal citrus cake — the tang of its simmering fruit filling the house with fragrance, orange skins gleaming in the pan — has become an annual treat. This lovely concoction, with its thick mixture of cooked and pulped oranges, stirred in with eggs, sugar, baking powder and ground almonds, is inspired by Nigella Lawson's Clementine Cake in *How to Eat*; but I adapt it to include a large measure of cinnamon and nutmeg for spice, and grated lemon zest for texture. Just put the whole lot into a cake tin and bake for an hour. Sprouts for Christmas dinner from the allotment by all means (and I do have a few tiny ones growing) — but citrus from overseas, I am afraid. I would be lost without oranges and lemons in December.

23 December Here is another seasonal essential. I always cook a ham for Christmas. Boiled in cider with peppercorns and onions, then studded with cloves, layered in mustard and brown sugar, and baked in the oven for some more richly associative Christmas smells, the ham is the herald of the feast. When Tim was alive,

313

and we spent Christmas at home, he would, without fail, take over the Big Turkey Meal. Timed with military precision, accompanied by a massive overload of sweat and stress, he still claimed to enjoy the process, and the result was always delicious. I was consigned to the lowly position of cabin crew — but chef's one concession was the baked ham, of which I was in sole charge. Probably because of that, it remains a firm favourite in my repertoire.

It is one week until we move, and things are still far from finished. I decide on a strategy of dogged perseverance, laced with denial. The truth is, I look dreadful and feel worse. But I have steered this boat out of harbour now and have to keep it afloat, whatever the cost. I move some more boxes. It is a bright, mild day. My old garden looks scuffed and worn. Apart from the trusty dogwood, and a smattering of berries here and there, all the colour has drained away.

For several years after we moved here, I planted up pots of winter pansies, blue and purple, and window boxes of gaudy polyanthus, yellow, red and blue. But the wind always wrecked the pansies, and the rain did for the polyanthus — leaving a thicket of squat, ugly foliage, and petals so weatherbeaten that all the colours leeched to brown. When I was new to gardening, I loved every plant, regardless. Now I know better, I dislike polyanthus (as opposed to the true yellow primula, which is a delight). I make do with berries and branches in winter, and look for the new tips of next year's flowers for my inspiration.

There is time for a miniature stroll in the new garden. I pull away the matted overgrowth on one of the borders, beneath the roses. To my delight, growing there are shoots by the hundred — snowdrops, crocus and bluebells — none of which have grown well for me before. In my tired and beleaguered state I am looking for reminders that the self-inflicted upheaval of this move is worthwhile. These shoots are the best sign yet.

24 December It is Christmas Eve, and I am doing the only thing possible at this stage — running away. Molly, Muffin and I drive up to Newcastle to spend three days with my sister-in-law Bridget and some of Tim's extended family. Bridget always provides a fine welcome, with plenty of food, drink and presents, and we spent many Christmases with her as a family, especially when Molly was small.

In my head, jumbled one inside another, are all the Christmases I spent with Tim during the fifteen years we were together: the early days in London, adults only, spent with friends, with lavish meals, copious drink and extravagant gifts; then the change of gear towards family, when Molly was born — the wonder of Christmas with a small child, the elaborate artifice of Santa Claus and magically filled stockings; the annual visits to both sets of grandparents; and the occasional escapes to Whitby, just us three, in a rented cottage, howling gales outside the window. My memory tends to be lateral, rather than linear, so these moments in my mind — some of them happy, some poignant — are rather chaotic, albeit colourful and rich; a box of decorations that I take out when the time is right, but do not always manage to pack neatly away.

In 2003, Tim's last Christmas of all, my parents came to stay. On Christmas Eve and the next day, Tim came home from the hospice, a Herculean effort in the final days of his life, and the best Christmas present he ever gave us. He was as weak as a kitten, fading fast, yet determined to celebrate. My father went with me on Christmas Eve to fetch him, and later, take him back for the night. Dad sat in the big armchair, as I helped Tim into his pyjamas and then into bed, the whole process lengthy, intensely laboured and intricate. Quietly my father waited, saying nothing, discreet as ever. Then he turned to me, as we were about to leave, saying softly:

"And they reckon that landing a man on the moon was an achievement."

25 December Christmas Day this year passed in the usual merry blur of unwrapping presents and stuffing our faces. I was shattered and fell asleep over my wine.

26 December Boxing Day is best spent by the sea in my opinion. So I drove off to the Northumberland coast, with just my dog for company, and took a windy walk by the lighthouse at Whitley Bay. The two of us roamed over the grassy headland, above the beautiful wide beaches, cold to the bone, Muffin running in circles of delight, her tail waving like a crazy feathered flag — free at last, after days of bored incarceration. Then I drove back to Newcastle — got hopelessly lost and had to be

316

rescued by helpful cousins, and was fed an enormous buffet as consolation when I finally arrived.

Boxing Day two years ago was spent at Tim's mum and dad's house, in Wetherby. I have a picture of Tim sitting in an armchair, his sister Philippa kneeling beside him, two oxygen cylinders standing to attention nearby, a breathing mask at his face, pulled down around his neck for the camera. He has that ludicrous Christmas hat perched on his head, and a genuinely happy smile on his face.

27 December Back to Leeds. Three days till we move in.

28 December It is hard to recognize the sunrise at the moment. Sometimes after eight, the sky lifts slightly, becomes a lighter shade of grey, and off we go. That passes for dawn. The day is spent in a manic round of business phone calls and meter readings, and a final filling of bin liners with the surplus of a life — coats, scarves, blankets and cushions — that wouldn't fit into packing cases or bags. At this stage, it feels like the last half hour of a jumble sale — Everything Must Go. Now.

29 December It is minus five degrees Centigrade. There is ice on the roads and frost on the verges. The electrician is *still* in the kitchen, wiring unfinished and no heating. He assures me it will be ready tomorrow, our first night of sleeping at the new address. I have never been more ready to kill someone in my life, but grit my teeth and trundle past him, with box after box — my whole life passing before his blank, indifferent gaze.

30 December Clare and Karen — two friends with big cars and willing dispositions — help me move mattresses into the bedrooms, so that there is something to sleep on tonight. The lights work, the heating is on — just a few small details to finish in the new year. We have done it: we are in. Somehow, in the chaos before Christmas, I remembered to bring the little pot of *Cotinus* cuttings I took from my mother's smoke bush plant and placed it in the covered porch at the new house for safekeeping. Today, I went to check the pot, and there, unexpected, were some tiny green leaves, sprouting prematurely from four skinny stems. I have no illusions — I do not expect these rather haphazard cuttings to survive, but at least they remain in strong heart, like a message from my mother, a good omen. I feel a little skip of excitement at the sight of those leaves. Something is over: something big, unforgettable and sad. Something else — uncertain and new — is beginning.

People look to me these days as some kind of expert on caring for someone with cancer, on bereavement and loss. They seem happy to defer — to give me the ultimate crown of suffering, saying, "Of course it's *nothing* to what you've been through", at the end of any complaint about their own lives. But this is nonsense. How can we hope to measure each other's

318

experience, in some macabre league table of distress, points scored for the most hospital visits made, the most funerals attended? Everyone struggles in their own way. And I am lost for words of wisdom or advice — still grappling to understand the ten years I went through with Tim, still bewildered.

But I do know what helped me, and helps me still. Three things. As the years went by, I stopped fighting the waves of strong emotion — the anger, fear and pain — that I felt daily, and began to be tempered in the fire of them, into someone more open, more relaxed, a little more accepting. Also, I started to appreciate the tiny details of life — a fat bud coming into flower, the particular way a shaft of sunlight pierced the window and made the room shine — and stopped looking for the bigger picture. Big is just a sum of all these tiny parts. And finally, I found my passion: the garden. Everyone has their own particular passion, their version of my pots and allotment, however it might manifest itself. The only important thing, the crucial thing, for survival of the spirit, is to look for that passion, and cleave to it with all your might. Then, somehow, everything will be all right.

31 December My least favourite day of the year is spent, in utter anticlimax, cleaning the old house from top to bottom. Each time I finish a room, I look around and say a silent goodbye. Then I go home to Molly, and we spend New Year's Eve in quietness. Just the two of us, together.

- Have a Christmas rose in your garden (they like to be under deciduous trees, for shade in the summer and light in the winter), as a subtle, shy alternative to the gaudy red poinsettias filling the supermarket shelves.
- Bake a ham. Delia Smith has the boiling-in-cider, bake-in-the-oven version I particularly like.
- Stick a few cloves in oranges. They will smell gorgeous and look festive.
- You have to get a real tree, if you celebrate Christmas, don't you? Nordman Fir, for a non-drop experience, or Norway Spruce for the lovely aroma.
- Plant two holly bushes — one male and one female — if you want your own supply of leaves and berries in years to come.
- Celebrate the Winter Solstice, 21 December, even if you only light a candle to the lost light — and to the light that is returning.
- Make a cake: a Christmas cake for fruitiness, or — better, in my opinion — a citrus cake for fragrance (see page 313).
- Walk in the garden, if you have one, and just watch it sleeping. Then put your feet up, and do the same.

Acknowledgements

When one person has cancer, a whole community of friends, colleagues, relatives and neighbours is affected. When that person is ill for as long as Tim was, the network becomes even more intricate. Some of the people who helped Tim, Molly and me are woven into the fabric of this story (some with their names changed to protect their identity): the majority are not. I call on a few of them now.

To the doctors and nurses at the Royal Marsden and Royal Brompton hospitals in London; St James's, Cookridge and Leeds General Infirmary in Leeds; Bradford Cancer Support Centre, in Bradford; and St Gemma's Hospice, in Leeds: your help was immeasurable.

Thank you to Robert Freeburn and Duncan Sones, Tim's employers, for being such kind and understanding men.

Both extended families, the McGees and the Bardsleys, stood by us magnificently.

Thank you to all our friends for their gifts of time, love, money and food — and a special mention for Lyall, who helped us find a car; for Vanessa, whose generous gift helped us to move house; and Adrienne — who keeps sending cheques. Thanks to my allotment pals for all the free advice and plants (and hot tea).

I bow before my agent, Jane Turnbull, who came and found me, with a smile on her face. Thank you to my editor and publisher, Roland Philipps — who made me work harder and think more deeply; to Rowan Yapp, who tactfully banged those deadlines home; and my meticulous copy-editor, Howard Davies.

Melissa Benn, dear friend, you got me back on my professional feet, with your unerring skill and warmth.

Molly McGee — my lovely daughter — you show me the way forward.

Finally, in memory of Kathleen Bardsley, and with gratitude to Catherine McGee: two strong, loving and remarkable mothers.

Remembering Babs Farnden, Bill Preston and Pickles the rescue dog, who all died during the writing of this book.